BEYOND
good intentions

A JOURNEY INTO THE REALITIES
OF INTERNATIONAL AID

TORI HOGAN

SEAL PRESS

BEYOND GOOD INTENTIONS
A Journey into the Realities of International Aid

Copyright © 2012 by Tori Hogan

Published by
Seal Press
A Member of the Perseus Books Group
1700 Fourth Street
Berkeley, California

Library of Congress Cataloging-in-Publication Data

Hogan, Tori, 1982-
  Beyond good intentions : a journey into the realities of international aid
/ Tori Hogan.
     p. cm.
  Includes bibliographical references and index.
  ISBN 978-1-58005-434-8 (alk. paper)
  1. Hogan, Tori, 1982- 2. Save the Children (U.S.) 3. International
relief. 4. Humanitarian assistance. 5. Nongovernmental organizations. 6.
Refugees—Africa. 7. Refugee children—Africa. I. Title.
  HV589.H64 2012
  362.77'914577092—dc23
  [B]
                                    2012008987

Cover design by Erin Seaward-Hiatt
Interior design by Domini Dragoone
Printed in the United States of America
Distributed by Publishers Group West

FOR MY MOM

You are my rock, my inspiration, and my greatest role model on how to live life with a compassionate heart and a determined spirit.

PROLOGUE

SOMETIMES A SINGLE moment is all it takes for our lives to change course. My own life has been punctuated by several such instances. Those simple moments of clarity and truth had the power to both derail my best-laid plans and inspire a sudden shift in my perspective of the world.

I was in a Palestinian refugee camp in Beirut at the tender age of nineteen when one of these flashes of insight struck me hard. I had been invited to spend the night in the camp by an old woman named Umm Hashem whom I had connected with during my brief stint as a researcher and volunteer in Shatilla refugee camp. I gratefully accepted her offer, and as I lay awake on the thin mattress in her one-room concrete "unit" that night, surrounded by three other members of her family, I had a sudden realization that was obvious, yet profound: *They can't go home.* In my head I already knew this fact, but in that moment the truth settled into my heart. The injustice of this family's situation felt unreal compared to my staggering privilege. I could have easily gone back to the hotel that night with my classmates, I had a return plane ticket home, and the American passport I carried with me granted a degree of freedom and access that others could only dream of. It didn't seem fair.

A single night immersed in Umm Hashem's world was obviously not enough for me to even pretend that I understood the reality of her situation. Even if I stayed with her for decades, I still wouldn't fully comprehend what it's like to be in her shoes. Empathy has its limitations. Yet, I knew in my gut that something wasn't right. There was an undeniable sense of injustice surging through me. I wanted to do something. I wanted to make her life better. I wanted to *help*.

And so it was there, on the floor of that tiny concrete room, as I listened to the sounds of the camp and the inner churning of my conscience, that I decided to dedicate my life to humanitarian work.

I came home from that trip and called my mom to tell her, "Guess what, Mom? I'm not going to be a geneticist after all." The life of a research scientist, which I had already been grooming myself for as an overachieving teenager with complicated research projects in the field of cancer genetics, was no longer my ambition. I think my Mom was only half shocked. I had, after all, always had a heart for service. I'd been volunteering since childhood, I passed up a second summer of research at Oxford in high school to work at an orphanage in Togo instead, and I'd spent the previous summer enthusiastically teaching English in a rural village in China. But up until then, I always assumed that helping others could only be a hobby. Suddenly it felt like a calling.

It was with that preciously naive "I wanna change the world" enthusiasm that I signed up to intern for Save the Children during the summer of 2002. I was assigned to assist the regional child protection officer in Kenya with some assessments on child protection needs in Dadaab refugee camp on the Somali border and in several repatriation camps in Somaliland. However, as you'll see in the pages that follow, that summer in East Africa at the age of twenty, and my subsequent study abroad semester in Uganda, made it glaringly obvious that the world of international aid wasn't all that it was cracked up to be. During that time I would face a second turning point in my path, in yet another refugee camp, and my naive impressions of humanitarian aid would get a serious reality check.

Transitioning from a bleeding heart to a critic of the humanitarian regime was not an easy process. There were very few people who were willing to speak honestly with me about the subject. Fortunately, after graduating from Duke University with a degree in global health and human development, and a research specialization in aid effectiveness for refugees, I spent a year studying as a Fulbright Scholar with a pioneering aid critic and anthropologist named Barbara Harrell-Bond. Barbara was, and continues to be, a woman who is loved, feared, and hated within the circles of international aid, probably in equal measure. She has ruffled more feathers than most, and she doesn't apologize for it. Not even for a second. Her book *Imposing Aid* was arguably one of the first of its kind when it was published in 1986, finally saying what nobody had been brave enough to say before about the shortcomings of international aid. I felt lucky to be under her mentorship during my year at the American University of Cairo while earning a diploma in forced migration and refugee studies. In many ways it was Barbara who gave me the go-ahead to start speaking out against the failures I was seeing in the aid world. The more time I spent working with refugee communities in Cairo who were being let down by well-intentioned aid agencies, the more I knew I had found my cause.

I returned to the United States for a year to work with resettled refugees in San Diego, while also working as a nanny to save up for my next big project. By that point I was completely fed up with the failures of international aid. "Jaded" would have been putting my condition lightly. Throughout my travels I had continued to see endless examples of how our good intentions to "save" the world were not only falling short but in some cases doing more harm than good. In 2006, fueled by my frustrations, I started an organization called Beyond Good Intentions and traveled solo around the world for a year to ten different countries to produce a film series on what really works in international aid. My 'round-the-world journey took me to Colombia, Peru, Argentina, Indonesia, Cambodia, Laos, India, Madagascar, Mozambique, and South Africa. Along the way, I met with sixty-three aid organizations and hundreds of individuals, who all helped me gain enormous perspective on both the failures and successes of international aid.

In the year that followed, I went back to graduate school for a master's in international education policy at Harvard University where I served as a Reynolds Fellow in social entrepreneurship and had the unique opportunity to interact with some of the leading players in the world of social change. Soon after graduating, I released the ten-part *Beyond Good Intentions* film series, which helped spark a much-needed dialogue about aid effectiveness and was viewed in more than 165 countries by over 100,000 people. During that time I also began offering educational programs and giving speeches about the various ways the aid industry should be transformed to serve recipients better. My endless curiosity about the world led me to immerse myself in more than seventy-five countries on every continent. In short, I'd become a global nomad with a passion for waking people up about the realities of international aid.

I share this background of the past eight years only to provide some necessary context. Because when I looked back at my life recently, I saw a path that was completely different, and undeniably more purposeful than I ever could have imagined. And it was thanks in large part to two distinct moments: the first in Lebanon, and the second in a camp on the Somali border when a refugee boy's comments changed me forever.

This book follows the true story of my return to East Africa in search of that refugee boy who turned my naive assumptions about humanitarian aid upside down. The return trip occurred between May and July 2010, and all the events, people, and organizations I write about are real, though some have asked for their names to be changed to protect their privacy. The opinions I express in this memoir are my own, and are based on my personal experiences, biases, and reflections.

I already know that some of the truths about aid I reveal in this book are not going to make me a popular person in certain circles. Many people, especially those inside the system, would rather not question the so-called "helping industry" at all. But I feel compelled to tell my story for the sake of the countless individuals I've met along my path who have been at the mercy of ineffective aid projects. This book is for them. I hope that my story serves as both a wake-up call and a source of inspiration on how we can more effectively change the world.

KENYA

CHAPTER 1

THE STEWARDESS IS remarkably alert compared to the half-asleep passengers on board this morning's 6 AM charter flight. Her hair is carefully pulled back in a tight updo, her navy skirt and vest are perfectly ironed, and the white and blue silk scarf tied around her neck brings an air of French couture that seems out of place. I watch her squirming in the jump seat as the plane begins its descent, crossing and uncrossing her ankles, attempting to find the most dignified way to sit in a clearly uncomfortable chair. The green and brown Kenyan grassland we had been flying over has now turned into an endless expanse of red and yellow sand, dotted with clumps of parched brush and a few herds of goats and camels being marched along by persistent women in colorful veils. The stewardess puts her hand up to smooth out her hair, which hasn't moved an inch the entire flight, to compensate for a particularly bumpy landing on the dirt airstrip. As the plane slows to a stop, she picks up the microphone and, amidst the screeching feedback from a PA system that has seen better days, she instantly transitions into perky stewardess mode and sweetly says, "We wish you a pleasant stay in Dadaab."

I try to suppress my laugh. We have just arrived at the largest refugee camp in the world, and we are being encouraged by our lovely Kenyan stewardess to have a "pleasant" stay. I'm guessing they don't tell the refugees the same thing when they arrive here.

She pushes the plane door open and lowers the stairs and I'm suddenly hit by the intense heat of the dry desert air, the kind of all-encompassing warmth that makes you secretly yearn for a bit of moisturizer and a frozen drink. I'm also enveloped by a wave of déjà vu. Not much seems to have changed since I last disembarked here eight years ago. A sea of white SUVs with massive antennas sticking out like tentacles have swarmed the airstrip awaiting their cargo of twenty-five "do-gooders" who are coming to heal wounds, write reports, and take photos of a forgotten Somali refugee population that has been forced to live in this makeshift desert community for the past eighteen years. Make that twenty-four "do-gooders." I myself am not exactly here to save the world—or at least not this time around. That was me eight years ago: a twenty-year-old intern for Save the Children, naively arriving at this camp full of grand humanitarian aspirations to improve the lives of refugees.

Save the Children. The name alone conjured up images of goodness and virtue to me back then. Or at least it conjured up images of Sally Struthers and others who spent much of the eighties and nineties trying to convince me in between my favorite television shows that for the price of a cup of coffee a day, I could save a child's life. I fell for it. But at the end of my time working in this camp, my virtuous dreams were dashed by the reality of the situation: I obviously hadn't saved a single kid. Not one. Not even close. In fact, I left this camp back in 2002 wondering if my presence here had actually done more harm than good.

At that time, I thought I would never see this dirt airstrip again. I vowed to myself after leaving the camp that instead of being an aid worker I would try to transform the aid regime and all of its obvious failures. However, uncovering this calling hadn't merely been a result of a summer full of vague challenges and disappointments. It was the result of a single moment; a single comment, in fact, spoken by a refugee boy when I was in this camp. In that instant, standing in front of a classroom of secondary school students, I faced what some would call a "moment of obligation" and my life would never be the same.

◆　◆　◆

The day had started out like any other as I was making my rounds, conducting interviews with groups of orphans, students, and refugee leaders for a report funded by the U.S. Agency for International Development (USAID). I was working alongside a Swiss consultant who had been hired by Save the Children to write the report. Having never worked with children or refugees before, it seemed her only apparent qualification for the job was being the girlfriend of the United Nations's chief protection officer in Nairobi. As a result, I ended up having to take on much more responsibility than I expected as an intern, leading the majority of the interviews myself. It was a difficult assignment. We had been sent to Dadaab to investigate the issue of child protection in response to a West African report that uncovered numerous allegations of aid workers demanding sex from children in exchange for food and other assistance. We were tasked with making sure the same thing wasn't happening in East Africa.

I believed strongly in the importance of the investigation, but I also sensed that it was just a report being done for the sake of reporting. By that time I was two months into my summer internship with Save the Children, having spent a few weeks at the D.C. office and a few weeks helping to set up a new post in Nairobi. Disenchantment was starting to creep in. On top of all the waste I'd seen in the budget documents and the questionable decisions made in fancy offices far away, I'd also spent hours filing countless field reports that I'm pretty sure nobody had ever read. Even if Save the Children wanted to implement new protection programs as a result of our findings, I could already tell they would have ended up locked in a nasty turf war with CARE, another large-scale international aid organization that had established supreme reign over the camp at the time. However, I was delighted to finally be out of the office and on my first field assignment, so I dutifully blocked out my concerns and gave the research my best effort.

As I walked through the gate of Hagadera Secondary School that afternoon, already fatigued from five days of interviewing, I was accosted with walls of American patriotism. Lining every surface of the administrative building of the school were flattened cans of donated vegetable oil, prominently marked with "USA" in bold blue lettering, flanked by three red stripes on either side, and the USAID logo with the cautionary statement below: NOT TO BE SOLD OR EXCHANGED. Although impressed by the school's ability to recycle these materials into aluminum siding, I was embarrassed to see my country's name and symbols plastered all over the place. If I saw another building in the camp painted with the words A GIFT FROM THE AMERICAN PEOPLE I was going to go crazy.

The principal greeted me with a firm handshake and graciously welcomed us to the school. We did the necessary introductions and, in a way that indicated an excessive familiarity with meeting the endless demands of visiting aid workers, he forced a look of willing cooperation and said, "How can we help you with your research today, Miss Hogan?"

I felt guilty for wasting the students' and administrators' time. But our orders were to get as much feedback as possible, from as many stakeholders as we could find. By that point we had already heard horrifying accounts of abuse and neglect from orphans, confirmed the existence of child labor in the camp, and met young girls who were enduring forced marriages and female circumcision, but we hadn't found any evidence of sexual exploitation of children by aid workers. It might have been happening, but nobody was talking about it. On that afternoon, out of sheer curiosity, I decided to broaden the scope of the research to see if I might get new insights about the general challenges facing children in the camp. After a quick tour of the grounds, the principal escorted me to one of the dark, mud-brick classrooms to interview a group of fifty-three first-year high school students, while the Swiss consultant went to speak with a group of girls in the courtyard. The teacher stepped outside and the students put down their math assignments, listening quietly to my introduction.

"Good afternoon. My name is Tori and I come from the United States," I said cheerfully. A few students looked amused and a couple of whispers reverberated through the room. I suddenly realized that with just a few words I had already aligned myself with the wall of tin, and likely the dollar signs and expectations that accompanied it. I pressed on. "I'm here to conduct some research for Save the Children. We are interested in hearing about the problems you are facing in the camp. Is anyone willing to share some of their opinions about the challenges you're dealing with here?" It felt awkward to be posing such a vague question, but I had a glimmer of hope that it might produce insightful responses.

Silence.

After a few awkward stares from one student to the next, one boy finally stood up, dressed in a uniform of dark blue pants and a crisp white button-up shirt, and said, "Madame, there is a lack of basic needs such as shelter and food. The rations are not good, and there is the problem of malnutrition here in the camp." He then boldly added, "We would benefit from a feeding program here at the school sponsored by your organization."

Next a female student in a long white veil rose, speaking softly from the back of the room, "The rate of girls in the secondary schools here in the refugee camp is very low compared to primary schools because of family problems and social beliefs."

"And the teachers do not receive enough training," another voice added.

"Miss, we are grateful for your presence in our class today, and we would like to tell you that there are many problems faced by refugee children in the camp," another boy started with a concerned face.

I waited, hopeful that this boy might finally be the one to address the deeper issues at stake. But those hopes were dashed when he explained with surprising formality, "Our greatest challenges include a lack of learning materials like textbooks and incomplete laboratory supplies for practical experiments."

Their responses were predictable. I jotted them down and asked follow-up questions in an attempt to pull more details out of them. In a well-choreographed ballet, the students took turns politely standing up behind their wooden desks and addressing their various grievances to me. It was as if they were reading from a script, a riveting play titled *What to Tell the Aid Workers*. I'm not saying that the concerns they mentioned weren't real or highly legitimate, but I could sense they were only telling me what they thought I wanted to hear, or perhaps what my organization might be willing to fund.

I wrapped up the discussion with the students and thanked them for their feedback. I had already met with three principals, sixteen parents, and eighty-one students that day, but I didn't feel as if any of those conversations had tapped in to the core issues at stake, like why these problems existed in the first place, or why they hadn't been fixed. The principal met me outside the classroom and energetically informed me, "Miss, there is one more class, the year-two students, who you should visit." He motioned for me to follow, and I reluctantly trailed behind as I tried to think up an excuse, *any* excuse, to skip interviewing the next class and call it a day. I couldn't think of an exit strategy fast enough, though, so there I was, standing in front of another blackboard with forty-eight sets of curious eyes staring at me.

The conversation with the next class of students began the same way as the previous one, with predictable and rehearsed responses. During a moment of prolonged silence, I scanned the room with an almost desperate "cut the crap" look on my face, eager for someone to be brave enough to tell me the truth. A tall Somali boy sitting in the last row slowly rose, cleared his throat, and looked down for an instant with a slight degree of uncertainty, shifting his weight before staring directly into my eyes and boldly saying, "A lot of aid workers come and go, but nothing changes. If the aid projects were effective, we wouldn't still be living like this after all these years. Do you really think you have the answer to our problems?"

You recognize truth when you hear it. This boy was finally saying what I'd been longing to hear. Something that hadn't been rehearsed. Something real. He was calling me out in front of the entire class, and he was absolutely right. Who did I think I was? Who did we think we were? Even if I was willing to listen to their various grievances, I didn't have the magic answer to their problems. In fact, I was beginning to suspect that I was *part* of the problem.

That single comment opened up the floodgates of discussion, and the rest of the students suddenly found the courage to reveal the deeper realities of life in the camp and their impressions of the aid being offered. They told me about the false promises made when "white ladies" like me came around, the lack of power refugees have in decision-making in the camp, and the waste, corruption, and distrust they witnessed from the aid organizations on a daily basis. It turned out the issue of sexual exploitation of children by aid workers was only a surface example of a deeper web of problems in which the international aid agencies were failing to serve and protect the very people they were there to help. It was one of the most humbling conversations of my life.

Later that night, back at the UN compound, the boy's comment echoed in my head. As I lay in the stifling heat, tossing and turning and listening to a persistent mosquito outside my net, I kept trying to justify my work. "At least I'm doing *something*!" But it was impossible to convince myself that being part of something that was ineffective, or that was even potentially harmful, was better than doing nothing at all. I knew it wasn't. But up until now, nobody ever had the guts to inform me that my good intentions to help weren't actually good enough.

My naive dreams of "saving Africa" were shattered that day, forcing me to swallow a heavy dose of humility and realism. I had originally planned to pursue a career as a globe-trotting, world-saving aid worker, but after my summer with Save the Children and my subsequent study abroad semester in Uganda and Rwanda, I threw those plans away. I couldn't pretend I hadn't seen what I'd seen, or hadn't heard what that boy had told me. I felt a deep obligation to share the truth about aid with others and to uncover how the "helping industry" could be reformed. The past eight years have been an intense and rewarding journey as I've established myself as a filmmaker, educator, and advocate on the issue of aid effectiveness. At age twenty I never could have anticipated the path I would end up taking. All I knew back then was that a fire had been lit within me, and I had to respond. But when I recently reflected on my life's journey so far, I was overwhelmed by a deep sense of gratitude for that catalytic turning point that happened in Dadaab so many years ago.

So now I find myself back at this refugee camp, on the same airstrip once again, for a simple purpose: gratitude. I have returned here to find the boy who was courageous enough to tell me the truth. The one who changed the course of my life. I want to see what has happened to him and his community, and to say "thanks."

◆ ◆ ◆

As I arrive at the bottom of the wobbly plane stairs, I am confronted with the sea of drivers standing next to their bright white vehicles with large blue labels and logos painted on the hood and doors. "Ah, yes, the white Land Cruisers," I sigh under my breath. They have become a supreme symbol of aid. In fact, if there are any groups that have truly benefited from international aid in the past few decades, I think chief among them must be Toyota. The Land Cruiser and development projects seem to be inseparable bedmates. It's almost as if a project just isn't credible unless there is a fleet of Land Cruisers involved, whether they are needed or not. And the unwritten code (and in some cases, the *explicitly* written code) is that the decals of the organization's name and logo should be displayed as large as humanly possible on the vehicles.

I am shuffled between a few drivers before finally finding a UN vehicle that is heading to the United Nations High Commissioner for Refugees (UNHCR) compound. I hoist my backpack onto my lap, straddling the middle seat between a photographer and a fuel efficiency expert. The drive from the airstrip to the UN compound takes only a few minutes, but it's long enough to become immersed in the crazy world you're getting yourself into. The smell of dependency wafts in the air.

The only required swerving en route is for goats and other Land Cruisers, both of which are plentiful here.

We approach the heavily protected UN compound with its multiple checkpoints and rows of barbed wire. A sign outside the gate prominently displays the names of some of the organizations that now maintain residence inside the compound. Instead of the mere four that operated here in 2002, there are now over twenty organizations working in the camp. It seems the "donor fatigue" I witnessed back then has ended and Dadaab has become sexy once again.

"The compound will probably look different than you remember it," the young fuel efficiency expert leans over to tell me as we pull in through the final set of gates. "It just keeps expanding." At first glance, the compound doesn't appear to have changed much. The lines of brand-new UN vehicles still wait expectantly under the makeshift carports, the dusty courtyard surrounded by air-conditioned offices has only had a face-lift with new paint, and the logistics guys still lazily recline on the benches outside their office, radios in hand, waiting for something interesting to do.

I eventually find the camp manager's office, where I'm told I can get the key to my guest room. I'm greeted by a gorgeous, young Spanish guy with deep brown eyes, a scruffy beard, and lightly gelled hair, wearing a gray T-shirt and jeans. He looks like the Calvin Klein model of the humanitarian world.

"Hi, I'm Tori," I tell him, smiling and offering my hand.

"Hi, Armando." He shakes my hand and welcomes me to the compound, shooting a cute smile my way. But he looks puzzled, tilting his head trying to figure out who I am and why I'm here.

"Tori, Tori, hmm . . ." He strides over to his computer and checks the lists. "And you're representing which organization exactly?"

"None," I say. "I'm a, eh, journalist." That isn't exactly true. In fact, I've never been a journalist. But labeling myself as such was the only possible way I could have access to the camp again. It turned out the category of "Just Want to Say Thanks to a Kid" wasn't an option on the application form.

"Oh right. Ghost Writer!" He can sense I'm not following. "That's what we've been calling you around here," he explains. "We knew that a journalist was coming today, but the people at headquarters didn't tell us your name or any information, so we gave you a nickname instead."

He hands me the key to my room and begins to brief me on the policies and procedures of the compound and the camp. An armed escort convoy leaves the compound for the three camps every morning at 8:00 and 9:45. As a visitor, I will have to pay for my food and accommodations while here. The bar is located at the back of the compound in the event that I need a cold beer at any point. He then leans back against his desk and scans me from top to bottom before saying, "Walking around the camp is at your own risk. But you are uh"—he motions toward his face and raises his eyebrows—"a juicy target."

"I'll take that as a compliment." I laugh, amused by his concern.

"A young, blond American woman would be a perfect grab for any extremist operating here. I don't recommend you going anywhere without the UN vehicles."

"Yeah, the blond hair is never helpful," I say, my mind flashing back to challenging encounters in places like India and Morocco where my blond hair not only made me a walking freak show but a target for harassment. "Thanks for the warning." We shake hands again and I leave the comfort of his ice-cold air-conditioned office, back into the blistering desert sun.

I look down at the map of the camp that Mr. Calvin Klein

gave me, but the glare of the sun on the white paper temporarily blinds me. When my eyes adjust to the light, I am able to see what the fuel efficiency guy was talking about: The compound really *has* expanded. Now, instead of a manageable cluster of simple buildings, the map reveals 148 little rectangles, each representing a different room or building in the compound. There are new offices, countless new residences for field workers, and even a large new gym and tennis court. The UN's effectiveness in assisting the refugees is still up for debate, but you can't deny they certainly know how to build things.

Before I start my extensive tour around UN Land, I head to my guest room to drop off my backpack. It's a simple concrete room with a bed, a desk, an armoire, and a family of feisty cockroaches. The place smells strongly of cleaning fluid, though I prefer that smell to the multitude of other smells I could be faced with in here. A nap would be lovely right about now, but the excitement of being here again after all these years forces me back into the oppressive heat to explore my new neighborhood.

I decide to head first to the back of the compound to the infamous Pumzika Club. The large, open-air thatched structure is the holy grail of the compound for most of the aid workers. With about fifty plastic chairs, eleven tables, and twelve mismatched bar stools, it dwarfs the CARE compound's bar and, with its colorful disco ball hanging from the rafters, it even gives the old Borehole bar nearby a run for its money. It's the place where you can savor a cold Tusker beer, hit on the newly arrived consultant who is only here for a few days, and sit around with colleagues either complaining about what happened in the field that day or drinking enough to forget.

I continue down the sandy walkways, which now have fancy painted street signs to guide your way around the large compound and rows of cute white stones lining the path for aesthetics. After passing by the tennis court, the impressive gym, and the nice private residences where the aid workers live, I come across a room that was a sore spot for me my last time here: the television lounge. And, worse yet, confronting me here on the first floor of the thatched two-story rotunda is the culprit itself: the forty-nine-inch LG Digital Flatron with Dolby surround sound.

The story of my distaste for this particular electrical appliance dates back to the summer of 2002, when the aid workers living here at the compound insisted it was inhumane to expect them to watch the FIFA World Cup on the existing large television set. It was decided the only way to correct this hardship was to order the largest, most state-of-the-art television from Nairobi for the rumored price of $4,000. The decision made me furious because at that time our refugee neighbors had just had their rations cut significantly due to lack of donor funding. The decision to buy the big-screen television seemed unnecessary and extravagant, and it served as a reminder to me of the habits of waste and escapism that seemed to plague the aid world.

Now the bane of my existence from my last visit is staring me in the face once again, a 175-pound paperweight. The television probably hasn't been able to be turned on for a while. The electronic components are likely filled with desert sand. But I guess nobody is sure what to do with such a large piece of trash here. Worry not, though, because upstairs in the newly appointed lounge this behemoth has been replaced with a brand-new big-screen plasma television. The shiny black model stands proudly in front of the eight black leather couches that form rows of semicircles around this beacon of the compound, which lovingly plays Kenyan and Filipino soap operas all day long.

"Do you want to join?" A Kenyan aid worker motions me to sit on one of the black couches to watch a show. I shrug an indifferent "okay" and feel guilty as I slide onto the soft leather and think about the luxury of life within these heavily guarded walls compared to the lives of the refugees nearby.

CHAPTER 2

A SLIVER OF light is already peeking through the dusty curtains as my feet hit the concrete floor. I sit on the edge of the bed blindly shuffling underneath it in search of my black flip-flops, hoping that the spiders and cockroaches haven't taken up residence under there. Still in a haze, I look around the room and it takes me a second to remember where I am. I know I should keep sleeping so I can be well rested for my search today in the camp, but my mind is restless, consumed with the sinking feeling that despite the euphoria of my quest for this refugee boy, my world might be crashing down around me. Slumping forward while clumsily pushing away the mosquito net, I place my head in my hands and exhale in pure exasperation. In a whisper directed to the world-at-large, I sigh. "Why does this have to be so hard?"

It's too early in the day to start up the tears again. I'm still physically exhausted from the emotional release I had yesterday evening while getting ready for bed. I usually pride myself on being really strong, but lately I've become a mess of fragile emotions thanks to the one thing I always hoped wouldn't be able to make me come so unglued: *some guy.*

But, in reality, this isn't exactly just *some guy*. It's *my* guy, or at least he was my guy. The precarious on-again, off-again relationship of a year and a half with my Dutch boyfriend, Mark, is hanging delicately in the balance at the moment, and it could tip in either direction.

I take a swig of bottled water, along with my malaria pill, and walk outside to contemplate life from the comfort of a white plastic chair in front of my guest room. As I take a seat it strikes me as unfair that here, in the middle of the open desert, I am unable to see the sun coming up over the horizon. There are too many imposing buildings, water tanks, and fences here on the UN compound to be able to see this natural wonder.

I prop my feet up on a nearby post and allow my body to slump into the chair in a posture that matches my mood. The unfortunate exchange between Mark and me back in Nairobi plays over and over again in my mind as I stare blankly at the sky, mindlessly passing my water bottle from one hand to the other. It doesn't seem fair that love has to be so damn hard.

It wasn't always this way for me and Mark. In fact, our love story started out as a fairy tale, complete with the backdrop of an exotic destination, the bliss of a deeply soulful connection, and months of beautiful love letters written from all over the world. When I arrived at that cute little hacienda in Chilean wine country a year and a half ago, I had no idea my life was about to change. I was on a two-week stopover in Chile before I needed to get myself to Ushuaia, Argentina, where I would catch a boat to Antarctica, of all places. I had been hired to do some freelance photography for a polar expedition company, and I was glad to have a brief sojourn in a warm destination in between a Boston winter and an Antarctic "summer." So there I was, seemingly in the middle of nowhere, surrounded by end-less expanses of gorgeous vineyards, swimming in the pool and enjoying the pure ignorance that in one minute my whole world was going to be turned upside down.

Suddenly, there he was, the future love of my life, swimming in the same pool. In fact, he swam right into me by accident, which is how our first conversation began with the words, "Oh sorry." This tall, redheaded, adorable Dutchman was intriguing from the start. We ran through the usual "tell me who you are, where you've been, and where you're going" dialogue that becomes a staple conversation when you're backpacking. He explained that he was on a six-month trip around the world, and he had just made his way through Patagonia.

I had no logical explanation for it, but within two minutes of hearing him speak, my heart was racing out of control. He was only talking about typical things like his remaining travel plans and his previous work as a sustainable investor, but something in me was physically reacting to his presence. Soon I was no longer breathing properly, and I seemed to have trouble correctly formulating sentences. I was in trouble.

The next few days unfolded like a dream: bike rides through the vineyards, late night conversations under the stars where we revealed the deepest truths of our souls to each other, and long strolls in the town nearby with its tree-lined streets and romantic plazas. In fact, it was on one of those gorgeous Chilean tree-lined streets that this whole beautiful mess began. We had just finished a wonderful lunch, during which I revealed to him that I wasn't sure if I should extend my bus ticket to stay longer because, as I bluntly put it, "I think I might like you, and staying longer would only make it harder to say goodbye." As we walked down the street, approaching the town plaza, I gushed at the impeccable scenery before us. "This is *so* wonderful," I sighed.

He stopped walking all of a sudden, pulled me toward him,

and leaned in. "No, *you* are so wonderful." My green eyes met his big brown eyes and the world seemed to melt away as he kissed me for the first time.

I extended my bus ticket immediately. The days that followed were the most blissful of my entire life. I was falling in love.

I'm a total romantic, so I secretly hoped that when I finally met the man of my dreams it would play out like a classic romance film: me as Audrey Hepburn, him as Humphrey Bogart. But this was better than I imagined. I had found a guy who I was beginning to think might not even exist on this planet. A guy who kissed me so tenderly, made me laugh all the time, was eager to explore the world by my side, and could make me melt by looking at me with eyes of total adoration. Not to mention he was also smart and sensitive and totally cute. When it was finally time to part ways, we were faced with a challenging question: How do we maintain this level of intensity over distance and time? Our burgeoning love seemed too special for modern predictability, so we decided instead of writing emails, we would write love letters. *Real* love letters. The kind with a pen, paper, airmail sticker, and stamp. And that's what we did. For four months, as he finished up his travels around the world, I would post letters to his next destination several times per week and he would send his profoundly romantic testimonies of love to my Boston apartment. (We would occasionally cheat and opt for Skype calls and G-chat, but it was the letters we cherished most.)

We reunited in June, and Amsterdam's Schiphol Airport instantly became one of my favorite places on earth, because it was there that I was finally able to run into the arms of the man I loved. Our summer together passed by beautifully with lazy days strolling along Amsterdam's charming canals, a long road trip through Ireland, and several weeks of touring through mainland

Europe in Mark's camper van. I should stop for a moment here and inform you that if you ever need to put your relationship to the test, try going on a camper van trip through Europe together. Living in such close quarters is bound to bring up all the painful intricacies of your relationship and, if you can survive it, I'm pretty sure you're meant to last. We, unfortunately, didn't survive it as perfectly as I had hoped. But even if I could ignore the camper van–induced challenges we faced, there was something deeper that was triggering some worries or doubt about our long-term potential.

If I had to be honest with myself, the arrival of some challenges in our relationship could have been predicted from day one. I knowingly fell for a guy who brought with him more baggage than most. When Mark was twenty-five years old, he fell deeply for a Dutch woman named Sofie. But his euphoria soon got a reality check when three months into their newly budding relationship she was diagnosed with a serious blood disease. It wasn't clear what the path might look like, but the prognosis was bleak. Yet when faced with this difficult situation at the prime of his life, Mark cast aside any shred of selfishness and promised Sofie from the bottom of his heart, "I'm there 'til the end." The next eight years were filled with many long hospital stays, debilitating treatments, and a deeply soulful bond between the two of them that somehow kept them smiling through all the pain. She finally lost her battle with the disease in 2007, with Mark by her side. I met him one year later, which we soon discovered was far too soon for either of us.

The love between Mark and I was profound, but I also knew he still had a significant amount of grieving to do, and my presence wasn't helping. We were starting to get signs that the closer I was getting to his heart, the more he was unconsciously pushing me away. He hadn't sufficiently dealt with his past to be able to open up fully again to ultimate love. The lyrics of a Ben Harper song kept playing over in my head: "They say if you love somebody, then you have got to set them free." It was the hardest decision of my life, but setting Mark free to tackle his grief head-on was the most loving thing I could do for him. The tears were flowing as we hugged each other goodbye on a street corner in Berlin last fall, terminating our ten-month relationship. And as I turned to head down the street, I had a sinking feeling that I might be walking away from the only man I'd ever love.

I distracted my heart for a few months with work and travels, and in many ways it felt like I was moving on. But a nagging uncertainty about our decision just wouldn't go away. When I couldn't stand the silence any longer, I gave Mark a call to see how he was doing. It was immediately clear that the uncertainty was mutual. We soon reunited and spent one of the most blissful weekends of our lives together, prompting us to decide to get back together and give it another try. I told him about my plans to return to East Africa in search of the refugee kid who changed my life. And, much to my surprise, Mark informed me that he'd recently accepted a new job in agricultural finance, and he would be in East Africa for the summer, as well. I took it as a sign that fate was bringing us back together.

◆　◆　◆

Ever since Mark and I got to Nairobi ten days ago we've fluctuated between total serenity and needless arguing. The unfortunate big fight that ensued the night before I left for the camp was at the far end of needless arguing. He was in a pissy mood after a hard day at work, and my attempts to cheer him up were apparently the opposite of what he needed. The disagreement escalated and his rather unkind words and aggressive tone left me in tears. I found myself on familiar terrain: Had I made the wrong decision in getting back together with him? I kind of want to blame him for it all, but I am self-aware enough to know that I need to spend some time considering my own culpability here.

Wallowing in my current romantic melodrama is probably not the best use of my time on such an important day. I've come so far to find this boy. I need to be in the right frame of mind for my search. Now the sun is almost ready to show itself over the nearby buildings, but sunrise from a tin roof doesn't have as much appeal to me compared to seeing it crest over the horizon. I take another swig of water and go inside to get ready for breakfast.

◆ ◆ ◆

I start picking at my simple breakfast of toast and hard-boiled eggs, while watching a trickle of aid workers file into the mess hall rubbing sleep from their eyes. It looks like it might take a few cups of coffee before some of them are ready for whatever's on their agenda today. Fortunately, I've always been a morning person, and I'm grateful to be feeling functional at this time of day.

I look up from my eggs and a tall, brown-haired man in khaki pants and a blue button-up safari shirt is approaching. "Mind if I join you?" he says in a kindly British accent.

"Of course, feel free," I say, motioning to the chair across from me.

"Hi, I'm Tori," I say, offering my hand.

"Pleasure. I'm Richard. Did you just arrive?"

"Yes, I came on the charter flight from Nairobi yesterday. The last time I was here was eight years ago when I was working for Save the Children," I say as I peel my egg.

"Eight years, huh? Well, you might be surprised to find that a lot has stayed the same. There are more refugees here, though. About 260,000 now, which is almost double what it was the last time you were here. That's a noticeable difference. And it's a problem we're trying to deal with every day because the existing space has been exhausted. This camp was only built to accommodate 90,000 refugees but the problems in Somalia continue." I give a sympathetic nod as he continues, "We're desperate for more land, and we are currently negotiating with the Kenyan government. There is some concern from them that if we add a fourth camp it could attract more refugees. But as I see it, if we had more space we would be able to organize everyone better."

He takes a sip of coffee, nods good morning to an aid worker who just sat down nearby, and continues, "We've tried everything. We even had Angelina Jolie here last September. But unfortunately, the 'Angelina factor' didn't help our efforts. We hoped her presence in Dadaab would allow us to bring attention to the land issue, but it didn't really work."

I stay silent, holding back my own cynical beliefs about the so-called Angelina factor.

"It seems celebrities often have more impact in donor countries than in the countries they're trying to help," he adds. "In Kenya using more formal and official channels can be more effective."

As the conversation progresses, I soon discover that I'm sitting with the UN director for the entire refugee camp. But this fiftysomething British man who has spent the past two decades working for UNHCR in both the field and at headquarters certainly doesn't strike me as director material at first glance. He's too nice. I later discover that it's rare to ever see Richard not smiling. He has a positivity that seems unreal in light of his demanding job.

"So, are you coming to Quiz Night this evening?" he asks with raised, hopeful eyebrows.

"Quiz Night?" I reply.

"It will be in the Pumzika Club after dinner. It's just a chance for us to relax and have fun while testing our trivia knowledge. It's usually a fairly good time."

"Sure, it sounds like fun," I say.

"You know, the UN considers Dadaab a 'hardship post,' but when you're in the compound, it rarely feels that way," he says, wiping the crumbs from his toast back onto his plate.

"Yeah, it sounds like the only thing you're missing here is a swimming pool," I joke.

He laughs. "Yeah, we often daydream on those really hot days about how great it would be to have a pool on the compound. But can you imagine the backlash we'd get as soon as the first journalists got photos of something like that?" He stands up to take his plate to the dish area, turning briefly with a big grin. "Nice to talk with you, Tori. I'll see you at Quiz Night."

◆　◆　◆

I put my empty dishes away and start heading toward the front of the compound where the convoy of Land Cruisers will depart for the camp. I'm still too early, so I walk slowly down the sandy path, lost in thought. It bothers me that Richard has indicated so little has changed in the camp over the years, but it matches the feedback I received yesterday afternoon from the senior operations officer, a bright and compassionate man from Malawi named Bornwell Kantande. By total chance, Bornwell was the first person I'd interviewed in 2002, and back then he told me the problems in the camp included a lack of teachers, low educational standards, poor health facilities, inadequate rations, problems with water access, and cases of rape when the women would go into the bush to collect firewood. When I asked him yesterday how things had changed since we last sat across from each other, he bluntly informed me, "It's worse."

Bornwell revealed that some of the hospitals and schools are now collapsing due to age and lack of upkeep, the influx of new refugees has led to an incredible strain on the camp's resources, the quality of education has gone down with only 15 percent of the current teachers having been trained, rape cases persist, and now camp managers are dealing with a new set of challenges including solid waste management issues and seasonal flooding. It sounds bleak.

It doesn't surprise me to hear this, unfortunately. Dadaab has always been treated as an emergency situation, and as a result, the camp administrators are only able to submit budget requests year-to-year. But this "emergency" has been going on for eighteen years now, with no end in sight. An entire generation of refugee children has grown up here, knowing nothing but this camp. Yet even in this protracted situation, camp officials are not given the opportunity to strategically plan for the possibility of having to carry out this mission a decade from now. It sometimes feels as if the United Nations hopes that if they don't plan ahead too far, maybe the refugees will go home tomorrow.

I hear the Land Cruisers starting up as I approach the loading area for the eight o'clock armed convoy to the camp. The first step is to find the correct vehicle because, although Dadaab is the name used to refer to this refugee camp, it's technically only the name of the nearby Kenyan village. The "camp" itself, which is situated in the semiarid Kenyan desert about sixty miles from the Somali border, is actually composed of three separate large camps: Hagadera, Ifo, and Dagahaley, each with their own systems, leadership, and structures. The camps are located within an eleven-mile radius of the UN compound, with Ifo being the farthest, requiring a forty-minute ride. Today I'm heading to Hagadera camp, the site of my fateful encounter eight years ago.

Usually when people imagine a refugee camp, they conjure up visions of endless rows of white tents and fragile people standing in line for a bowl of food. But Dadaab hasn't been like that since the very early days. The camp has turned into three desert towns of sorts, each one complete with semipermanent houses, open air markets, small stores, a police station, schools, and a hospital. However, in contrast to their Kenyan neighbors, the refugees are officially not allowed to work—other than helping out the Non-Governmental Organizations (NGOs)— movement outside the three camps is not allowed, and their basic needs are provided for by international aid organizations. The camp's population is made of up 95 percent Somalis, but in many ways it looks and feels like any Kenyan town. The UN is the coordinating body for all camp activities, although the actual aid work, like distributing rations or running the schools and hospitals, is carried out by contracted international NGOs who typically get their funding from large donors like the US Agency for International Development (USAID). It's a complicated and imperfect system that, as far as I can tell, hasn't changed much since I was last here.

I eventually locate the right vehicle and I jump in the back of the covered truck, which has padded benches on either side and capacity for eight of us. Two UN workers are already in there, and I take my place next to a protection officer reading a newspaper. My excitement is building.

As I sit here waiting for the rest of the truck to load, I have a flashback to my first day on the job back in 2002. The Swiss consultant I was assisting had explained to me as we sat in the truck, "When they start shooting at us, you need to get down like this, okay?" as she demonstrated the best way to protect myself from gunfire in a moving vehicle. *When* they start shooting? I hoped she meant *if.* It being my first day in the field, I would have preferred simply being told where the water cooler was instead of how to protect myself from a hostile attack. But her concerns weren't unfounded. There had been a lot of violence and security concerns around the compound and camp at the time, including some threats against aid workers. In fact, at one point during our stay some disgruntled locals set fire to the fence surrounding the UN compound while we were inside. Fortunately, no one got hurt.

I get the impression that security issues have lessened significantly here these days. As the truck approaches the convoy staging area, joining four other vehicles from the UN, World Food Program, CARE, and Handicap International, I discover the convoy is a lot less "armed" than I remember. Eight years ago, we had to closely follow a Kenyan police unit that posted vehicles in the front and back of our convoy, including one with six men standing in the truck on lookout with seriously big guns in hand. It always felt like an attack was imminent. But today, I only see one police vehicle with two guys in the cab of the truck, and one guy lazily sitting in the back. He likely has a weapon somewhere, but I can't see it. Though it doesn't really matter how well armed the convoy is because I honestly doubt that these police patrols would ever take a bullet for the aid workers. They're probably not paid enough for that.

We hit the road for the ten-minute ride to Hagadera camp, following a plume of white dust stirred up by the convoy, and my heart starts to beat faster as I prepare myself for what I hope will be a reunion with the boy I'm looking for. I start counting the camels we pass by to distract myself from my nervous excitement.

CHAPTER 3

It feels strange to be in the camp again, though technically I've only seen its perimeter so far. The convoy dropped me off at the very edge of Hagadera in front of the CARE compound, and I was immediately whisked inside behind the big metal gates. I fidget with anticipation as I sit on the concrete ledge outside of the education office, waiting for Osman to arrive. Eight years is a long time ago, now that I think about it, and certainly my memory won't be perfect when it comes to recognizing the students from 2002. Not to mention these aren't kids anymore, they're now men in their mid-twenties. But as a tall Somali man with prominent ears and serious eyes strides across the courtyard toward me, I can't help but think that his face looks vaguely familiar.

I have been connected to Osman through a student named Bashir, who was also a member of the 2002 class. Bashir has since returned to Somalia, where he works as an aid worker, but I have had intermittent email contact with him on two or three occasions in the past few years as he had been looking for advice on scholarship programs. When I told Bashir that I was returning to Dadaab to try to meet up with his old classmates, he gave me the number of his friend Osman. I called him yesterday, and Osman said he was happy to put together a meeting for me with some of the students from that original class, though I didn't explicitly tell him the motive for my return.

"Hello, are you Osman?" I ask, standing up as he approaches.

"Yes, Tori, hi," he says as he shakes my hand, his serious eyes melting with a broad smile.

"It's great to see you after all these years," I say enthusiastically as I start pondering whether or not Osman might, in fact, be the ex-student I'm here to find. "Do you remember me?"

"Of course we remember you," another man says as he approaches from behind and extends his hand. It does strike me as a little odd that they both claim to remember me so well, since our previous interaction was so short. Maybe they're just being nice. He introduces himself as Abdirahim, and my mind starts churning as I ask myself, *Could it be him I'm looking for?* The uncertainty of my search is starting to bug me. I have no idea who made the comment, I only vaguely recall where in the classroom he was sitting.

"I've arranged a place for you to meet with some other members of the class. We can walk there now," Osman says. As we approach the exit, the guard of the CARE compound pulls hard on the metal rod that locks the large red gate, allowing us to slip past the assumed protection of the fortressed courtyard into the real world of the camp.

There's a combined sense of freedom and stubborn defiance sweeping over me as we head down the road toward the market. I know I'm not supposed to be walking around in the camp. Armando already warned me of my status as a "juicy target" for the extremists that may or may not be operating here. But at this moment, I really don't care. My conversation with Osman and Abdirahim is flowing as we walk, and it's worth whatever risk I'm facing to be able to authentically reconnect with these guys. The people passing by and those sitting alongside the road selling goods are giving me looks of surprise. Despite the high concentration of aid workers in Dadaab, it's more likely to spot them behind a heavily barbed wire compound fence or passing by in a flashy air-conditioned Land Cruiser than walking by foot along the dusty roads.

"The UN staff told me I shouldn't walk around here. They say it's not safe for someone like me. What do you think?" I ask my escorts as we pass by a row of men waiting on donkey carts to pick up latrine parts from a German aid organization.

They both chuckle and Osman replies, "It's not a problem. They say that, but nothing ever happens."

"Besides, we are strong enough to protect you!" Abdirahim adds assuredly, flexing his arm.

I smile in response, feeling confident in the abilities of my personal security detail. It's disconcerting that there's such a lack of trust on the part of the aid workers toward the refugee community. With such a feeling of separateness here between the helpers and the aid recipients, however, it's not surprising that problems could arise. It's a chicken-and-egg scenario. When you treat people like criminals, it's not uncommon for them to eventually start fulfilling the role. Though, according to Osman, the security concerns might be more imagined than real. And whether or not it's a safe decision I'm making right now, I'd rather not be part of continuing the trend of suspicion and separation. At the moment, aside from a mildly heightened awareness due to the warnings I received, I feel safe.

Besides, no matter where I am in the world, I always prefer walking to any other form of transport. There's no better way to experience the sights, smells, and sounds of a place than for your feet to hit the pavement. Or, in this case, the sand. The hot desert sand is filtering in through my sandals with every step, and my attempts to fix the problem by adding a slight shake every time my foot raises is proving futile. I should just embrace this free exfoliation treatment, even if the sand, which is occasionally a mix of burnt trash and goat poop, might not be so hygienic.

◆　◆　◆

We arrive at a small one-room community library across a sandy road from the primary school. I conducted a few meetings in this library during my last visit, and the place still looks exactly the same. A few shelves of donated books and an aging map of the world greet us as we sit down at one of the large wooden tables. After a flurry of cell phone calls and some coordination in Somali, I'm thrilled to have six of the original forty-eight class members surrounding me at this table. There's Osman and Abdirahim, who brought me here, plus Mowlid, Farah, Ismail, and Abukar.

The last time I saw them they were adolescent boys, but now they are all grown up, each one sporting facial hair and more wisdom in their eyes. It turns out that, for a variety of reasons, they all started school at different ages, so they actually now range in age from twenty-four to twenty-nine.

"It's great to see you all here today," I start in. "My name is Tori and I visited your class in July of 2002. Do you remember when I came?"

"Yes, of course," Abukar says, as the rest nod confidently. "Your visit stood out. You were young like us, and you listened to what we were saying," he says. I'm touched. But then he adds, "Also, you were the only visitor who came to our class that year. Most of the aid workers and other foreigners went to visit the year-four students."

I had briefly contemplated building up to the gratitude part, but for some reason I feel like just putting it out there right off the bat. "The reason I came back here is because I wanted to say 'thank you.'"

A wave of smiles appears as the guys look around at each other, trying to figure out if the person next to them knows what I'm thanking them for.

I continue, "Your class changed my life. It was just a one-hour conversation, but my whole life was different after I met with you. So I came here to say 'thank you,' and this was the whole purpose of the trip, to sit here at this table and look you in the eyes and say 'thanks.'"

They seem to be moved, nodding with a sense of pride, eager for more details. I tell the story from where we left off eight years ago. I share with them the feelings I was grappling with the night after meeting them, the decision to dedicate myself to reforming the aid industry, and the series of twists and turns my life has taken since my stint with Save the Children.

"I was originally on a path to become one of those expats in the barbed wire compounds," I say, "but because of our conversation, I went a different direction and became an aid critic instead. Now through the films I've made and the educational programs I run, I'm trying to wake people up to the ways that aid often fails to be effective and how it can be better."

"This is wonderful to hear, Tori," Osman says with a big smile on his face.

There's a different energy in the room, an openness that I recognize from my first visit with them when the floodgates were unleashed and they willingly told me what they thought about the aid organizations. Starting off with my expression of gratitude might not have been the worst idea, after all. Though, the "thank you" isn't over yet. Because while I definitely wanted to thank the class at large, I more specifically am hoping to find the young man who made the specific life-changing comment. But I push aside the search for the time being and ask them to reflect on how their lives were back when we met and how they are now.

Mowlid, who is sitting to my left wearing a blue and white pinstriped shirt with the sleeves rolled up to his elbows, is the first to respond. "We have all been here since 1992, for almost nineteen years. Life was still really harsh back when we met you—both the economic and social life of the people was down beyond belief. It still is, really."

"And the aid agencies weren't that effective, so nothing ever improved," Osman adds.

Everyone nods. The conversation heats up as the men around the table start adding in their two cents about why the aid agencies are less than stellar.

"Do you get the impression that the aid agencies care?" I ask.

"No, it's not a matter of caring," Ismail replies. "To them it's only a matter of survival. Their only job is to keep us alive." He looks annoyed, then adds, "Because when they give you only fifteen kilograms of rations for a whole month for a large family, it's not enough. And when it comes to something like work, you might be working for the aid organizations the whole day, like twelve hours, and you're only paid an incentive salary of two hundred shillings per day, less than one hundred dollars per month. Even if you have a master's and you are a refugee, it's because of your status you won't be paid a real wage like the other people. A Kenyan with only a secondary school diploma will be paid something like a thousand U.S. dollars a month, and a refugee with a master's is paid like only a hundred dollars. When we ask them what is the difference, they tell us that because of our refugee status what they are giving us is an *incentive* to work, not a salary."

The topic strikes a chord with everyone around the table and ignites a heated discussion about the agencies' decision not to pay the refugees legitimate wages for their work. The administrators I was speaking to yesterday defended the idea by saying it wouldn't be right to give the refugees a real salary because they already have their basic needs taken care of, such as food, shelter, and water. The incentive pay is merely seen as "pocket money" in their minds.

But how can the UN officials defend that stance when they are living in free housing themselves, eating free food every day, and having access to unlimited free water and electricity? They have zero expenses while staying at the compound, and in many cases their families have UN-sponsored housing back in Nairobi or elsewhere. To top it all off, they also receive a special bonus payment for working in a "hardship" post, on top of their already high salaries. The policy of incentive pay to refugees sounds inappropriate and hypocritical.

"The way you're treated matters a lot," Abdirahim adds. "When it comes to delivering services, we provide the lion's share here in the camp, but when it comes to *trust*, it's something very less. They won't even trust you to take a pen from one place to another."

"What?" I blurt out in surprise.

He continues, "But what other choice do we have? Because at the end of the day, the UNHCR will tell you that you cannot go back to Somalia because if you go there your life will be in danger. And you cannot go around Kenya because between here and Garissa there's a checkpoint and the police will be on your neck, so you cannot move from here. And it seems as if we just move in a cage. We can only rotate in the three Dadaab camps, we cannot go outside. And yet when it comes to responsibility, we are all responsible—"

"Accountable," Abukar interjects.

"Accountable, yeah. Again, so when you think about this idea of incentive pay, it's degrading really. Somewhat demoralizing."

"Yeah, I agree with you, absolutely. It sounds awful," I concur.

"Yeah, like slaves," Ismail says, looking down for a moment as the weight of that word hangs in the air.

"So when you look at the life here, it's very stressy," Ismail eventually says, breaking the silence. "But when you compare it to the life back in Somalia, it's a situation of 'if you can't beat them, join them' because you don't have anywhere else to go. You just have to stay and bear the situation as it is," he says with dejection.

"Some of your classmates have decided to return to Somalia, though. Do you want to go back there?" I ask.

Ismail shakes his head. "Me? No. The life is even worse in Somalia. So it's better that you stay here, and earn your one hundred dollars." He looks around at his fellow classmates. "Compared to the life in Somalia, this place is okay. But when you look at the TV or read the magazines and the newspapers, when you compare your life with the life of the other people, you say, 'Ah! I am a human being. Am I supposed to be living like this?'"

We expand the conversation beyond the work issue and they divulge the other problems that are plaguing the camp: there are too few secondary schools to meet the demand, dropout rates are high, youth gangs roam the camp at night, and new arrivals aren't receiving shelter. They also mention the endless difficulties in the resettlement process with long waits, horrifying bureaucracy, and no feedback when cases are stalled. But they're quick to point out that for most of them, resettlement to another country like the United States or Canada will never happen. Only about 2 percent of Dadaab's refugees are selected through a lottery system each year for third-country resettlement. For most of the people living here, their only option is to wait in this hellish limbo, praying for peace in Somalia so they can one day go back home.

It feels like déjà vu, as I'm overwhelmed with the long lists of challenges they face. After a brief pause, Osman smiles at me and says, "It's really wonderful to have you back in Dadaab."

Mowlid jumps in. "It's not typical for people to come back. We are used to seeing people who come the first time, and they are very cooperative when they want to write their books, their research, but they never come back. That's the first and the last time you see them. Today for your coming back, and even for sharing with us the good things that you've done for improving aid, we really appreciate it."

Farah clears his throat and gestures with his hand for emphasis. "Okay, let me say on top of that, the whole world is full of challenges. Even those that are in America, Europe, Africa, wherever, we all have challenges. And it's good that you always face the challenges. Like now you are using your money, your time, whatever to help change the world. So let me say this: never give up. Just continue." He leans in to the table, pausing for effect. "Even if it doesn't change immediately, it can change sometime later, some twenty or thirty years to come because of whatever now you are doing. One day the world will change. And then we will meet somewhere, and even if you have not changed anything, at least you have tried. Not only you, but all of us, we have at least tried to change the world."

"Yeah, I hope we do," I say, impressed with his pep talk.

"And at this time, we have voted," Mowlid says confidently, "and we are now adding you to our group. We were forty-eight, but now we are forty-nine." A wave of consensus surrounds me.

"You are part of us," Osman says, "the Tsunami Class." He explains that their class gave themselves that nickname because as they were preparing for their graduation, the 2004 Indian Ocean tsunami occurred. They felt such deep sympathy and concern for the people of Indonesia and the other affected countries that they wanted to honor the tragedy by naming their graduating class after the event. I find it remarkable that a group of refugee students, who face their own challenges on a daily basis, had such strong empathy and concern for the plight of others around the world.

It's going to take a long time before my smile goes away. I'm touched to now be an honorary member of the Tsunami Class. But in the midst of my joy, I realize I had been so pulled into the conversation that I forgot about my search. As we get ready to leave the library, I decide to ask.

"You know, there was a comment that was made when I last visited, and I'm still trying to find out who it was that said it. Maybe it was one of you." I recite from memory what the boy said to me that day: "A lot of aid workers come and go, but nothing changes. If the aid projects were effective, we wouldn't still be living like this after all these years. Do you really think you have the answer to our problems?" I look from one man to the next, "Did any of you say that?"

They are speaking quickly to each other in Somali.

"Was it Bashir?" I propose.

"No, it wasn't Bashir," Farah says. More rapid mumbling. "I think it was Ahmed Abdulahi Abdi."

"Yeah, it was him," Mowlid confirms, nodding his head.

"Ahmed?" I echo. "Where was he sitting in the classroom?"

We reconstruct the classroom and determine that Ahmed was sitting in the back right corner, next to the only two girls in the class, right where I remember the comment coming from. It was definitely him.

"Great! So where can I find him? Is he around?" I ask.

They all look at each other and Ismail shakes his head. "No."

"He has been resettled," Farah says.

"To America," Ismail adds.

My heart sinks. I've come all this way to find him, and it turns out he is one of the very few refugees who got a golden ticket out of the camp. I naively assumed he'd still be here, or at least in nearby Somalia, where I was prepared to go if I needed to track him down there. I traveled all this way only to find out he was in my own backyard. This wasn't the outcome I had expected, but at least there's still a chance of finding him back at home.

◆ ◆ ◆

As I walk back from Quiz Night at the UN compound, my flashlight guides the way to the guesthouse as I alternate between looking up at the brilliant stars, then looking down for scorpions, then back up at the stars. These stars are breathtaking, even with the full moon overwhelming their brilliance.

I turn on the light in my room and grab my green journal from the table as I flop on the bed with my back against the cold concrete wall. Tapping the pen against my knee, I try to make sense of my confused emotions. There's an exhilarating joy pulsing through me as a result of the depth and openness of my encounter with the guys today, but also a crushing sense of defeat. I had such high expectations for being able to track down the boy who made the comment to me. I will definitely do my best to find Ahmed once I'm back in the United States, but I still have two more months left in East Africa, and I want to use them well. I stare up at the ceiling, letting out a long exhale as I think it through.

I could always just hang out with Mark for the summer, I guess. But something about that doesn't feel right given the way things have been going lately, not to mention how busy he'll be with work. Plus, I'm pretty sure that spending two months playing Suzy Homemaker at our apartment in Nairobi, anxiously waiting for my man to come home from work each night, doesn't suit me. I need a better plan.

Suddenly I hear Ahmed's words echoing in my head: "Do you really think you have the answer to our problems?" It dawns on me that in my eight years of being an aid critic, I've been predominantly focused on the *problems*, on all the things *not* working, and less focused on the *answers*. Maybe now is my chance to change that.

The ideas are flowing as I open my journal and start scrawling my brainstorm for how to spend the next two months. Within minutes it's clear: I'm going to embark on my own mini-quest for answers, in honor of Ahmed and his question. I'll follow the same path I took in 2002 when I spent seven months working and studying in East Africa: an overland journey across Kenya, Uganda, and Rwanda. I won't plan out the details too much. I'll let myself be guided by a general curiosity to uncover answers about how aid can be more effective. I put down my journal and pull my knees to my chest. "This feels right," I say softly, resting my chin on my knees.

I have six more days left here in the camp, and I intend to spend them as a curious observer, looking into the aid being offered here. Osman has already invited me to visit the secondary school where he teaches tomorrow, so I'll start there. Once I'm back in Nairobi, I'll somehow make my way west on a spontaneous see-where-the-world-takes-me journey. Hopefully this trip will give me answers to share with Ahmed, if I ever end up finding him.

◆　◆　◆

After getting ready for bed, I pick up my journal again and my thoughts shift from my new summer plans and the ongoing search for Ahmed to my feelings about Mark. I haven't been able to get him off my mind all day.

As I start to write, I realize that the ups and downs of our relationship have taught me one thing for sure: soul mate love can suck. There are days when the heart-wrenching emotion of being in a relationship this deep actually makes me yearn for a little mediocrity with some "average Joe." What they don't reveal to us in *Cosmo* magazine is that once you find that kind of deep, soulful love, you better be ready for your life to come unhinged. Because the dynamic of a soul mate, and this is probably a decent litmus test for whether or not you've found one, is that they reflect your own soul back like a perfect and occasionally painful mirror. Sometimes their presence enables you to radiate your soul more fully, while at other times it prompts an arduous journey of self-growth that you're pretty sure you didn't sign up for.

Dating Mark hasn't always been easy, but there's also no denying that our love is real. When you're deeply in love there's no guesswork involved: you just *know*. But what I'm also starting to realize is that just because someone is undeniably a soul mate, it doesn't necessarily mean you're a good fit when it comes to the practicalities of daily life. Mark and I have the soulful love part figured out. Deep down I want to believe that that's enough and that the details will work themselves out, but lately I'm not so sure. However, as painful as it is to go through this period of uncertainty and strain, I'm grateful to be experiencing the ups and downs of love because, before Mark, my heart wasn't always so open.

I had a wise mentor in college who told me that the majority of the world tends to live their lives on a plus-one/minus-one scale, playing it safe with little joys and little sorrows. But he encouraged me to think differently. He said, "Tori, if you really want to *live*, you need to be willing to live on a plus-ten/minus-ten scale. But for all the intense bliss you experience along the way, you better be ready for the intense sorrow as well." Living life to the extremes was a scary proposition at that time. Couldn't I simply opt for plus-five/minus-five? Wasn't that sufficient?

Because, if I had to be honest at that stage, minus ten scared the hell out of me. For years I avoided opening up my guarded heart because I was too afraid to be hurt by love. I promised I wouldn't let any guy break my heart, so I dated at a distance, never letting anyone get too close.

This all changed in December 2007 when my dad went in for what was seemingly a routine bypass surgery just before Christmas, and he didn't survive. In the days following his death, it literally felt as if my heart was torn in two. Both the physical and emotional feelings of my intense grief were unbelievable. But soon after the dust settled and the reality of the loss had sunk in, I had an epiphany. "So *this* is what minus ten feels like." A huge smile spontaneously took over my entire face as I realized an important thing: I had experienced the depth of human pain, and I still woke up the next day. I survived it. If anything, the intensity of the grief made me feel more alive than ever before: I felt ready for *plus* ten. In a strange way, the grief of losing my dad had expanded my heart, taken down my guard, and opened me up to experiencing true love. Thirteen months later, Mark came into my life.

I feel the bliss of plus-ten with Mark so often, but it's the increasing frequency of days spent on the opposite end of the scale that is making me worry.

CHAPTER 4

FLASHBACKS TO NINTH-GRADE geometry do not occur often in my life, but with my knees crammed under this wooden desk and an elaborate description of how to find the area of a rhombus going on in front of me, I feel like I'm right back in Mrs. Paladinetti's freshman class. The only difference this time around is that the teacher standing at the front of the classroom is from Somalia, the room is crammed with nearly fifty students, and a noisy goat outside is interrupting my concentration. But otherwise it's totally the same. It's a good thing that Osman is reminding me and this classroom full of bright-eyed secondary school students what the hell a rhombus is, because after some rather traumatic advanced calculus experiences, I have attempted to block out most math concepts from my memory.

Armed with only a tiny piece of chalk and a dusty board, Osman is patiently and clearly explaining how you divide a rhombus into two equal triangles to easily find the area. As I watch him drawing one diamond-like diagram after another and taking the students through a few sample problems, I am overcome with a sense of deep respect and pride for where his life has taken him. Osman hadn't intended to become a teacher, and he was never trained as one, either. But when the refugee leaders in the camp became frustrated by the fact that, despite the high demand, the UN was not making any move to add another secondary school in Hagadera camp, the community took it upon themselves to fundraise and build the school on their own. Soon after the Community Secondary School was finished, they asked Osman to be the vice principal and math teacher. So here I am now, in yet another classroom with him eight years later, only this time he's at the front of the room and I'm the one sitting in the cramped desk.

I look over to my neighbors here in the back row of the classroom. After a lifetime of being the overachieving goody-two-shoes student up front, I'm not used to being with the slackers in the back, but I'm enjoying it today. One of the boys near me is using a shabby math textbook that is being shared between three students. I'm amused to see he has taken the time to cover the book in newspaper, the same way our teachers used to make us cover ours in brown paper bags. But on second glance I notice the partial headline on the back cover reads, "shot dead in the night". That wouldn't have been my first choice of newspaper pages to use, but perhaps the other pages didn't have much good news on them, either.

"How do you find the area of a rhombus if you are only given the length of the diagonal?" Osman asks as he draws the figure on the board. He tells them to solve the problem in their notebooks and to let him know when they have the answer so he can come and check it. The students start working furiously.

"Yes, Teacher!" The first hand flies up.

"Yes!" The second.

There's obviously a competition between the students to see who can finish first. I remember those days. Osman strolls down the aisles and checks each student's answer as they finish. Most of them get a checkmark over their answer with a blue pen. For a few he has to tell them, "Try again."

The girl diagonal from me tends to get the answers before most of the boys, but her voice is so soft Osman doesn't notice immediately. Another girl shows him her answer and Osman patiently and sweetly corrects her attempt. His demeanor with the students is much different from what I'm used to seeing. He carries only a piece of chalk and a pen, no stick like many of the other teachers in the camp. The atmosphere in Osman's classroom is one of respect and exploration. He has a measurable interest in the students' success, and he seems to try hard to make the learning process enjoyable. The students are lucky to have him.

After some more explanations on the board and a few more rounds of sample problems, a bell rings outside to indicate the start of break time. The students lift up the wooden tops of their desks and place their tattered notebooks and pens inside before heading outside to briefly relax before science class.

◆　◆　◆

Osman and I cross the sandy courtyard and enter the administrative office of the school, which runs parallel to the classrooms. A lonely stool sits in one corner of the office and an old bookshelf occupies the opposite corner, sparsely filled with ancient workbooks that are still used for instruction. There's no other furniture in this concrete room. The emptiness is symbolic, in a way, as it reinforces the fact that this school is being conceived from big dreams but restricted community resources. Osman goes to a neighboring room to find another stool so we can both sit down. We begin filling each other in on the details of our lives, and I ask him to tell me how he ended up here in the first place.

"We used to live in Somalia as pastoralists, moving from

one area to another with our many cattle. We were very rich when it comes to cows!" he says with a beaming smile, which soon disappears. "But then my father was killed and all those animals were looted by gangs. Without the cattle, my mother had nothing."

He pauses, and I resist any urge to fill the silence with meaningless commentary. I can tell he is replaying the faint memories of his childhood in his mind as he pieces his past together. "There was so much brutality in Somalia back then. So many of the females were raped. The rebels all had guns and they could easily tie her up to a tree and use her forcibly without her will."

"Is that what happened in your community?" I ask, wary of the response.

"Yeah, that's what happened. In fact, many years later I found out one lady nearby was raped by twenty men. Twenty men! And once it was finally over, she could not even walk. Some people in this world are so hostile," he says as he looks down at the floor. "They don't care for your life, they just want to hurt or kill anybody. Sometimes they would even tie your legs together, and then drag you behind a vehicle until you died. Those were the sort of problems that were going on in Somalia."

"And what happened to your family?"

"After my father was killed, and the cows were looted, there was nothing left for us. We had no family nearby, so the neighbors helped as they could, but they were struggling, too, and we all lived in fear of attacks. Things were so dangerous at the time that we decided to flee. I was only five years old. We were part of the first group to escape Somalia in 1991 when the troubles started. Some of our neighbors helped us to flee, and they even took some of us children on their backs to the border because there was no vehicle, we had no transportation. That's how we came to the camp."

"How long did it take to get here?"

"It was about ten days on foot to the border. We were in a transitional camp for a short time, where we were given food and shelter, and then we were brought here to Hagadera."

Osman recounts the few memories he has from the early days in the camp. But the one that stands out the most to him is the sudden death of his mother due to an unknown illness only two years after their arrival. He was seven years old. His oldest sister, who was only sixteen at the time, became the head of the family, in charge of her four younger siblings.

"She became the mother of the family. She took all the responsibility for us," he explains. "She's the one who cared for us, who took us to school. When our school asked for us to bring our parents, we used to take her." He pauses and smiles. "She was a very good sister. She was always encouraging us to stay in school. She said even with the expenses of school, we can still survive. She used to give us hope."

"And now you're passing that hope on to your students?" I ask.

"Yeah, I am trying to share that hope with them," he says. "I was in their position not too long ago, and I try to be a role model. They need to see that it is possible to cope in difficult circumstances without giving up. Teaching here isn't an easy job. The school is struggling a lot since it is supported exclusively by the community. I even went four months without pay. I know I could get a better job, but the students like me, and I'm proud to be helping them learn." I'm impressed by his selfless dedication to teaching, especially when he's already explained that his dream job would be in business management.

Osman looks down at his cell phone to check the time and sees that break is over. He picks up the stool to take it back to the next room, but stops at the door and turns to ask, "Would you like to go ask the students a few questions? It might be informative to compare their answers to what we told you eight years ago."

"Sure, that would be great," I say, delighted at the suggestion. We meet up in the courtyard and cross over to one of the classrooms as we watch the last few stragglers file into class, just in time.

We start in a classroom of third-year students. Osman introduces me to the class and I present them with the open-ended offer to share any of their concerns with me. I look around the room and I can tell this class is shy. Finally, a boy named Hassan raises his hand.

"The challenge of secondary schools here in the camp is that we still have no practical lessons; we have no labs for chemistry or physics."

The issue of not having any practical materials for science experiments is a complaint that hasn't disappeared in the past eight years. It blows my mind that such a simple request still hasn't been granted by this point, but Richard explained to me at breakfast that lab supplies are rarely a priority for donors. He concedes that being exposed to practical experiments in the classroom is essential for the students to perform well on the Kenyan national exams. Yet, when it comes to educational spending, Richard confirmed my suspicions when he informed me that UNHCR is only expected to report the total percentage of children attending school to the donors, not the results achieved. For most donors, it's only about numbers enrolled.

The tendency for donors and relief agencies to only focus on easily quantifiable results such as the number of students, rations distributed, and shelters built, is a classic downfall of the aid system. Provision of assistance is often reduced to a single check box, and the issue at hand is rarely ever the *quality* of the services and materials being offered. So, as a result, these students are forced to learn from untrained teachers, they share out-of-date textbooks, purchase their own school supplies and uniforms, and are expected to learn complicated concepts without the benefit of any learning materials.

The cost of training a teacher here is a mere $50, according to Richard. He agrees with me that teacher training is important, but he says that nine hundred teachers being trained for $50 each would be prohibitively expensive for the donors: $45,000 for nine hundred well-trained teachers. In the United States $45,000 would only cover the tuition expenses for a standard two-year teaching degree for *one* person!

I write down the request for lab equipment as Hassan continues, "And the food rations are insufficient. We are only given three kilograms of flour that is supposed to last for fifteen days. How do they expect a human to survive on that?" His list continues and includes issues such as the number of patients who are too sick to get to the hospitals and the water shortage that is affecting several areas of the camp.

Another boy named Shafa stands up to mention the lack of employment opportunities. Only a few secondary school graduates will be lucky enough to be hired by any of the aid organizations; the rest have no opportunities for work. I can feel his frustration as he asks me, "What will my parents think if I've finished secondary school and I'm still sitting around the home with my father?"

"We're losing our morale," a soft-spoken girl in the front of the class stands up to inform me. "Why should we continue to study when there are so few opportunities for any of us to attend university?" I'm encouraged by the level of honesty that is coming out of this discussion. It reminds me of my original talk with the Tsunami Class. I'm grateful that Osman has encouraged his students to speak freely with me.

"Really, our only hope is resettlement with UNHCR," Shafa adds. "But that isn't possible for many of us. Only a small percentage of families are ever resettled to another country. So, while we wait, we need to busy ourselves. You escape any reason of staying home, which means going to school instead. But we are paying 2,900 shillings to attend school, so it becomes an expensive escape mechanism."

I look down at the list, feeling disheartened. "Okay, so no higher education or work opportunities, limited learning materials, insufficient rations, health issues, and water shortages," I say as I reread what I wrote. "But have you seen any changes here over the years?" I ask the students, searching for a little hope.

Hassan stands up and replies bluntly, "We all came here when we were young"—he gestures to his classmates—"and now we're old. That's the only change we've seen in the camp." His comment is funny at first, until you realize the truth behind it. Very little has changed. Few services and opportunities have improved. These students have endured a lifetime of a relatively stagnant existence.

Osman and I visit two more classrooms to get some feedback from the students. The complaints are mostly the same: expensive school fees, water and sanitation problems, lack of firewood, poor teacher training, poor health facilities, and lack of support from UNHCR and the NGOs.

As we prepare to leave the third classroom, a boy named Abdul Hassan stands up and says to me with a shrug, "Challenges are a part of life, but what we see in the camp is that perhaps some challenges cannot be solved." My heart drops. The inadequacy of the aid response over the past two decades has led the next generation to doubt possibility and progress. I refuse to believe these issues can't be solved. Perhaps that's just me and my middle-class American mentality of "you can do anything you set your mind to!" talking, but the issues they're mentioning are not impossible to tackle. Especially not if you have had eighteen years to work on them, plus millions of dollars in relief funding and an endless stream of organizations claiming they want to help. The aid organizations have failed these children. Or perhaps the global community has failed refugees in general. The whole policy of "warehousing" refugees in camps, forcing them to be dependent, and limiting their freedom to grow, work, and develop has had the effect of creating an entire generation of young people who shrug and say, "Maybe there's just no hope."

◆　◆　◆

Luckily, the members of the Tsunami Class in 2002 were full of hope, and they still are. Osman is no exception. As we stand outside the administrative building, leaning against the wall to take refuge from the hot afternoon sun, he turns to me and says, "One day we'll see our country at peace. What we're targeting is our future. That's why this school is so important to me and why I think university education is essential for Somali refugees. One day these students might be leading the country." He stares out into the courtyard and then looks back to me, flashing a bright smile as he says, "It's a long-term plan."

Since his opportunities for advancement are so limited here in the camp, he is setting his sights on resettlement. He tells me that he has recently been selected, along with his sister and her husband, as a candidate in the resettlement lottery. They still need to go through several rounds of interviews, background checks, and health inspections before the U.S. government will give the go-ahead, but he's hopeful the process will move quickly. "It's all fate. Some people wait for ten years, some two years, others leave within six months. Hopefully we can leave within this year, and I can join you in the United States."

"That would be great," I say.

"Yeah, it's good, but I'm also realistic about what to expect.

You know, when you are here, you think life in the USA is paradise. But my friends who have been resettled say that things are different. It's not easy like we all assume. When you go there it's true that you can earn money; it's true, but you need to work hard. That's what they're telling me. So the money is there, but you need to work for it very hard."

Though hard work is not new for Osman. He is already used to long days. He works from early in the morning here at the school, and then his day continues into the night as a private tutor for secondary school students who are in need of additional instruction.

I turn toward him, pushing my shoulder into the cool concrete wall. "Osman, when you look at your life, do you think it's difficult and hard, or do you see it differently?" I ask.

"Some people cannot resist stress," he replies. "But I am not stressful. I believe that when you encounter problems, you need to have the ambition to go ahead. I never lose hope." He shakes his head slowly and says again, "I never lose hope."

He puts his hands on the ledge of the window behind him. "I've been here for eighteen years. We are surviving, and we have the courage to keep surviving." He looks me in the eyes and pauses for a moment before continuing, "As a refugee it's good that you have hope inside here"—he points to his chest. "Without hope, it will kill you psychologically . . . I have hope."

CHAPTER 5

"Cocktail?" John points at me with a raised eyebrow as I walk in through the screened door to a birthday party that has just gotten underway at his residence here on the UN compound.

"He makes an excellent gin and tonic," the camp's logistics coordinator leans over to inform me, toasting his glass in my direction.

A fruity martini would probably be asking too much, I surmise. "Wonderful, a gin and tonic it is, then. Thanks, John." He scurries off to his small kitchen, looking delighted and confident in his role as official host for the evening.

I take a seat in John's living room, but my presence isn't yet noticed by the three new faces I see sitting on the couch, passionately engaged in a flurry of conversation. "Did you see the toilet he has? It's amazing," a woman from South America with long brown hair and hoop earrings exclaims to the others. "It flushes!"

"I know. And these couches are unbelievable. They're so much more comfortable than our lousy broken plastic chairs. And, seriously, look at that TV! I'm trying not to be jealous," a woman says as she points to the television set across the room while still stroking the soft fabric of the couch. "I could get used to this."

"Did you say a *real* toilet?" The man sitting across from me gets up to go check it out. But first, leaning across the coffee table as he rises, he sees me and offers his hand. "Hi, I'm Duncan."

"Hey, I'm Tori. Nice to meet you. You're the birthday boy, right?"

"Yeah, that's right. We've come for a weekend visit to this nearby utopia to celebrate my forty-fifth. This place is amazing compared to where we live." He rounds the corner to check out the bedroom and bathroom, letting out a few audible "wow"s, clearly impressed with what he sees.

It turns out they are from Doctors Without Borders (more commonly known internationally by the French translation, *Médecins Sans Frontières*, or just MSF). I discover that the MSF folks are the only aid workers here who actually live *in* the camp at a compound next to one of the hospitals where they provide medical services to the refugees. And, from their current reactions to John's place, I'm guessing their living conditions are austere.

The sweet-looking woman sitting next to me, who appears to be in her mid-thirties, shakes my hand and introduces herself as Jane, from England. She tucks a tuft of dark curly hair behind her ear and smiles. "I'm Duncan's wife and one of the MSF doctors here."

We begin to chat, and I resist the temptation to ask her what she thinks of the organization she's working for. I'm learning these days to keep my mouth shut more and more when the urge to add my critique emerges. But if I am asked to be purely honest about my impressions of MSF based on my previous experiences with the organization, I'd have to admit that I wasn't so amazed by them the last time I was here.

I vividly remember being taken around the MSF facilities in 2002 by a French doctor who seemed to be interested in little else than the bragging rights and prestige of being an MSF doc. The woman nonchalantly strode through the therapeutic feeding center for severely malnourished children casually gesturing right and left, dropping comments like, "That kid probably won't make it much longer." As I watched her work, there was zero eye contact with the nearby mothers, no sense of empathy or even tact. I can understand the need to harden yourself so you don't get overly affected emotionally, but she seemed to be taking that too far, treating her patients from an almost subhuman perspective.

Another issue that bothered me was that the foreign MSF staff I met then were not engaged in any form of training to build the capacity of the local refugee staff. In my opinion, it would be infinitely cheaper and more culturally appropriate to train Somali or Kenyan medical workers instead of continuing to import foreign doctors for years on end.

To make matters worse, I had heard from others that this French doctor would often dismiss the advice of local Somali staff who tried to advise her on cultural appropriateness, especially when dealing with sensitive medical cases. She was approaching her daily practice in the camp as if she were still in Paris, and that simply wasn't what the refugees needed. But what did I expect from her? She was only on a standard four- to six-month volunteer contract, she made zero effort to learn the Somali language, and, in her opinion, she was doing her part to valiantly save the world.

I am keeping my opinion to myself, though, because I get an entirely different vibe from this group, especially from Jane. She seems open and empathetic and so far she hasn't condescendingly referred to the refugees she works with as "these people." I recognize that my existing opinion of MSF was based on a limited set of interactions with only one team of volunteers. It's possible that that French doctor and her colleagues were a couple of bad eggs, tainting my perspective of the entire organization. Keeping an open mind is essential this time around.

◆ ◆ ◆

I decided early on that life is too short to put up with superficial conversations. So I developed strategies for encouraging people to open up about the deeper quandaries of life and living. It's not that I'm nosy and want to hear people's darkest secrets; it's more of a case that I am bored by small talk and I have an endless curiosity about what really makes people tick. So, it doesn't surprise me that within only a few minutes of conversing, Dr. Jane and I are already talking in hushed tones about one of my favorite subjects: love.

She reveals to me that she and Duncan met in Liverpool through mutual friends at the School of Tropical Medicine and were instantly amazed at how well aligned their dreams for life were. After years of searching, she suddenly found herself with this kindhearted man in his forties who had never been married, had a perfect sense of humor, and had a zest for life that matched her own. She tells me the nine-year age difference between them is actually a positive thing, which I'm glad to hear because Mark happens to be eight years older than me.

She goes on to explain that prior to meeting Duncan, she had gotten to the point where, after a string of failed relationships, she settled into the possibility of never finding anyone to spend her life with. She wasn't willing to lower her standards, but as she inched toward her mid-thirties she couldn't help but think that all the good guys might be taken. Then Duncan appeared in her life, and the rest is history. They've been married for just over a year now, and she glows every time she says his name.

I fill her in on the bullet points of my romantic saga with Mark. Like most women, she gushes over the fairy tale parts. But when I get to the more serious stuff, the "something's missing" and "we're having problems" part, she sighs and shakes her head. "Isn't it horrible that our hearts sometimes allow us to love people who totally aren't right for us?"

I nod slowly. But, wait, is she saying that Mark isn't right for me? How can she say so? What about all the good stuff I mentioned? Clearly I'm having a hard time even considering the possibility that he isn't the one for me.

She continues, "I spent nearly two years in a relationship with a man who, in my heart, I knew wasn't right for me."

"From the start, you sensed that?" I ask.

"Yes, pretty close to the beginning of the relationship I had twinges of doubt, but I became very good at ignoring those instincts," Jane admits.

"Why did you stick it out, then?"

"I made the classic mistake of seeing the fact that I loved him as a sign of our fit." She shrugs as she finishes off her last sip of wine. "It took a while before I realized that sometimes our hearts lead us astray."

I've heard this story countless times before. It seems tragic that so many women end up wasting precious years of their lives with men who aren't right for them. But I find myself making the same argument these days: why would I walk away from Mark when I obviously still love him? Perhaps this is what people mean when they say that love is necessary but not sufficient.

But isn't it a damn shame that as soon as you find a guy who's halfway decent you also find yourself fearing that you might never find someone better? I bet so many women settle for half-assed relationships because they think, *Maybe this is as good as it gets?* I don't want to fall into that trap. But if Mark's not the one, then the next person has some seriously big shoes to fill.

Jane looks over and interrupts my spiraling thoughts. "It does eventually work itself out," she says as she holds out her wineglass while John pours her another drink. "You might have to go through some hell to get where you want to be, but if you listen to your gut, you eventually find your answer." She glances over to Duncan with a bright smile.

Then her face turns more serious, and she looks me in the eyes and says, "But, Tori, if you have deep feelings of uncertainty about this Dutch guy, you need to listen to them. Hold out for the right person. I promise, he will eventually come."

I take another sip of my gin and tonic and try desperately to relax into the belief that it will all work itself out, one way or another.

◆ ◆ ◆

It's early Monday morning and the MSF hospital in Daga-haley camp is already abuzz with activity. Duncan and Jane encouraged me to come by to see the hospital, and I gladly accepted their gracious offer. I'm sitting on a wooden bench next to an elderly refugee woman in a red and black veil who is waiting to be seen. Two young girls are settling themselves in for a long wait on the ground nearby, setting out the food and water they brought to sustain them through the day. The buildings around us are a hodgepodge of designs, ranging from a food storage building that is made of tarp covered with a tin roof, a handful of old crumbling wooden buildings that were built in the early nineties, and a smattering of new concrete structures that are slowly being built, one at a time.

I spot Nicole, an energetic American woman from Phoenix who I met at the airport in Nairobi. She was returning from a week of rest and relaxation in Mombasa, and had briefly told me about her experiences with MSF and her role as the nursing and pharmaceutical supervisor.

As we approach each other she hugs me and says, "Tori, it's great to see you again! How is your search going?"

"Well, I managed to track down some members of the class I was looking for, but I haven't found the young man who made the comment yet. It turns out he was resettled," I say, still with a feeling of disappointment that my grand plan to find him was thwarted so soon.

"You'll find him," she says assuredly. A young Italian medical worker approaches us, waving a paper in the air. "Oh, you found the sheet. Yes!" Nicole exclaims, looking relieved.

"Yes," the woman replies in a thick Italian accent. "But I was on the phone with him and he says the Kenyan Ministry of Health cannot provide us with the vaccine, because—why?—just because he don't receive the data sheet. But I sent three times! Three times! The vaccine is there, but they don't provide MSF with it!"

"Just because of the paper?" I ask.

"Just because of the paper. And we have a lot of people, they wait for the vaccine," she replies.

Nicole mutters and sighs, "Oh my God." Then she tells the Italian woman, "*Respira, respira!* Breathe. At least we've got it now and we can send it again."

"Just another Monday, huh?" I say in a sympathetic and joking tone.

"Yeah, ugh, some Mondays I want to burn my eyes out," Nicole says with a quick laugh. "The bureaucracy in this country can be unnerving. MSF could have easily provided enough vaccines to vaccinate the camp five times over with one phone call to Bordeaux," she sighs. "But because of national regulations we're blocked from using our own vaccines. We can only use vaccines provided by the Kenyan Ministry of Health, and so we're completely dependent on them for deliveries."

"How frustrating," I say.

Nicole nods with a resigned look on her face. Within seconds her smile reappears as she sweetly asks, "I'm free for a little while, would you like to have a tour of the place?"

"Yeah, sure, that would be great." We say goodbye to the Italian woman and head down the path toward the back of the hospital compound. We enter the surgery building and I follow Nicole's lead to take off my shoes. "We try to keep it as sterile as possible in here," she says as she steps over a small concrete ledge and pulls back the curtain that prevents the desert sand from blowing into the ward. There is a flurry of conversation with a Kenyan nurse, named Mary, regarding surgery schedules. The phone rings, another request, another problem. I'm impressed to watch the way Nicole transitions from one issue to the next, giving everyone her full attention and doing what she can to help find solutions. I've only been hanging out with her for a few minutes and I already feel exhausted by the onslaught of things she has to deal with.

"Oh, by the way, we are still waiting for that mother, because she declined again the caesarean section," Mary informs Nicole as we emerge from the bare, but functional operating room.

"But she's been in labor for forty-eight hours, he's *not* coming out that way," Nicole says with an exasperated voice.

"Yes, I know. But she is still having hope it will come," the nurse replies.

"Oh my gosssh . . ." Nicole's voice trails off and she scrunches up her face, putting her hand up to her forehead. She knows they can't force the woman to accept surgery, but the baby could die if they don't get it out soon. She explains to me that there have been a lot of rumors circulating around the camp about caesarean sections lately. Ever since MSF built the concrete walkway connecting the maternity ward to the surgery building, it has become assumed that if you go to the hospital to deliver, they *will* operate on you.

After a brief visit to the pharmacy, piled high with over 700 different kinds of drugs and medical supplies that are sourced both locally and abroad, we head to the other side of the camp to meet with Nicole's boyfriend, the hospital's logistics coordinator.

Lorenzo, a scruffy Spaniard with dark blond hair and a five o'clock shadow, approaches us as we're walking and asks Nicole for an impromptu meeting about the various tasks she needs him to do. The two have been dating for two field placements now, after having met in Cameroon and then requesting to be placed together in Dadaab. We sit down and Nicole pulls out a laundry list of "to dos" as she explains in a mix of Spanish and English that she needs a mobile light in the maternity ward, better electrical function for the blood centrifuge in the lab, spare uniforms for the maternity nurses, and mosquito nets in the adult ward. Listening to them speak is rather amusing because Nicole has managed to learn grammatically perfect Spanish with the thickest American accent possible. Though perhaps I sound the same when I attempt to speak Dutch with Mark. Maybe a sign of true love in bicultural relationships is not laughing too much when your partner tries to speak your language.

Lorenzo's phone rings and he's suddenly entrenched in a heated discussion with someone on the other end. It's about air conditioning, and he's pissed. "I don't think any of the vehicles except the ambulance need AC. It uses up too much fuel. It just doesn't make sense. It's not needed!" he insists.

Nicole leans over and whispers to me, "Only one of the

vehicles still has AC, but apparently they've been running it at full blast and he's ticked. He wants to cut the wires." She laughs, amused by his passion for the subject.

Wait, I have to pinch myself: an international aid worker is actually taking steps to *reduce* frivolous spending? I'm impressed. My thoughts about MSF are improving by the minute.

◆　◆　◆

"Now this little boy—we don't know how old, but to me he's at least eighteen months—is here with his grandmother because his mother has died," Jane explains to me as she stands next to one of the beds in the pediatrics ward, clipboard in hand and her brown hair pulled up in a loose bun. "And he's only ever had milk, he's never had proper food. And so he's anemic. His hemoglobin is 5.1, which is really bad."

She discusses the situation with the pediatric nurse, a Somali man named Abdul, and asks him to explain to the grandmother that the boy needs foods like liver, eggs, and dark green vegetables in order to heal. But then she turns to me and says quietly, "Never gonna happen."

These sorts of foods are not included in the standard rations, and the refugees don't have access to them unless they have found some way to earn income to buy meat and produce at the unofficial food market in the camp.

"We have a supplement we can give him that is high in iron, so we'll give him that," she says.

We move on to the next patient: a cute one-year-old Somali girl with big eyes and short curly hair who is suffering from severe diarrhea. The mother, who is sitting with the baby trying to comfort her, informs Abdul that she stopped breastfeeding as soon as she found out she was pregnant with another baby. Jane sees my confused expression and explains, "There is a common myth that if you are pregnant and you breastfeed, then the fetus poisons the milk and it gives the child diarrhea."

The mother also tells Abdul that she exclusively breastfed her firstborn child, but she believes the baby took all the nutrients from the fetus (the baby in front of us), and she doesn't want that to happen again.

Jane thinks for a moment, then replies with remarkable calm, "Tell her that mothers are magical and she will have enough milk for this one and also to nurture the fetus. Tell her that some women have twins or even triplets and they still manage to feed them all." Abdul does his best to kindly relay the message in Somali.

"So what does she give the child instead?" Jane asks.

"Tea," Abdul replies.

"Tea." Amazingly Jane jots this down without reacting, despite the fact that this woman has essentially only been giving her baby flavored water with a dash of milk for the past three months. "Okay, she's really going to have to stop giving the tea. Can she give formula or ultra-high-temperature boxed milk?" she asks Abdul. She turns to me again. "They tend to give camel or goat milk, but of course it's not boiled and there's all kinds of germs in it, so it's actually safer to give cow's milk or UHT, but they usually can't afford it."

Another nurse comes in and taps Jane on the shoulder. She's needed in the therapeutic feeding center for a baby whose condition is worsening. She excuses herself and asks Abdul to explain infant nutrition to the mother while she's gone.

As we enter the therapeutic feeding ward next door, we're greeted by the faint cries of several tiny babies and the desperate looks of parents sitting on beds who hope we're there to attend to their children. One father even motions me to come over to check on his baby, assuming I'm part of the white doctor contingent. There are thirteen malnourished babies here at the moment, most with IVs connected to their tiny hands. The baby we've been called in to check on is one of the tiniest infants I've ever seen. This three-week-old has been fighting for life since day one. His small chest protrudes as he takes short gasps of air, his wrinkled skin is dangling on his skeleton, and he has a clubfoot that gives his body a contorted and pained look. It breaks my heart to see the mother's sad, concerned face as she stands next to the bed watching her precious newborn struggling for life.

The nurse fills Jane in on the updated stats for the infant, and hands her the chart. "Oxygen saturation, seventy-eight percent?" Jane reads with a surprised tone. "Did somebody *really* write oxygen at seventy-eight and then do nothing about it?" She looks up for answers. The two nurses on hand feign a mumbled explanation, but Jane immediately jumps into solution mode and asks, "Is it possible to get the oxygen saturation machine now?"

I watch Jane's face melt from momentary exasperation to calm presence. She seems to have taken a deep breath and moved on from the nurse's mistake. You can't let things like this slow you down too much, or you'd never get anything done here. Nicole already informed me that while they do have issues like this arising from time to time, she is spending a lot of her time conducting training sessions for the nursing staff in hopes of raising the caliber of care and enabling them to run the show in the future without so much international assistance. And whether the nurses attend the daily trainings primarily because they're held in one of the only rooms on the hospital compound with an air-conditioner or because they're legitimately interested in what is being taught remains to be seen. But the trainings are happening, and they seem to be helpful.

The baby's lips are blue. "They've been like that since he was born," Jane informs me. She works with the mother to try to get the baby to suck either a bottle or the breast, but the infant is barely able to do so. The oxygen saturation machine arrives and Jane carefully tries to attach the sensor to the baby's little foot. "This foot is cold, so it's going to give you a low reading," Jane explains to the nurses. "But now it doesn't seem to give a reading at all." For several minutes she tries again and again to reposition the sensor in order to get a correct reading amid an endless string of beeps from the machine. Finally, a more positive-sounding beep. "Okay, ninety-two percent. It's low, but it's acceptable. It doesn't appear that the baby is in any kind of respiratory distress, but we need to keep a close eye on him."

Jane maintains a professional demeanor with the nurses, but as we walk away she confesses to me that she's not entirely sure what is causing this infant's condition. "The baby appears to have a congenital syndrome, but not a common one I can put a name on," she says. I can tell that she desperately wants to be able to perfectly diagnose every child she sees, and it seems like she doesn't cut herself enough slack when her own limitations enter the picture.

As a casual observer who's just hanging out at the hospital for a day, I know it's impossible for me to get a full sense of MSF's work, especially when it comes to patient outcomes or the efficacy of the medical team. I'm only able to base my opinions on what I'm seeing in front of me. But the impression I get so far is that this is a compassionate team of professionals who are providing first-rate medical care to the people of Dadaab. And, according to what Nicole told me earlier, MSF's track record in successfully treating patients is apparently strong.

We return to the pediatrics ward and Jane wraps up her assessment of the baby who has been drinking tea instead of breast milk. Jane looks like a pro as she leans over the bed and gently examines the baby's tender stomach. Despite the fact that she was never officially trained as a pediatrics specialist, her calm demeanor and her patience with the children makes her look like a natural. "She might have tuberculosis," Jane says quietly, as she wraps up her clinical notes. She prescribes an antibiotic for the intestinal infection that is causing the diarrhea and gives the nurse detailed instructions for the mother to keep an eye out for potential symptoms of TB.

The stagnant smells of the ward are starting to make me feel ill. It's a combination of body smells and strong cleaning solutions, made more intense by the extreme heat. I don't know how Jane is able to work so effectively in these conditions. It must take some time to get used to. Her pediatric rounds appear to me as a seamless dance, slowly moving from one sick child to the next, spending plenty of time calmly listening to the parents, examining each kid, digging deeper for alternative diagnoses, and never losing her positive attitude and bright smile. This woman was born for this job. She attends to the wound of a boy who has been bitten by a snake, deals with another little boy who has developed severe asthma, and talks with a family whose three-month-old baby has been having seizures. I'm trying not to idealize her, but this is exactly the kind of doctor I dreamed of being back in college, before I became possessed with a vision to reform the aid world and dropped my premed track entirely.

I probably made the right choice, though, because I doubt I could ever muster up Jane's level of patience.

◆　◆　◆

Before leaving the hospital in the afternoon, I swing by the crowded and chaotic outpatient clinic where Jane is seated next to a large wooden desk covered with an assortment of medical supplies and notes. I watch her as she uses a small light to look inside a six-year-old boy's mouth.

"What's his condition?" I ask.

"He's bleeding as a result of an unsuccessful uvulectomy," she informs me.

"A what?" I ask, not surprised that my few years of premed training never introduced me to this word.

"There is a belief in Somali culture that the uvula—the thing that hangs down in the back of your throat—irritates the throat and causes a persistent cough. So, when this boy's cough wouldn't subside, his family decided to simply take a razor and cut out his uvula." I look at her in disbelief.

"It used to be much more common, actually," Abdul adds. "Though it is practiced less these days. I had it done as a child, too."

"Oh yeah?" Jane says to him with a sweet smile as if he's just informed her that he used to own a puppy as a kid. She has zero judgment in her voice about the seemingly bizarre cultural practice of cutting out the uvula. She continues, "But unfortunately, this boy's wound didn't heal properly and now it's infected and bleeding heavily. We'll need to treat the infection and see what we can do about the bleeding in the meantime."

Jane is rising near the top of my Mother Teresa–ranking scale.

She finishes treating the boy and sweetly touches his face, smiling at him before turning to write a prescription. I can't help but ask, "Jane, you seem to possess the amazing ability to treat your patients with such grace and respect at every moment. But isn't this work so much harder than what you're used to at home?"

"Medicine is the same the world over—they're all human beings," she says, as she looks up at the next patient coming through the door.

CHAPTER 6

PERHAPS IF I close my eyes and inhale deeply I can be transported to the cornfields of Iowa. Nope, it just smells like hot desert air in here. But the "goodwill" of Iowa and its neighboring states surrounds me as I carefully walk along a narrow path through one of the massive World Food Program (WFP) storage tents. Bags of flour and cornmeal tower over me twenty feet in the air, awaiting their turn to be distributed. These sacks of food have come an incredibly long distance—for an incredibly high transport cost—to aid the refugees of Dadaab.

Samir, a Kenyan WFP supervisor, looks back at me as we walk past the cornmeal stacks. "We have 4,500 metric tons of food. That's the maximum amount we can fit in our nine tent warehouses at any time. It sounds like a lot, but that's only enough to feed Ifo camp for a few months, I think."

"Where does it all come from?" I ask.

"Mombasa Port."

"And before that?"

"More than ninety-five percent of the food comes from the United States. Sometimes we get vegetable oil from Indonesia, and maybe some other goods from elsewhere, but it's mostly from America," he says as he dusts off some flour from a USAID logo on one of the bags next to us.

"But what about getting local food supplies from the region to stimulate the East African economy?" I ask, perplexed by the inefficiency of a food aid system that hasn't changed for decades.

"No, it's extremely rare for us to purchase food locally," he says as he shakes his head.

As we exit the large tent, Samir leads me over to another warehouse tent nearby where he's supervising the unloading of a recently arrived truck full of imported flour. I watch as eight men take turns carefully crossing the makeshift bridge between the truck and the top of the stacks, carrying the heavy sacks of American flour on their backs. They look ghostly, their black skin covered with a thin layer of white flour and sweat. It looks like difficult work as they trudge back and forth under the weight of the sacks, but they are making it tolerable by singing lively songs as a group.

"What are they singing?" I ask Samir as we lean against the truck.

"Well, they caught sight of you, so now they are singing a song to me about you." He laughs. "The line they just sang translates to, 'She's your sister, don't give her to the hyenas.'" He laughs again.

I'm not entirely sure what the lyrics refer to, though I'm confident that Samir has no plans of throwing me to any hyenas. I wouldn't blame him for considering it, though. The next song they sing is a call-and-respond number, led by one of the workers. I can't imagine hauling those heavy sacks, but it seems the singing helps a lot.

"Thanks for showing me around, Samir," I say with appreciation.

"Sure, no problem," he says with a smile as he returns to his supervising duties.

I walk away from the storage tents toward the distribution center. I'm glad Osman encouraged me to come here today to see this for myself. Today is food distribution day for anyone who has a family size of one. That typically means teenage orphans, widows, single adults, and anyone who creatively cheats the system by registering separately from their large families so the food supply can be more consistent. Tomorrow will be families with two people, and anyone with large families won't collect food until next week. The food is meant to last for two weeks, but every refugee I've talked to says this never happens. The rations are too small and most families struggle to even make the donations last a week.

I pass by a man standing on a chair who is using an old rag to erase the whiteboard that displays the food distribution amounts. I watch as he changes this week's cornmeal rations from 3.31 kilograms to 3.15 kilograms. For people with a family size of one, the board now prominently displays the following reduced rations: wheat flour (3.15 kg), yellow maize (0 kg), cornmeal (3.15 kg), pulses (beans) (0.9 kg), oil (0.45 L), corn soya blend (0.675 kg), salt (0.075 kg), and soap (0 kg). No meat, no dairy, no vegetables, no fruit, and limited sources of any vitamins and minerals. I dare anyone to try this diet for eighteen years straight and see how they feel.

Unfortunately, the refugees have little choice when it comes to accepting these paltry rations, so once every two weeks a representative of each family must come to pick up the food that is bestowed upon them from the farmlands of America. It's no surprise that the refugees who are able to earn extra income through the informal and formal job sectors use that money to buy better food at the small outdoor food markets in the camp, which have products that are apparently sourced with the help of local Kenyan merchants. There they can find things like milk, vegetables, and cuts of goat, cow, and camel.

I take a right and walk down the outdoor corridor lined with barbed wire on either side that leads from what I call the "holding pen" to the distribution area. Of course the term "holding pen" sounds incredibly derogatory to describe the area where the refugees are corralled to wait in long lines in a cramped wood structure until it's their turn to collect their rations, but when you see the lack of dignity in the design of the process, the term fits. I approach the waiting area and there are suddenly hundreds of eyes on me. Six rows of men and two rows of women, separated by gender for cultural reasons. The people in front are seated on the dirt floor under the covered wooden structure, while the rest are standing behind, anxiously waiting for the line to move. This is only a fraction of the 10,000 refugees who will come through the food distribution site today.

There doesn't appear to be any sort of security detail here, but the WFP workers do what they can to maintain order. I'm amazed that there aren't more problems given the stress of having to wait in the heat for so long for your chance to collect rations.

"Straighten this line out!" one of the WFP guys yells loudly in Somali as he approaches one of the lines. "You know how you are supposed to line up." As he walks down the line, with a stick in hand, a wave of comments from the refugees, who appear to be mocking him, erupts.

"What are you two doing here? You know you're not supposed to be here!" The man has spotted two boys in one of the lines and he makes a scene, physically removing them from the waiting area. The boys are pleading their cases, but the man doesn't seem to be listening. Understandably, the boys are pissed. Whoever they're collecting rations for today is counting on them to bring the food home. I'm not entirely sure if they've decided to enforce the rules just because I'm around. However, I'm glad to see that kids aren't being allowed to collect the rations given the cases of exploitation that were seen elsewhere in the past. It's better if the kids aren't put in such a position.

The man returns to the front and says to me, "We don't want small kids here." I nod.

Suddenly I hear a sound so loud it makes me jump. *Bam!* It happens again. I look around to see where the noise is coming from, but before I have a chance to identify it, the WFP worker says to me, "Quickly, you need to get under there for protection!" He motions me toward the wooden structure.

I join everyone under the covered holding pen as the loud noises continue. It turns out the pissed-off boys are now throwing rocks at the WFP staffers from over the fence. Most of the rocks are landing on the tin roof, luckily, but a few get close to hitting people.

"Have you ever been hit?" I ask one of the WFP monitors after the rocks stop flying.

He shrugs. "Yeah, I've been hit before. This happens from time to time."

◆　◆　◆

"Victoria! Victoria!" I hear a young woman's voice say as I turn around to see who could be calling me by my real name. I only occasionally introduce myself as Victoria, usually after getting a confused look from the person I'm meeting as they try to repeat the word *Tori*, but I must have done it recently.

In a sea of colorful veils, I see a familiar face walking toward me along with thirty other women who are now being called to take their turn collecting rations. It's Fatima, a twenty-year-old girl I met a few days ago while spending time in the housing blocks of Ifo camp. She had been so welcoming during my visit to her "neighborhood" and had taken me to meet some newly arrived refugees who were working on building a mud and stick house for their family. It's easy to recognize her because today she's wearing the same peach-colored veil with a flowered patterned band underneath that she wore the other day.

"Fatima! Wow, I didn't expect to see you here. What a nice surprise," I say. "How long have you been waiting?"

"Since six o'clock," she says. I look down at my watch. It's nearly 9 AM. "I will need to go through the line three times today because I have to collect rations for my sister-in-law who is pregnant and another person who couldn't come today." She has three ration cards tied on a string around her wrist. The rules state that she can only do one at a time, since each of these people has technically registered as a family of one. It's going to be a long day for her.

"Do you mind if I join you?" I ask, curious to see what the collection process is like.

"No, not at all. Come with me!" She takes my hand and leads me through the mass of women who are making their way along the barbed wire corridor, now in a half-run, toward the distribution area. The process feels chaotic already as we approach one of the seven lines that lead into the collection buildings. We wait patiently for a while in one of the lines to have her ration number marked off, but when we get to the front we're told we're supposed to be in another line instead. Fatima gives the guy a "you've gotta be kidding me" look, but then turns to me and shrugs with an expression that seems to say, "This is the way it is here."

As we approach the next line over, a CARE official stops me, putting his hand up as he approaches. "Miss, you can't go in there."

"Why not?" I ask.

"Because visitors are not allowed through the collection. It's for security," he says.

"I am willing to risk my safety. I don't mind," I say stubbornly.

"Well, you just can't go through. Visitors don't go through," he insists.

"But I'm with her. It won't be a problem," I say, gesturing toward Fatima. He continues to shake his head no. But my determination persists.

"Rashid, can you come here for a moment?" I call out to one of the UNHCR workers I befriended back at the compound. "He's saying that I'm not allowed into the collection area because I'm a visitor. I have already said I will accept the risks."

Rashid turns to the CARE worker. "It shouldn't be a problem. She has accepted the risks. Are you trying to hide something?" I'm impressed that Rashid has my back. The CARE guy mumbles a response and motions us to proceed to the line. My curiosity is even higher now. There must have been a reason that he was so vehemently opposed to me seeing whatever I'm about to see.

We get into the new line and inch up toward a Somali man in a red and black soccer jersey who is seated at a small wooden desk where he checks the ration numbers and marks it off with a pen on the manifest. People are pushing and crowding him and it appears as if the only way for you to get your number marked off is to shove your card in front of his face. Luckily the women are lined up on one side and the men on the other, so the amount of pushing around us is less. But the ration card checker is ignoring the women's line altogether. The pushy men are dominating here. Eventually Fatima, who strikes me as being rather feisty and determined herself, shoves her card in front of the man, while pointing to me for extra clout as if to say, "Look, I have a foreigner with me so stop being a jerk and let us in." He looks up at me with surprise, and marks her number off on the manifest while motioning with a quick head nod in the direction of the collection area, indicating we're cleared to go.

Another line awaits us. But this time it's even worse. All I can see is a mass of people, both men and women mixed together, crammed between two fences in a covered structure that, again, looks more appropriate for corralling livestock than distributing food rations. Fatima points to a small square opening in the fence a foot off the ground as she informs me, "We start here for the CSB (corn-soya blend)." I look down at the little opening that is just big enough for a small metal bowl to fit through. Fatima stoops down and puts a white plastic bag at the square opening while a veiled woman sitting on a stool behind the fence scoops the corn-soya blend with a bowl and dumps what looks like three or four cups of light yellow powder into Fatima's plastic bag. The measurements aren't perfect, but hopefully Fatima is getting as close as possible to the 0.675 kilograms of CSB she's allotted.

We move a few more feet down the narrow fenced corridor and come to another small opening in the fence, this time for cornmeal distribution. The same scene unfolds as before, and I'm impressed with Fatima's level of patience as the people around us start packing in on all sides. With the cornmeal safely packed away in another plastic bag, and placed in her larger collection sack, we start nudging our way into the thick of the crowd in order to get to the opening in the fence where the flour will be given out. Within seconds we're surrounded on all sides by people pushing their way forward. The heat in here is stifling, and the body smells of so many people in such close proximity are overpowering. It feels like we only gain a few inches at a time as we shuffle closer. To make matters worse, there is a white fog hanging in the air caused by the flour particles becoming airborne while being distributed. I look down and find that I already have a thin layer of white flour dust covering my feet, clothes, and arms.

A teenage guy in an orange shirt who had earlier tried to cut in front of us is now being pushed into us from behind. I strike up a conversation with him, and discover that his name is Amir. "Hey, shouldn't you be in school now?" I ask him.

"Yeah, I'm in my last year of secondary school, but I can never go to school on food distribution day. It's impossible." He explains that, like Fatima, he will have to come through this line today more than once to collect rations for others who aren't able to come. Though he also reveals to me that he's sometimes able to cut the line and collect his rations from behind the fence because he has made friends with some of the people who work here. It's obviously not fair, but I can understand the urge to exploit any available loopholes out of self-interest.

I look over to the adjacent collection building that is separated from our fenced corridor by a small open space of two or three feet. Over there the scene is the same: people crowding the small openings in the fences trying to collect their rations while dealing with the heat, smells, and poor air quality. Two women hang on the fence looking out toward our building, probably trying to get a few breaths of the fresh air that occasionally breezes in between the two structures. They look tired, but one of them still gives me a half smile before turning back to push through the crowd for flour.

It takes us nearly ten minutes in the middle of the flour mosh pit before we find our way to the opening where Fatima can collect her 3.15 kilograms. The Somali man distributing the flour appears to be in his late forties and is wearing a bright green shirt, a white turban on his head, and a breathing mask that, instead of being used for its intended purpose of protecting his lungs from the fog of flour particles, is positioned on top of his turban. He looks like a tough guy and never cracks a smile, but he also looks like one of the better-fed people I've met. His protruding belly is a rare sight here. Apparently if you know the right people and can find a way to work as a food distributor, you and your family can end up being relatively well fed.

He dips a large metal bowl into a nearby wooden bin that

is filled with flour and is littered on top with empty sacks. His hands are completely white and his pants and shirt are covered in flour, too. Fatima is ready with a white sack at the opening in the fence as he pours in the contents of the bowl. If I remember my kilograms to pounds conversion right, she has received roughly seven pounds of flour. Her large white sack, filled with the individual plastic bags of rations, must be getting heavy as I can see her face straining as she lifts it over her shoulder to push back into the crowd. It's now clear to me why the WFP worker was hesitant about me going through the collection process. I have never experienced such inhumane circumstances before. We're only halfway done, but we're already tired, sweaty, hot, covered in flour, barely able to breathe, and pushing our way through a mass of people who are all experiencing the same hellish process.

"Can you stand this heat?" I look up to see Amir, the teenager we ran into earlier.

"It's really hot," I say as I wipe a mix of pasty flour and sweat off my forehead. "But I figure that you have to do this twice a month, and you've been enduring it for years and years. I can at least survive it for one day." He nods and gives an appreciative smile.

"Yeah, understanding the conditions we're facing is the first step to be able to advocate for improvements, no?" he says.

He's absolutely right. A Kenyan friend of mine named Pete Ondeng once told me it's impossible for someone from outside the box to transform the lives of people inside the box without actually stepping in it themselves. Yet so many aid decisions seem to be made from the comfort of air-conditioned offices in Europe and America instead of from the sweat-stained, flour-covered trenches of reality here in the camp.

I had assumed the bottleneck was only centered around the flour area, but the crowd persists as Fatima collects her rations of beans, sorghum, and salt. We finally come to the last stage of the ration collections process: the cooking oil. Fatima has come prepared with her small yellow jerry can, and a woman dips a red plastic mug into a large bucket filled with oil, pouring it into Fatima's can through an orange funnel. The woman is taking her time for some reason, and she doesn't respond well to anyone encouraging her to hurry. Surely there are *much* more efficient ways to distribute the rations.

The end is near, and I can start to feel some fresh air wafting from the exit a few feet in front of us. But first a man needs to weigh Fatima's sack to ensure she didn't get too much or too little. She's under, so he adds a scoop of flour to bring her closer to the correct amount. Finally we stop at another checkpoint, where a man sitting on a wooden stool asks to see Fatima's ration card again as he marks off a second copy of the manifest. I get the impression that all this bookkeeping is done more for protocol than anything else. I'm doubtful that much of the information is used, let alone checked for accuracy. I can only imagine the millions of ways people have figured out how to cheat the system. I've already heard of people going through the ration lines for dead relatives. I can't even be 100 percent sure that all three of the ration cards tied around Fatima's wrist are legitimate. But she doesn't give me any con-artist vibes, so I think it's probably fine.

◆　◆　◆

Air! Finally! The hot desert air fills my lungs as we exit the collection facility and I feel a sense of enormous relief and freedom. I look down at my watch: 9:50 AM. The collection process from start to finish took *fifty minutes*, and the corridor was at most only fifty feet long. Fatima's sack now weighs over twenty pounds, and she tugs it along, half-carrying and half-dragging it on the concrete walkway that leads out of the collection center.

"Time to do it again," she says with a shrug and a smile as she lifts her wrist displaying the other two cards she still has to collect for. I feel horrible that she has to endure that hell again and again. We say goodbye and I thank her for letting me experience the process with her.

As I approach the benches nearby where a few security guards and the WFP monitors lazily sit, I spot Rashid and he gives me a knowing look after seeing my exhausted face. "So, how was it?"

"Rashid, you and I both know that there isn't a shred of dignity in this process at all," I say as I brush flour off my shirt.

"Yeah, it's far from ideal. This structure was built when the refugees arrived in 1992, and it was only intended to accommodate thirty thousand. But now it's used by eighty-seven thousand refugees. It's not an excuse for what you've seen, I know." Rashid's empathetic tone is touching, but there's a hint of defeat in his voice.

Dignity. That's the word standing out in my mind most prominently right now. Who decided it was okay to corral people like cattle? Or that refugees should have to wait for hours just to have the opportunity to collect subpar food rations that are not only insufficient in quantity but also don't correspond to their preferred cultural diets or nutritional needs? Why should there be such room for error and personal manipulation depending on whether or not you are able to bribe the right people along the line? I can feel my blood starting to boil as the injustice of it all makes me outraged.

I take a deep breath and try to calm down, telling myself to be less reactionary. But just as I'm doing so, I catch sight of a pregnant woman, who looks ready to give birth at any moment, putting an arm out to steady an elderly woman as they both drag their heavy sacks along the concrete floor.

I start to get up to go help them, but Rashid instructs one of the security guards to go assist the women instead. The guard carries their sacks to the exit of the distribution center, but then they're on their own again to get the food all the way to their homes.

Rashid and I sit in silence on the bench for a while, listening to the sound of the sacks being drug along the ground and watching the stray goats who managed to sneak in and are licking up the bits of cornmeal and flour that have escaped from people's sacks. "I know there has to be a better way," Rashid finally says with a sigh.

"Yeah, so why have things stayed the same for so long?" I ask.

"I don't know. I guess it has just been accepted that this is the way it's done." He shrugs. "The refugees have found ways to improve the process over the years, but it's still within this basic, flawed structure. For example, you see that guy over there?" He points to a man in a white T-shirt who is standing behind one of the men weighing the rations. "He's a member of the food advisory committee, and he helps patrol the process on behalf of the community. His job is to deal with any conflicts that might arise, and to check to make sure everyone is getting the right amounts. It's not a perfect solution, but it's a start in the right direction."

"It seems like there's so much room for error and corruption, even with the monitors here," I say.

"Yeah, I can't deny that," Rashid replies.

A woman passes by the bench as she carries her bag toward the exit. She stops in front of me suddenly and looks me in the eyes as she says something passionately in Somali while gesturing to the sack. "What is she saying, Rashid?" I ask.

"She said, 'Look! We are given so little,'" he says softly with a sheepish expression.

The woman looks irritated. Twenty pounds of rations might

sound like a lot, but it's apparently hard to make it last. And yet the only reaction most of the WFP, CARE, and UNHCR workers can muster up when confronted like this is shrugged shoulders and a sentiment of "save your breath, there's nothing we can do." In a way, they're right. The big decisions aren't made here. They're made in Rome, where the World Food Program has its headquarters. And they're made on the floor of Congress in Washington, D.C., where the self-interested "generosity" of the American people politically dictates the food situation for refugees on the other side of the planet. But after seeing the process firsthand, it's clear to me that this *has* to change.

After stewing a little more, I turn to Rashid and say with exasperated enthusiasm, "There's so much room for innovation here, Rashid. Like, for instance, with today's technology, why would you still have to rely on physical ration cards to prove eligibility? Or why aren't you using specialized machinery to accurately and quickly dispense the proper ration amounts to avoid error and corruption? And why does there even need to be an old-school collection facility in the first place? What about pre-packaging the rations in reusable containers? Or starting a home-delivery system to ensure the food is making it to the right places and that the disabled and elderly are able to get their fair share? Or what about . . ." My voice trails off as I sense this rant is useless.

I can see from his face that he agrees with me. He is one of the more enlightened aid workers I've met who can acutely sense the reality of the challenges and can see the need for improvement, but I sense he feels powerless to do anything about it.

The CARE worker who originally attempted to prevent me from going through the collection process passes by, but he quickly diverts his eyes when he catches sight of me. He knows what I've seen.

CHAPTER 7

I ZIP UP my backpack and push it to the side as I collapse onto my bed. I'm now packed and ready for the 4 PM flight back to Nairobi, but it's only 2:24 and I still have time before the convoy leaves for the airstrip. I'm sad to leave this place. Though, once again, I find myself leaving Dadaab with mixed emotions. I'm grateful for the people I met this past week and for the glimmers of hope I saw, but the overwhelming feeling of frustration I still have is hard to shake. Eight years later, and most of the aid organizations here are *still* failing the refugees. But when I went back to the Community Secondary School this morning to say goodbye to Osman, his persistent hope reminded me that all is not lost.

I'm definitely going to miss being here. Though I'm also slightly embarrassed to admit that I'm sort of looking forward to the comforts that await me in Nairobi. I used to be *so* hardcore when it came to "roughing it" in difficult conditions. The harder the better! Rats brushing up against my arm as I slept on a thin mattress on the floor of a Ugandan hut? Who cares! Contracting a horrible parasite after eating custard in a Peruvian village? Totally worth it! Being crammed like a sardine in a local bus in Laos while the blood from a freshly killed fish in the luggage rack above my head drips down? Bring it on! But somewhere around the age of twenty-seven these types of things started to lose their appeal. I'm not saying I'm trading in my backpack for a roller suitcase yet, but to take a shower without any poisonous spiders joining me would be lovely.

I decide to pass my remaining time on the compound by saying goodbye to all the wonderful people I met during my stay here. I stop by the mess hall, the TV room, and the offices, thanking everyone for their kindness. As I return from saying goodbye to hunky Armando and giving my key back to him, I pass by something that has made me both laugh and scheme every time I caught sight of it this week: the UNHCR Suggestion Box.

The large white wooden box with a slit at the top, mounted outside one of the first rows of offices, seemed too perfect not to mess with. I thought about collecting the countless complaints that I'd heard from the refugees this past week and filling the box to the top. Or I also considered inserting my own "suggestions" for improvements like: (1) Spend more time with the refugees than in your air-conditioned offices, (2) Don't boast about "participation" and "including the refugees in decision-making" if it's nothing more than a show for the donors and your reports, (3) Try the word *dignity* on for size and start applying it to every program you oversee, and (4) Be innovative and solutions-oriented in your work instead of assuming that things must continue the same way they have for the past two decades. The list could have gone on and on. But I eventually decide not to bother submitting anything because I have a pretty strong sense that the key required to open the lock on the suggestion box disappeared years ago, and my "suggestions" would probably just be unearthed decades from now like the time capsule I buried in my backyard as a kid.

I guess that's one of the hardest parts about being an aid

critic: You can speak out and protest all you want, but there continues to be an overwhelming feeling that nobody really cares to listen. And when that sense of hopelessness is apparent from the enlightened few on the inside of these organizations, as well, you know it's going to be a long time before any change starts to happen. My feeling is that the only way real change is going to take place is either by way of a total shift in perspective of the entire donor community (I'm not holding my breath for that), or by a semirevolution on the part of the refugees to demand better quality from the organizations working on their behalf. One can hope.

I pick up my backpack and say farewell to the security guards as I load into one of the SUVs en route to the airstrip.

◆　◆　◆

I didn't realize how eager I must look standing at the bottom of the plane stairs, waiting for the stewardess to give the go-ahead for us to board. But as I wait, an Australian man dressed in a khaki field vest approaches me and asks, "Desperate to get out of here?"

I turn to him and confess, "No, not at all. It's just that, well, someone is waiting for me back in Nairobi, so I guess I'm just eager to see him."

"Oh?" he says with an intrigued look on his face.

"My boyfriend," I say by way of explanation. "He'll be at Wilson Airport waiting for me."

The stewardess appears at the top of the stairs and says, "You're welcome to board, ma'am."

I board the plane, taking a seat in the second row at the window and, soon after the Australian guy sits down next to me.

"I'm John," he says as he puts his hand out to shake.

"Hi, I'm Tori. Nice to meet you. So what were you here in Dadaab for?"

"Well, my most recent job was working as the head of treasury operations for the World Food Program. I'm usually based out of Rome," he says as he hands me a business card from his shirt pocket. I try not to make an inappropriate face in response. This guy is one of the head honchos in global food aid, and he probably has a hand in helping to make some of the less-than-stellar decisions that emerge from the boardrooms of the Rome office. But I guess he deserves a fair chance.

"Oh?" I say, matching his earlier intrigue. "How do you like that position?"

"I am still relatively new to it. Before this I was working in international corporate finance, but I found myself wanting to be involved in something more meaningful. At the moment, though, I'm filling in here as the head of finance for the WFP Kenya office. I'm only here for two months to bridge a gap until the position is filled by our new hire who's moving here from Pakistan soon. It's nice to be back in the field." He warmly smiles as he asks, "So what do you do?"

I give him the condensed version of the past eight years since my last trip to Dadaab, and he seems impressed to hear about my current role as a specialist in the field of aid effectiveness. Unlike many high-up aid officials that I meet, John doesn't seem turned off by the fact that my job description involves questioning the merits of his organization.

"Did you get a chance to see much of what's going on in Dadaab?" I ask.

"It was a short visit, but, yes, we checked out one of the new food distribution centers that's being built. It's going to be a much bigger, purpose-built steel and concrete collection center that should be a vast improvement on the wood and chicken wire structures they have now."

"Will it improve on the current approach to distribution?"

I ask, thinking back to my trip through the collection facility with Fatima the other day.

"What do you mean?" he asks.

"Well, I had the chance to experience the collection process myself, and I couldn't help but notice that the design of the buildings make for a truly undignified experience," I reply bluntly.

"Is that right?" he says, with a curious and surprised look on his face. "I'm not sure if it will change the process, but it will be a bigger version of what is in place now to accommodate the growing population of refugees."

"I was stunned by the conditions," I inform him. He asks me to elaborate, and I explain the details of what I saw in the collection facility and the ideas I shared with Rashid the other day about how the process could be improved. He listens with great interest, encouraging me to take my concerns to the top. As we start to taxi down the dirt airstrip, I try desperately to dig for dirt on the finances and the management of his organization, but his answers are excessively diplomatic. I can't seem to get anything juicy out of him. I look out the window as the plane takes off and the village of Dadaab gets smaller and smaller in the distance.

As I root around my bag for a pen and my journal, John turns to me and asks, "So what is it about this boyfriend of yours that makes you so eager to get back to Nairobi?"

"Oh man, what can I say? It's a complicated situation," I reply, hoping I might be able to get away with being as vague and diplomatic as he was. But he keeps his gaze on me with a look of total curiosity that seems to say, "Go on . . ."

Maybe against my better judgment, I divulge the woes of my relationship to the head of finance for the Kenyan office of the World Food Program. He is fascinated by the way Mark and I met, and the ups and downs the relationship has taken. His comments and questions are spot-on, which only encourages me to go deeper. There is a dynamism in our connection, and for reasons beyond my understanding, I trust him. Perhaps it's the kindness in his eyes. John explains to me some of the similarities he experienced with his own wife, and the way things seemed to work out in the end.

He shifts his body to face me as he asks, "So how are things going between you two now?"

"Not so good, to be honest. We keep having stupid fights, and I'm stuck in this dynamic of constantly trying to assess whether or not he's 'the one,' but I really can't be sure. I feel like I've been putting him under a microscope lately, which, as you can imagine, doesn't produce the most healthy results." He nods in agreement. I go on, "A part of me desperately wants him to be the guy I spend the rest of my life with. Most days are so blissful. But some days I don't feel confident about the match at all. It's like an endless cycle of certainty and uncertainty," I say.

"That must be exhausting for both of you," he says with kindness and empathy in his voice.

"Yeah, it is. I'm not sure what to do, to be honest," I reply.

"Be patient," he says with a smile. "It will become clear."

"Patience," I repeat with a long exhale. "That's not exactly my forte."

He smiles as he turns to pick up his book from the seat pocket and begins to read. I put the tray table down to write in my journal about my anxious thoughts in hopes of making the hour-long flight pass by more quickly.

◆　◆　◆

The plane has barely stopped but my seat belt is already off, and one hand is on the strap of my backpack, ready to dart off the plane as soon as the door opens. The only thing I can think of is reuniting with Mark. We start to file off, and a sense of hesitant anticipation is circulating through my body as I start to walk down the stairs of the plane.

"Tori, wait. There's one more thing I thought I should mention," John says, as I step down onto the tarmac, swinging my backpack over my shoulder. "When it comes to love, sometimes you're never really *sure*. My mother recently admitted to me that on the day of their wedding she wasn't certain they were making the right choice. But a year ago they celebrated their fiftieth anniversary, and they have been deeply in love throughout all those years."

I look over to him and smile as we walk across the tarmac together, approaching the exit of Wilson Airport. "That's beautiful," I say.

"I don't think you ever *really* know for sure," he says. "You might just have to take a chance and trust in it. . . . Life goes quickly." He puts out his hand. "It was a pleasure to meet you, Tori."

"You, too, John. Thanks for the words of wisdom," I say as we shake hands and part ways.

My heart is beating fast as I get ready to see Mark again. But when I emerge from the exit gate into the parking area of Wilson Airport, my redheaded love is nowhere to be seen. I scan the group of people waiting and all the drivers holding signs, but he's not there. I walk a little farther toward the road. Every second that passes feels like an eternity, but I try to push back any thoughts about the possibility that he has changed his mind and has decided not to be here to greet me. But maybe the fight last week was too terrible, or maybe he had a change of heart? Or maybe he's just stuck in traffic. Or maybe he forgot me? Ugh. Runaway thoughts have a tendency to pull me off track pretty quickly. I desperately need to stop this. He's coming, Tori. Believe that he's coming.

A minute has passed, but before I have a chance to invent any further potential negative scenarios, I look behind me and there he is, walking quickly in my direction. My face lights up, and so does his as we both start running toward each other. I drop my backpack to the ground and he throws his arms around me, holding me close in a tight embrace. We both look at each other with tears in the corners of our eyes as we whisper in unison, "I love you!" He kisses me and then holds me tighter, apologizing for the way he acted before I left, then he strokes my hair as he kisses the top of my head. The world seems to stand still as we hold each other in the parking lot.

◆　◆　◆

The past week together in Nairobi has been absolutely beautiful, without a single problem, in fact, which is why it feels strange to be waking up this morning with resurfacing doubts, only hours before my bus is scheduled to leave for my two-month overland journey. It's only seven o'clock, but I've already been awake for hours, lying in bed consumed with thoughts about our relationship. It's hard to put my finger on the exact cause of my uncertainty. But I've been mulling it over, and my best guess is that I don't feel like myself in this relationship. The spark for life I used to have has faded.

I look over to Mark, who is peacefully sleeping next to me. I adore this man. How can I be having these thoughts? I close my eyes and try to be still, praying for some clarity. Then it dawns on me: I've been trying to figure out the source of this "something's missing" feeling between us, but perhaps what's missing is *me*.

I sit with this for a moment. If I don't feel myself in this relationship, then I either have some intense personal transformations to undertake or I'm with the wrong person. The real pisser is that I genuinely love Mark. But maybe Dr. Jane was right . . . maybe love's not enough. The thought of not being with him seems catastrophic, but the thought of staying with him given the current conditions and regular disagreements seems unfair to both of us.

Mark starts to move a little, and I look over to see those big brown eyes smiling at me as he says in a sleepy voice, "Hi, my love."

"Hi," I say with a long, sweet sigh.

"What are you doing up so early?" he asks as he rolls over toward me.

"Just thinking," I reply.

"About what?"

"About us. Me. Life. You know, the big stuff," I say. Before he has time to ask for more details I quickly say, "I'm going to go make some tea. You want some?"

"Sure," he says as he rubs his eyes.

I come back into the room and he's sitting up in bed, looking adorable as ever. He always has such a boyish sweetness about him in the mornings. "Thanks," he says as I hand him a cup of tea. "So what are you thinking exactly?"

Damn, how do I say this? I know he has been thinking similar things lately, but the whole "it's not you, it's me" discussion feels unbearable. I take a sip of tea to buy some more time. "Well . . ." Another sip. I have to do this. "We both know something is off between us. We are on an intense roller coaster with the highest of highs, but also the lowest of lows. It's like we aren't capable of any middle ground: it's either bliss or heartbreak for us."

"Yeah, it's true," he says with a disheartened face. "It's always been like that for us. There's a certain friction that comes and goes, disrupting the peace."

"Yeah, like that last fight," I say. "But it's more than just our disagreements." I explain to him the insights I had this morning—that I don't feel myself lately in this relationship, that I feel unauthentic, like I'm trying to conform to some sort of role or be somebody I'm not. I went from being this strong, independent woman to an "oh, whatever you want, dear" kind of girl. I look down, unable to continue staring into his understanding but noticeably sad eyes as I add, "I feel like I've lost myself."

He takes a moment to soak in what I've said and then says, "To me a big part of true love is being yourself around the other person, and to be able to accept that person exactly as they are. I don't want to be in a relationship with someone who can't be authentic with me."

I know what he is saying, and I completely agree. I wouldn't want to be with someone who didn't feel like himself around me, either. And I shouldn't want to stay in a relationship where I feel like that. The only trouble is that even though I know something isn't right, I don't feel confident walking away from the relationship forever.

"I obviously need to do some soul-searching." I pause for a moment before hesitantly suggesting, "What about us taking a break for a little while, at least for the next two months while I'm on my trip through Uganda and Rwanda? And then we can reassess where our feelings are when I get back at the end of July." I can already tell he's not a big fan of the idea based on his facial expression, but I press on, "I just need some time and space to figure these issues out in my head and my heart."

He exhales loudly. "We can't keep doing this, Tori."

"I know, but I need some time to process my feelings and figure out what's missing. And I think I need some space to do it."

We talk it over for a while, and we finally agree we'll try a temporary break. A break that can serve as an emotional reset button for the relationship. But it has to be the last one. I agree we can't keep this on-again, off-again relationship going. It isn't healthy.

A silence descends for a few moments as we both stare out in front of us. Then, in unison we look into each other's eyes. "I'm gonna miss you," he says as he puts his arms around me and pulls me close.

"I'm going to miss you, too. I hope we find our answer soon," I say, my eyes tearing up.

Mark watches me with sadness as I start packing up my things. I know this trip is what I need right now, but it doesn't feel easy.

Just as I'm getting ready to shut down my computer and store it away in Mark's apartment, an email arrives from John. It's a response to a message I sent him yesterday thanking him for his sage advice that reads:

Dear Tori,
Seeing the two of you together, and the way he ran into your
arms, and the way the two of you only had eyes for each other,
I don't think that there's much doubt at all.
I was going to say that to you if I had a chance but we left
in a car before you left his clinch!
BRgds,
John

I do my best to ignore the email as I head off to the bus station.

CHAPTER 8

WITH THE IMPRESSIVE Rift Valley on my left and an endless string of villages and oddities on the right (including bizarre things like the "Bubbles Butchery" and some guys selling thick Russian fur hats . . . in Africa), my bus blunders along the pothole-filled road as I make my way west. There's not really a defined plan for this westward journey, but I'm confident that the details will work themselves out as I go. In my ideal world I would be heading to Somalia right about now to track down Ahmed, but he isn't there. Where he is, exactly, I'm still not sure. But I have some feelers out among a few refugee agencies in the United States, and I'm hoping something will turn up soon. In the meantime, I'm doing this overland journey on his behalf. I'm hopeful that I'll gain clarity along the way so I can finally put to rest my eight-year quest for answers to Ahmed's question. Right now the only certainty I have is that this bus I'm on is heading to the town of Kitale, Kenya. A friend has connected me to a highly respected international NGO working with AIDS orphans there, and they've offered to host me and show me around.

I spend the bus ride staring out the window in a mindless

daze, watching the Rift Valley give way to the hot pink shores of Lake Nakuru that are lined with hundreds of thousands of flamingos, and later to the sprawling farms and rolling green hills near Eldoret. Occasionally the slight gasps of excitement by three *muzungus* (the Swahili term for "foreigners") sitting a few rows in front of me snaps me out of my fog. They're heading to Kitale, too, to work as medical volunteers for seven weeks. They told me at the rest stop that it's not only their first *time* in Africa, it's their first *day*. I try to remember my first day on this continent in 1999, and I long for that sense of awe and wonder and newness I had back then. The quirky things like squat toilets, unidentifiable street food, and random animals by the road are all commonplace for me now, and rarely warrant a second thought. But on their first day in Africa, these three are utterly captivated by it all. Part of me wishes I could bottle their excitement and enthusiasm.

Before long I find myself sitting on the back of a bicycle being driven around Kitale in search of my home-stay house. I balance myself on the padded seat behind the driver, admiring the fact that he's ever-so-boldly wearing a flowery blouse that looks like it was donated from a church lady in Des Moines. A brief but powerful rain has just subsided and the sun is starting to go down, but not before producing a massive double rainbow all the way across the sky that almost looks close enough to make it worth searching for that mythical pot of gold. He maneuvers around the puddles as we pass by all the other bicycle taxis in one of the loveliest "rush hours" I've ever seen. I look up again at the rainbow and the dramatic clouds nearby. It's moments like this that keep me addicted to this part of the world. The hassles of my search for Ahmed and the complications of my relationship seem to disappear for a moment as me and my flower-clad driver navigate through town.

◆ ◆ ◆

I already feel warmly welcomed by the staff within minutes of arriving at the modest headquarters of the Kenyan AIDS Relief Association (KARA), an international NGO that was started by an American woman a few years ago. I just finished up a brief introductory meeting with the organization's local director, a Kenyan man named Bernard who has a remarkable degree of reflectiveness and insight. As I wait for my next meeting with a woman named Judith, I pass the time flipping through KARA's annual report to get a better sense of the organization.

I glance down at the cover of the glossy report and see a photo of a sad and dirty-looking girl standing outside a hut holding a doll. In my work I always get irritated with this kind of "poverty porn." As I flip through the pages I count nine of the twenty-nine photos depicting the local people looking completely miserable and needy. Another four have "Thanks, KARA" written in Swahili somewhere in the photo (apparently done by the photographer)—including on walls and even on a goat! But the fact that a whopping sixteen photos show happy, smiling, functional people is actually impressive compared to most NGO publications I've seen.

I go back through the report and browse the prior year's expenditures, the number of beneficiaries reached, specific success stories, quantifiable achievements, and a handful of bar graphs depicting their progress and future outlook. Based on the report, the organization's growth looks strong and the impact thus far is impressive. But I know better than to make opinions based on annual reports. Before I have a chance to look deeper into the financials listed on page twenty-one, a Kenyan woman emerges from a nearby office and motions me to join her.

"Hi, Tori, I'm Judith. Please, come in."

I enter her office and sit across from her at her desk. "Can I get you some tea?" she asks, motioning to the door.

"No, thanks. I'm fine," I reply.

"Okay, well . . ." She hands me a copy of their organization's brochure as she smiles enthusiastically and says, "Let me tell you about us!"

Judith goes on to carefully outline the numerous projects that KARA runs in the areas of nutrition, health, psychosocial support, child rights, economic security, and education. Technically their specialization is in helping children affected by HIV and AIDS, but their approach is holistic, focused not only on the child but on the entire household. They even offer programs like agricultural training for AIDS patients and access to income-generating activities. Judith is a perfect spokeswoman, as she's currently making each program sound like an absolute gem of an idea. Most organizations have a person like her: someone who can really "sell" the concept to outsiders. But I've had enough experience evaluating the effectiveness of aid organizations to be skeptical of such eloquent "pitches." Still, that being said, KARA sounds like an innovative, thoughtful, and possibly even effective organization.

KARA is even taking time to participate in long-term research on their programs through partnerships with American universities. I highly support them in this initiative, as I think research is a missing link in most aid projects. The organization is also shockingly collaborative, a rarity in this industry, as Judith explains that, instead of reinventing the wheel, they're trying to strengthen the structures that already exist by partnering with other local NGOs and government ministries. Their intention is to eventually phase themselves out of this region over time by building up local community-based organizations to run the programs independently.

"Judith, you make KARA sound like a first-rate organization. What has the impact of all these efforts been?" I ask.

"Well, we'd love for you to see for yourself. We've arranged
a program for you to join Charles, one of our staff members,
in the field to visit several of our projects today and tomorrow,"
she informs me. This sounds like a perfect starting place for my
mini-quest. I gratefully accept her offer.

◆　◆　◆

"Welcome to the Wangari Academy," Charles says as we
descend from the truck onto the lawn of the school's courtyard.
"Academy" is a generous term for this shabby-looking primary
school consisting of an L-shaped collection of small mud, brick,
and concrete buildings. It's break time for the students, and a
few older girls are playing with a jump rope while some little
kids sit in small clusters watching them. But before I can get
too immersed in the kids, I'm shuffled toward the administrative office, where I'm greeted by Geofrey, a kind-looking Kenyan
man with a broad smile, who has graciously offered to take me
on a tour of the school.

Our first stop is in one of the dormitory rooms that is home
to eleven boys. It's hard to see anything in the room as we pull
the sheet back from the door because only a narrow sliver of light
is making its way through the tiny window and there is no electricity. Once my eyes adjust to the darkness I can make out the
brick walls covered with a smooth layer of mud and four sets of
bunk beds that line the walls, each covered with a tattered blan-
ket. I do the math quickly and turn to Geofrey, "Eight beds for
eleven kids?" I question.

"Ah, yes, some of the boys have to share," he replies. "We
unfortunately have too many orphans who have nowhere else to
live, so we have to do what we can with the space we have."

After checking out the girls dormitory, which is as dark and shabby as the boys', we enter a tiny mud-walled classroom with six wooden benches, and only three grade-four students sitting next to each other in the first row watching their teacher write some Swahili phrases on the board.

"Why are there so few students?" I ask Geofrey.

"The school tuition is only fifteen hundred shillings per term (which is less than twenty dollars), but most of the children in this area are unable to find that money. So we have a real problem with student numbers. We have maybe one hundred children registered in the school, though many of them we don't see regularly enough, and among those thirty are AIDS orphans. For them we have to rely on outside sponsors to cover their tuition expenses," he explains.

We pass the latrines and enter the kindergarten classroom, only to find the teacher in the back reading a newspaper, while the kids sit idly in their desks at the front of the room. She doesn't seem to care that we've caught her taking a personal break; in fact, she barely looks up at us. This classroom definitely stands out from the others, as it seems to have been the only one that benefited from a large donation of colorful poster board paper that have numbers and shapes drawn on them. A string of numbers from one to fifteen written on bright pink paper hangs from a string spanning the width of the classroom. The room has a cheery feel, but there doesn't seem to be an awful lot of learning going on at the moment.

The apathy of the teacher is disconcerting, but when I consider the comments Geofrey keeps making about the lack of funding, I start to wonder if the two are connected. As we step outside I ask Geofrey, "So how do you pay the teachers?"

"Uh . . . Well, that's a challenging subject at the moment . . ." He trails off.

"I'm curious . . ." I say.

"Most of the teachers here haven't been paid since March. They're paid from the school fees, which are sometimes diffi-cult to collect from such poor families. As the money trickles in slowly, slowly, we pay the teachers. My own salary is paid by KARA, and so is Joyce's, the art teacher."

"Wait, let me get this straight. These teachers have been working for four months without pay?" I ask with a shocked expression on my face, suddenly flashing back to my conversa-tion with Osman, who has been doing the same back in Dadaab. "How do they support their families? And why are they still willing to come to work each day?"

"It not an ideal situation, but I guess they stay because they want to help the kids, and because it's hard to find work around here, so even if the salaries aren't coming in they tend to stay, waiting for things to improve." He pauses. "We really hope maybe KARA will decide to pay their salaries," he hesitantly adds, avoiding direct eye contact with Charles.

My sentiments about the kindergarten teacher are soften-ing after hearing she's been working pro bono for a third of the year. I can understand it might be hard to stay highly moti-vated under such circumstances. But motivation doesn't seem to be a problem for Joyce, the pretty and stylish Kenyan art teacher who greets us at the door of the grade 6/7 split class-room, welcoming us to art class. As we enter the classroom I'm transported back to my childhood as I watch the twenty-seven students carefully mixing powdered tempera paints, which I haven't seen in use since the eighties.

"We're learning about color gradients today," Joyce says proudly as she holds up one of the students' papers with blue paint that evenly transitions from dark blue to light blue.

"Nice. How often do they attend art classes?" I ask.

"They have art twice a week. They seem to enjoy it, they're always asking me, 'When is art? When is art?'" Joyce says with a laugh.

As we continue to chat, I find out that Joyce has a college degree in art and she has been hired by KARA to run this program after they received specific funding from a Danish woman who is passionate about art. With the money from the the woman's donation, KARA is able to pay for the art supplies and Joyce's salary. While it's nice to see the kids enjoying the art class, a part of me wishes the woman had let the school choose what to use the money for. I'm guessing "art classes" was far down on their list of priorities when they currently have no electricity, unpaid teachers, zero textbooks, and minimal teacher training. However, I can't deny that the students look like they're having a good time, so it's certainly not causing any harm.

Still, the donor game drives me crazy. Whether it's individual donors like the well-intentioned Danish woman, or a large behemoth like USAID, the problems I see are often similar: assumptions about what's really needed, a strong leaning toward fun, "feel good" projects, and in most cases, a clear need for credit. In fact, as we were walking into the classroom a few minutes ago, I couldn't help but notice the shiny gold plaque on the wall outside advertising the fact that the classrooms had been built by KARA. A painted mural of a village on a nearby wall also oozes donor worship with the words *Thanks, KARA* written in Swahili in large black letters over the top. The sad part is that more often than not, these signs are put up by the donors themselves. Credit-seeking is one of the reasons donors love to build schools and drill wells and dedicate buildings—these are all things you can clearly put your name on and take pictures with.

I personally would like to start a campaign for donors to invest in unsexy aid. The less sexy, the better! I'm talking about high-impact efforts that you can't easily take credit for or physically put your name on. Things like teacher training and deworming and legal aid. In my experience, despite a recent explosion in well-intentioned corporate dropouts wanting to build schools around the world, it's generally the quality of the teaching, the health of the students, and the availability of instructional materials that make more of a difference than the four walls surrounding the kids. In fact, I've seen "schools" that took place under trees led by skilled teachers that were more effective than classes in the fanciest of donated buildings.

My wandering mind is interrupted when Charles asks the students if they have anything they would like to say to the visitor from America.

A boy stands up and says, "I would like to thank you because you sponsored this school." He promptly sits down. I hear nervous laughs from Charles and Geofrey behind me.

"Oh, I didn't sponsor it," I inform the boy. His face looks confused. Why else would a *muzungu* lady be here other than to check the outcomes of her valiant generosity?

Charles thanks the kids and Joyce for letting us visit and hurries us out of the classroom.

"Charles, didn't you say before that several of the teachers used to be KARA scholarship students?" I ask as we cross the courtyard.

"Yes, that's right. Five of the teachers here used to be part of our bursary program because they were AIDS orphans. Now they have decided to give back as teachers," he proudly explains.

"Wow, I'd love to hear more," I say.

During the next break I'm able to speak to all five of them to find out more about their motivations for wanting to "pay it forward." As AIDS orphans they were selected as bursary students years ago by KARA, enabling them to have their school fees covered by foreign sponsors. A few of them even attended the Wangari Academy as kids, and now serve as teachers here. Their personal stories are tragic to hear as we all sit around a table conversing in the dark administration room, but each of them starts beaming from ear to ear when they get to the part of the story about the day they were told that KARA's bursary program would be sponsoring their schooling.

When I ask Niara about it, she excitedly recounts, "I kept asking, 'Is it true? Are they really going to pay my school fees or are they kidding around?'"

"You can have a friend, you ask for a cup of tea and they don't give you," Anthony adds. "But then someone you don't know far away who maybe has only seen your picture gives you something, you think it's a miracle." The others nod.

Then Benson, whose class I visited earlier this morning, chimes in, "Some people just have the heart to give. I feel lucky to have been sponsored by somebody in the U.K., and it's a burden that I can offload by helping someone else here. I show my appreciation to my sponsor by giving back through my work as a teacher, and hopefully I can become a sponsor myself for other kids in the future."

"I think we all hope one day we will be able to be sponsors for someone else." Niara smiles.

"To be honest, by helping me, those sponsors have helped this community as a whole," Benson adds. "Because their investment in my success has led me to be able to share my knowledge with others, including the students I'm teaching here." He pauses for a moment. "I believe if you just train one child, later they will be able to help two or three or even more."

It's clear the ripple effect is working well in this case. "So what's next for you, Benson?" I ask.

A huge smile comes across his face as he proudly announces, "I've just been accepted to college."

◆ ◆ ◆

My heart aches for this school. You can tell it's full of eager little minds that are coming from the most challenging circumstances imaginable, as many of them are directly impacted by the AIDS epidemic that is ravaging this community. The students proudly arrive in their tattered uniforms every day and sit on wobbly benches, staring at a blackboard while highly passionate (but undertrained and hardly paid) teachers attempt to impart some knowledge to them without any learning materials to help in the process. The school's needs are clear, and not so costly. A little effort could go a long way here. Benson, Niara, and Anthony and all the other recipients of bursary funds are a living example of the way small investments can make a big difference.

"I'm really impressed by the bursary program," I say to Charles as we get back in the truck to leave.

"Yeah, the results have been wonderful. We only wish we could do more," he says. I turn to him and give a sympathetic nod.

As the truck pulls out of the school's gate and starts down the road, I look to my left and am struck by the sight of their nearest neighbor: the coffin makers. Lining the dirt strip between the school and the main road I watch a handful of carpenters carefully nailing and sanding down the wooden boxes that are apparently in high demand these days. It's a chilling reminder of the reality of the problem that these kids and their families are faced with. Whether it goes diagnosed or not, AIDS is devastating this community. As I look back over my shoulder to get another glimpse of the coffin makers, I see the school in the distance and I feel sorry for the fact that its presence, though an important effort, won't necessarily be putting the coffin makers out of business any time soon.

CHAPTER 9

"THESE GIRLS DON'T look too excited to see us," I whisper to Dafina as we are ushered into the large, dimly lit classroom of more than one hundred girls wearing gray uniforms.

"They're shy, I think," she whispers back.

Their faces look stoic and bored. They've clearly been through this drill before.

The teacher introduces us and encourages us to stand at the front of the room as she turns to the children, loudly asking them in a singsong voice, "How are you?"

"WE ARE FINE, THANK YOU," they yell at the top of their lungs in unison. No matter where I am in East Africa, this is always the response I hear. The louder the better. And always in unison, thanks to years of practice from an early age. I'm still waiting for the day when one of the kids decides to be honest and blurts out, "Well, I've actually been better . . . thanks for asking." It still hasn't happened.

The teacher nods. "These visitors are from KARA." She pauses for emphasis. "What has KARA ever done for you?" she asks them in a probing voice.

Silence. A few of the kids look around at their neighbors

for clues, but most of them just keep deadened stares on us as we stand there looking like idiots in the front of the classroom. It feels incredibly awkward.

The teacher helps with an additional prompt, "KARA gives you *what* on World AIDS Day?"

Eventually a few hands go up.

"Money!" one girl says as she stands proudly to answer.

Another girl stands up nearby. "And T-shirts."

"Bangles," a sweet-looking girl in the front adds softly.

A short pause. Another girl raises her hand, "Oh, and bags."

The teacher looks pleased as she nods in response to each answer. "Do they give you lunch?" she asks.

"YES," yelled in unison.

"Yes, shame on you for not remembering," the teacher says as she motions to Dafina to take over the session. I feel like leaving already. But I agreed to accompany Dafina, one of the KARA staff members, here to do a delivery of sanitary pads as part of a USAID-sponsored program. But before we can distribute them, she has to give the sanitary pad talk.

Dafina starts out by asking the girls to raise their hands if they are already menstruating. Only half hesitantly put their hands up, probably all sixth graders. Most of the girls look too young to even be close to starting their periods. She nods and continues her spiel.

"What did you use before KARA brought you sanitary towels?" she asks, clearly already aware of the answer. A few of the less shy girls inform her that they used to use cloth, cotton wool, or pieces of blankets.

Dafina goes on to explain to them that when they are menstruating they are supposed to change the pads and wash themselves three times a day. And she explains that if they have any problems, to talk to their teachers.

"Don't sell those pads," she adds. "Please keep them safely for your next menstruation cycle. Don't give them to your sister, because they are meant specifically for you. Any questions?" she asks as she scans the room of girls. They start snickering and whispering to each other. It seems this is a big joke, or perhaps the topic is too sensitive for such open conversation.

Finally one of the girls stands up and asks in a timid voice, "Is it okay to not follow a regular schedule? Is it okay that I sometimes miss a month?" Before she's done speaking, you can already tell that she is embarrassed. More snickering. A silent pause. A cow moos outside, and I'm wondering what's taking Dafina so long to respond.

"Tori, would you like to comment on this issue?"

I look at her with an "Are you kidding me?" expression on my face. I was only supposed to be here as an observer. But her face is urging me on in silent expectation.

"Umm, well. Sure. When you're young and just starting to menstruate, it's normal for your period to be irregular," I say to the girl. She looks pleased by my assurance. "In fact, it took me a few years before I was on a regular schedule," I add.

Dafina smiles at me and nods as she pulls out a calendar and encourages the girls to count the twenty-eight days out loud with her. She then turns to me. "Tori, do you have anything else to say?"

Since when did I become the period advisor? "No," I reply, anxious for the one hundred sets of eyes to stop looking to me for menstrual insights.

The demonstration on how to use the pads is useful, but it is interrupted when the facilitating teacher swoops across the room to close the shutters after catching a few boys peeking inside to watch. When the demonstration is finished, the teacher steps forward and says, "Pauline, can you thank our visitors?"

Pauline, who appears to be the "head girl" of the school, stands respectfully and says to Dafina and me, "Thank you for coming and for the presents you are giving us." I cringe.

It's time for distribution. Dafina has the list of students' names, and the teacher, Josephine, is in charge of handing out the packs of pads and the underwear. I start helping out by unwrapping the packs of underwear that were sent by USAID for this month's distribution. I watch as Josephine hands one pair of underwear and one pack of pads to each girl. But the underwear comes in four different colors. I ask myself, *Why should getting a handout mean getting no choice?* I finish unwrapping the underwear packs and I arrange them on the table in stacks for each color.

"Josephine, I'm happy to take over the underwear distribution if you want to focus on the pads," I offer.

"Okay," she says.

The first girl who approaches my end of the table looks at me, waiting for me to hand her a pair. "You pick," I tell her.

She smiles and looks down, then up again to be sure I was serious, before picking up a pair of orange underwear. It's a simple thing, but the girls appear pleased to be able to choose their favorite color. Pink is the clear favorite, though there are plenty of takers for the green, yellow, and orange ones. The phrase "beggars can't be choosers" flashes through my head, and I wholeheartedly disagree. We've been operating from the "take this and be grateful" mentality for too long in aid. Though, to be honest, I'm not such a big fan of in-kind donations in the first place.

"Does every girl in the school get pads?" I ask as Dafina passes by with her clipboard.

"No, it's only given to the orphans and vulnerable children," she informs me.

I watch a girl standing by the door, trying to figure out a

way to discreetly hold the underwear and the pads before going out into the courtyard amidst all the boys. *How embarrassing,* I think to myself. Not only is it embarrassing enough to be carrying around sanitary pads, but then you add on the fact that if you're seen with these donated items, you are instantly marked as an orphan or "vulnerable" child. Talk about stigmatizing! Who needs the popular girls to ruin your ability to fit in at school when you have USAID?

Half of these girls don't even have their periods yet. I'm curious to know how many of these packs of sanitary pads are going to be sold by tomorrow on the market.

Dafina is carefully writing down the names and girls' identification information for the list. She also has to get a few signatures from the teacher and principal for verification purposes.

"It looks like you have to be meticulous with the reporting," I say as I watch her writing.

"Yes, USAID requires very specific reports on who received donations. The program is quite restrictive. We do procurement from USAID three to five times per year, but we rotate over time to different schools. So last time I gave them four packs, this month I'm only giving them one, next month I'll give them three packs. I think I'll be back in January to give them another three."

"Why one pack this month when they already had four packs last time?" I question.

"Because I had to fill the blank space in the quarterly report due on the twenty-eighth for USAID. I have to send the lists to Nairobi and we have to have given out the full amount for the quarter or else they won't give us money for another distribution," she explains.

"Is it more trouble than it's worth to deal with USAID's demands?" I ask.

She shrugs. "We're used to it."

The distribution is finally finished, and 112 packs of pads and underwear have been given out today. "What percentage of the girls in the school are covered under this program?" I ask as she puts away the distribution list in her bag.

"We think there are four hundred girls of menstruating age in the school, but, as I said, only the orphans and vulnerable children get pads," she says.

"Isn't that stigmatizing?" I ask as we start walking across the courtyard toward the truck.

Dafina laughs. "No, actually some of them think it's more of an advantage to be an orphan because they're given presents and money and T-shirts! One girl recently said to me, 'I wish my parents had died so I could be taken care of like this!'"

My eyebrows rise as I look at her in disbelief. Is this what the aid is doing? I'm at a loss for words.

◆　◆　◆

"So, what do you think so far?" Judith asks me as we sit with Edwin, KARA's monitoring and evaluation officer, on the outdoor terrace of a restaurant, waiting for our lunch to arrive.

"You have some good programs, for sure. I enjoyed speaking with the teachers at the Wangari Academy who used to be sponsored as bursary students and are now giving back. I think the bursary program has impressed me the most so far. And the sanitary pad distribution was, well, eye-opening," I say as diplomatically as possible.

"In what way?" Edwin asks.

"I wasn't entirely sure how it ties in with KARA's core mission, and I couldn't help but notice how rigid the program is in terms of USAID's demands for distribution and reporting. How do you deal with the challenges of meeting the donors' needs?" I ask.

"It can be a real difficulty to manage this sort of thing. USAID, in particular, is extremely strict with their reporting. They are the only ones that require monthly reporting," Judith explains.

"It's time-consuming," Edwin adds.

"But USAID feels like it has to be 'watertight' since they feel there is too much corruption in Kenya," Judith explains. "And sometimes they're right. For example, when we heard that World Vision was receiving PEPFAR money, we decided to try to partner with them. We gave them the list of orphans and vulnerable children needing school uniforms, but a year later they still weren't delivered, despite the fact that World Vision had reported them as delivered!"

I shake my head, though it doesn't surprise me to hear this. "Yeah, I can understand USAID's reasoning for transparent reporting," I say, "but monthly reports sound like a lot of unnecessary work."

"Yes, unfortunately." Edwin nods. "And for each donor we are required to comply with different standards and expectations regarding the type of information we have to collect and the exact way that it has to be written out. It's a big challenge. And it makes you think twice before agreeing to take small amounts of money from a highly demanding donor. It might not be worth the effort in some cases."

"Beans and chapati?" the waiter asks.

"Here," I say as he places the plate in front of me. "*Asante.*"

"The donors still seem to have all the power," Edwin continues as he picks up his fork. "They're the ones setting the agenda. But it's hard for the donors to understand the realities of what's needed on the ground, since they're usually far away in some Western country."

"Very true," I sigh.

Judith looks up from her meal and says, "You know, this is our third round of USAID funding, which is a badge of honor in this field."

"Really, why?" I ask.

"It shows that we're good at reporting," she says, laughing. "Some grant-making organizations like the Elton John AIDS Foundation won't even consider your application if you have not previously received USAID type of funding because they aren't confident in your reporting abilities. That means a lot of smaller, effective organizations aren't considered for big grants."

"But if you had to be honest, did you really want to do something like the sanitary pads program, or was it just an opportunity to qualify for available funding?" I ask, hoping for some continued candor.

Judith looks up and moves her head right to left as she thinks of the best answer. "Well . . . It's a difficult question," she says, pausing a bit longer. "We don't agree to any funding that is *completely* out of line with our mission and vision for the organization. But fundraising lately has become harder and harder. You have to be open to opportunities, even if it wasn't what you might have planned."

"So basically you have to see what the donors are willing to fund and then alter your projects to fit that?" I ask.

"To a degree. Yes, that's kind of how it works sometimes," she says with a hesitant look.

There's a term for this: It's called *mission creep*. I see it happen all the time in aid organizations. An NGO can start with the most brilliant vision and clarified goals that are perfectly aligned with the needs and desires of their target population, but the donors won't be interested in funding that particular vision. Instead the donors will only show interest in funding whatever their sexy topic *du jour* might be, let's say girls' education, and the next thing you know an agriculture NGO is bending their focus to start up an after-school tutoring program for girls. They have no expertise in education, but they wing it because that's the only way the salaries can get paid. It's a vicious cycle. Eventually you end up with a "jack of all trades" type of overstretched and underspecialized organization that is hardly effective at any of the projects it's running due to a lack of demand from the community and the absence of specific expertise among the staff.

"Are you afraid KARA might be losing its way by having to follow the whims of the donors?" I ask.

Judith takes a sip of tea before responding. "We try to stay focused on our goals, but we have a large staff that we need to keep employed. And in difficult economic times like these, you can't be too picky. You have to take whatever funding you can get."

The sad reality is that once an aid organization reaches a certain size, their primary goal tends to shift from fulfilling their mission to keeping the paychecks coming. "Institutional survival," it's called. And it sounds like KARA isn't immune to this tendency. According to their annual report they are currently involved in agriculture, nutrition, income-generating activities, child rights and welfare, child-to-child education, AIDS counseling and testing, psychosocial support, school support, bursary programs, and direct aid donations in the form of blankets, clothes, food, and shelter. Some might call it "holistic"; others might call it "donor coddling."

"Ready to go?" Edwin asks as we finish settling up the bill. "We have much more to show you."

❖　❖　❖

"I think we'll have to walk the rest of the way from here," Charles says after talking it over with the driver.

The truck can't go any farther due to the muddy road conditions, so we'll have to go by foot. Day two of the "program" with KARA has proven even more ambitious than the first, as today we've ventured deep into the rural countryside to visit some of their projects that are two or three hours away from Kitale.

"I don't mind," I say as I jump down from the truck, narrowly avoiding a puddle.

After fifteen minutes of walking along the muddy path between two fields, we approach the house of a KARA recipient named Katiku. I've already been briefed by Charles during our walk that Katiku is HIV-positive, and so is his wife, Grace, along with their five-year-old son, who is the youngest of six kids. It looks like Katiku has been anxiously waiting all day for our arrival as he hurries toward us to shake hands and welcome us to his home. We follow him up a slight hill along the edge of a cornfield, past two cows, and into the living area that consists of a crumbling circular hut where the family used to live, and a brand-new rectangular mud house that was built by KARA.

"Please, come in," he says proudly.

Katiku and Grace sit across from Charles and me in wooden chairs behind a large table in what appears to be the living room of the new house. Grace has a quiet, gentle look about her, and Katiku has concerned and tired eyes, which he's trying to mask with a smile. After the introductions and pleasantries, I ask Katiku, "So, how did you find out about KARA?"

"They found me, actually. I was in the local AIDS support group and KARA found me that way. I received counseling from KARA at first. Then they built this house where we're sitting right now. I'm also getting nutritional flour from them. And I got help growing some kale and spinach, but the rains have been too much lately, so I don't think it's working."

"And the income-generating project," Charles interjects.

"Oh yes, KARA set up a pond over there for fish farming. It's very productive so far, and it benefits all thirty members of the support group."

"Do you get assistance from any other organizations?" I ask.

"Yes, AMPATH has provided some medical help, and PSI gave me these jerry cans for water." He points to two unused white plastic water jugs in the corner. "Oh, and also they gave nets and condoms, and WaterGuard solution," he adds. "It was a whole pack they give. And Forward Kenya gave me farming boots and fertilizer and seeds. And USAID gave us those chickens you see," he says, pointing outside.

"Wow, that's a lot of help you are receiving. How are you so lucky?" I ask with a smile.

Grace puts her hand up to her face and giggles, while Katiku gives an awkward smirk. "That's the love of God," he replies.

"Would you prefer to help yourself instead of relying on all these NGOs?" I ask, fully aware that this is a pretty loaded question.

"Yes, of course, it would be nice to be independent. We got that fish pond from KARA, so I can't say I'm independent." He pauses for reflection. "It's difficult, though," he continues, "to depend on someone if you don't know when he will be available. The NGOs come and they go. It's not always regular and you don't know what to expect. The help is appreciated . . . very much. But I have to do what I can for my own family and not expect it to come from another place."

He brings up a point that echoes Ahmed's original comment to me. We always talk about the "dependency syndrome" in aid, but in most cases NGOs are far from "dependable" at all.

I look to the door as Katiku's five-year-old son enters the room and hides behind his father's chair, checking us out at a distance, before climbing up onto his mom's lap. I have to be honest that when I first heard Katiku rambling down the list of all the stuff he's been given by various NGOs, I couldn't help but think that he was, well, to put it bluntly, an aid whore. You know, he had learned to work the system, tell his story in the right way to the right people, and end up with the lion's share of donations. God, I'm such a cynic sometimes. But as I watch this little boy leaning against his mother's chest with such innocence in his eyes, it strikes me that none of the three people sitting in front of me are going to live for many more years. With hardly any access to antiretrovirals, the chance of prolonging their lives is unlikely. A couple of chickens, some farming boots, and even a new house are all rather inconsequential in the long run. Luckily, I'm able to allow my inner aid critic to subside for a moment to just absorb the tragic humanity of the situation. All I can see in front of me are three precious people whose lives will be cut short.

As we continue to talk with each other in greater depth, it dawns on me that perhaps the real value these NGOs are offering is not by way of the stuff they bring as donations, but rather by the pure fact that they *come*. They sit, they listen, and for a short period of time, they give Katiku and Grace the message, "you matter."

I don't know which box that ticks on the USAID report, but it's probably the most valuable outcome of this work.

UGANDA

CHAPTER 10

I LOOK DOWN at the photo in my left hand and again at the tiny scrap of paper in my right that has the name of the village I stayed in when I was twenty years old scrawled on it in purple ink. We slow down as we pass by a familiar-looking village. I turn to the guy sitting next to me in the cramped minibus that has been slugging along the bumpy dirt road for an hour. "Is this Bududa?"

"No, a little longer still. I'm going there, too, actually. I'll let you know when we reach it," he assures me.

I look at the picture in my hand again. It's a photo of me at twenty, looking down with affection while holding a chubby Ugandan baby in my arms. It's horribly cheesy in its "white lady comforting the African baby" vibe, but it's unfortunately the only clue I have to track down the host family who I stayed with briefly eight years ago. In the photo I'm standing next to a doorway and half of a kid's body can be seen standing next to me, peeking around the door frame. He looks eight or nine years old, I'd guess. That kid, and the color of the paint in the house where I'm standing—a rather distinctive aqua color—are the only bits of information I have about this family. I stayed with them for only a week in 2002, and sadly I can't remember their names after all these years. But they made an impression on me back then, and I'm eager to reconnect with them.

I'm always up for a good adventure, but I'm not so confident this one is going to pan out. However, coming back here seemed like the natural next step in my quest for answers. My thoughts about aid were formed in various parts of East Africa eight years ago and, now that I've returned, I have a rare chance to step back and see where I've come since then in my own understanding of the field. I also want to see how the people and places that were so influential in shaping me during that time have changed.

Being back in the refugee camp was step one, I guess. Standing in that classroom again after all these years, I was able to relive the moment my world was broken open by Ahmed and I came to terms with my own assumptions about the "helping industry."

But if Dadaab was the birthplace of a new worldview, I guess Bududa was the birthplace of my jadedness. Maybe I just want to come back here to soften that stance. And this time I'm hoping all the hands won't be out, and that nobody will ask me to "save" them like they did during my last visit. I'm desperate to see a heavy dose of self-reliance among the villagers in Bududa. But the last time I was here, the place seemed to be consumed by dependency.

"This is us," the guy next to me says as he motions to the minibus conductor to have the driver stop.

I tug my backpack out from under the seat and pay the conductor. I don't recognize the place at all. What I remembered as being a tiny village with hardly anything going on now has its own "main drag" with a row of simple wooden shacks housing small shops, bars, and eateries. Things have definitely expanded here.

"So where are you staying?" the guy asks me as we stand next to each other on the side of the road.

"I'm actually not sure. I didn't make any plans," I say, hoping some halfway decent options exist.

"Well, there's this place here," he says as he points to a shabby-looking bar/guesthouse across the street, "but it has a . . . reputation." By "reputation," he probably means it's a prostitute hangout. That wouldn't be my first choice.

"There's another place farther down that might be more suitable. I'll walk you there," he says.

"Thanks, that's really nice of you. My name is Tori, by the way," I say as we shake hands.

"I'm Peter. Nice to meet you."

"Are you from Bududa?" I ask.

"No, I am just working here at the hospital as part of my residency program. I finished medical school in Kampala a few weeks ago and I was sent here to complete my practical training. Are you here to volunteer?" he asks.

"Volunteer? No, I'm not a volunteer."

"I assumed you were here to help out with the landslide victims. We've seen several *muzungus* coming through over the past few months since the Bududa tragedy," he explains.

"What landslide?" I ask, embarrassed to be so poorly informed.

"You didn't hear about it?" he looks at me, surprised. "It was terrible. A few hundred dead, many more homeless, all in a matter of minutes. It happened three months ago, about twenty minutes from here, and the camp for displaced people is overflowing."

"Man, I had no idea," I say, shocked by the news. I never expected the middle-of-nowhere district of Bududa would suddenly be put on the map by a major disaster.

"Here's the place," he says as we walk up to a guesthouse next to a field of banana trees. He chats briefly with the owner, who informs him that one of the two rooms is vacant and it will cost me the equivalent of $2.50 a night.

I thank Peter for his help and say goodbye as I follow the owner around back. He slides open the lock on the metal gate and leads me into a small hallway that separates his family's house from the guest rooms. The tiny room where I'll be sleeping is basic, which I expected. There's a thin red carpet on the floor, worn-out purple floral sheets covering the sagging mattress, dusty walls painted yellow, a dirty piece of lace covering the small window, and two chairs against the wall facing the bed. On top of the bed sits a television set, which the owner promptly unplugs and starts to carry out of the room.

"Are you sure it's not a problem that I stay in here?" I ask, aware that I am disrupting what has been turned into the TV room.

"No, no problem. No problem," he assures me as he lugs the TV to a storage room adjacent to his little shop out front.

"Thanks," I call out to him across the hall as I close the door and collapse onto the bed. It's been a long day with a lot of transit, so it feels delightful to be here. I'm tempted to take a short nap before heading out to find some dinner. But as I reach over to reposition the pillow, I feel something underneath. It's a DVD pack of *Playboy*'s *Extreme Enticement Sex* videos. Gross. It seems I've taken up residence in the local masturbation room. My personal sleep sheet will definitely be getting used tonight. But, really, what can you expect for $2.50 a night?

◆　◆　◆

I'm totally out of practice when it comes to bathing from a bucket. I used to be a pro at it, but I seem to have lost my touch. The morning air is cold, so every pour of water onto my bare skin is pure torture. *I heard Gandhi could bathe with a single cup of water*, I think to myself as I dump yet another cup on top of my head. *Yeah, but Gandhi didn't have hair!* Getting the shampoo out of my long hair is definitely the hardest part. I do the best I can and finally have to surrender to "good enough." It's time to start the search for my old host family.

After grabbing a banana and some fried dough that the neighbors are selling (which, I swear, could give Krispy Kreme a run for its money), I find the owner of the guesthouse out front and ask him if he knows where Namatiti sub-village in Bududa district is. He's never heard of it, but he knows a driver named Moses who might be able to help me search. He gives him a call and within minutes Moses arrives with his motorcycle, which in Uganda is referred to as a *boda-boda* (apparently because they can theoretically take you from "border" to "border").

As I approach the bike I ask him, "Have you ever heard of Namatiti?"

"Yes, yes, of course," he says confidently. "Come, I take you there." He motions for me to get on the back of the motorcycle and within seconds we're flying down the dirt road. I can't believe he actually knows the place. For some reason I assumed that this was going to be a difficult search.

I hang on tightly and lean forward as we make our way along the slippery mud roads. But I try not to inhale too deeply because Moses's winter jacket, something that is unnecessary in this warm weather, but serves as a status symbol around here, must have gotten left out in the rain and smells like a moldy life jacket.

Our first half hour together is filled with promise and bravado as Moses boldly takes me down a long muddy road where he's *sure* the village is. But soon we're met with a dead end. Then it's off to another dirt road, which is so steep and muddy the *boda-boda* can't climb it, so we have to go by foot. Along the way we show everybody we pass the photo of me and the baby, asking if they know who the boy in the photo is or where the house might be. Nobody has a clue, though the speculation is endless. An hour of walking up to the top of the hill to the local primary school is met with the assurance from the headmaster that it must be the sub-county chief's house, but he's all the way back down at the main road. We eventually find him drinking in the village bar (at ten o'clock in the morning, yes), and he thinks the boy *might* be his. What kind of father doesn't recognize his own son? But, then again, what kind of father is soused at this hour? The photo then gets passed along by the secondary school headmaster to a few classes, but nobody has any clue. At this point Moses and I both have mud all over us, thanks to our arduous climb, and after three hours of searching, we still have no leads.

"Maybe we try the district office," Moses suggests with a defeated shrug. "I am without other ideas."

"Yeah, maybe that will work. If they can't help us, I guess I'll have to call it quits," I say, feeling dejected.

We hop back on the motorcycle and blunder down the dirt road back into Bududa town where the new district office sits on a small hill. Moses apparently "knows a guy who knows a guy," and the next thing I know I'm sitting across the desk from Daniel, one of the district officials. I explain to him my quest, and I can see he's intensely interested. But he can't seem to figure out where the picture was taken or why we hadn't been able to find any better leads while on our search in the hills.

"I'll call in the parish chief of that area to see if he can help," Daniel says as he takes out his cell phone. After a short conversation he hangs up and informs me, "He's nearby and says he'll stop by soon. Out of curiosity, why is it exactly that you are interested in finding this family again?" he asks.

"When I came here last I was a study-abroad student at

Makerere University. Some of my classmates and I were sent here for a week to do something called a 'participatory rural appraisal,' in hopes of helping the local people figure out their own needs. We thought things were going well until the final meeting when we presented our findings. The guy whose house we were staying at stood up and said to us, 'Thank you for helping us to conduct this assessment, and now we need you to save us.' The appraisal was supposed to help them figure out how to help themselves, but for some reason they still figured they needed 'saving.' We all went back to Kampala annoyed and jaded, especially me."

"That kind of dependency has been around forever. It doesn't surprise me to hear this," Daniel admits.

"Are there any NGOs working here these days?" I ask.

"Umm . . ." A long pause as he tries to think. "No."

"So if there are no foreign NGOs operating here, why do the locals assume outsiders might save them?" I ask.

"We have a mentality when we look at your skin color. We associate it with many things. People will say, 'Ahh, help us, help us.' We don't have any NGOs at the moment, but still the people say 'help us' because they think the *muzungu* is the origin of resources," he explains.

"So is there still a cultural assumption that we're here to help or give things away?" I ask.

"Yes, we've had foreigners coming for years, especially missionaries, so the locals formed opinions over long periods," he says. "*Muzungus* are associated with the development of schools and health centers, donations of clothes and soap, child sponsorship, and other things. Most people know someone who has been sponsored and when they see whites they think the same might come to them."

"So when they see me they're consciously thinking, it's worth a shot to see if she'll give me something?"

"Yes, exactly. They have nothing to lose, so they try. But I don't like to see it because there is such a syndrome of dependency. No matter how hard we try to distance ourselves from it, it's a challenge to get rid of," he says.

"It's such a shame," I say with a sigh. "I wish things were different."

"We're making good progress on our own without foreign help lately. We're standing on our own feet. I think it will just take more time for these perceptions to change," he says with a patient and hopeful look in his eyes.

❖ ❖ ❖

"The parish chief has arrived, he will surely know the family you are looking for," Daniel says with excitement as we head outside to greet him.

"So you are the chief of Namatiti?" I ask the man after we've all been introduced.

"Where?" he responds with a confused look on his face.

"Namatiti. The village I'm looking for," I repeat.

Daniel looks at me with a surprised look. "Did you say *Nama*titi or *Bunabu*titi?"

"*Namatiti.*"

"Oh dear, Namatiti is another place! You were in the wrong direction," he exclaims. The pieces suddenly all fall into place—Moses, in his unshaken confidence, thought I had asked to go to Bunabutiti, a large village near Bududa, instead of Namatiti. And he'd passed the same information on to the district officials here. No wonder I've wasted an entire morning searching and not recognizing anyone or anything! As frustrating as it is to be exhausted and covered in mud from the crazy search, I can accept that things like this happen.

"Okay," I say, trying not to sound exasperated by the error. "Then do you know where *Namatiti* village is?"

The parish chief shakes his head. "No, there's no Namatiti. I think you mean Bunabutiti."

"No, I promise, the place was called Namatiti," I assure him. I don't bother to mention that the only reason I can accurately remember the village name is because one of the other five college girls who was conducting the research here eight years ago jokingly referred to the place as "Not *my* titty." Mature, I know. But it stuck in my mind, and I can't concede that it's Bunabutiti I'm looking for. I'm certain it's Namatiti. Yet we seem to be at a deadlock. Nobody has ever heard of Namatiti, and I've taken the search all the way from the mud pathways to the top of the district government. I'm not entirely sure what other options I have left.

"I have an idea," Daniel says as he heads down the hall toward his office. Within a minute he's back with a large three-ring binder in his hands. "In here is a list of every single village in the entire district—890 in total. Let's see if we can find it."

This seems like an impossible feat, I think, as he starts thumbing through the unalphabetized pages, one by one. His finger glides down every page, but after passing by several hundred village names, I'm starting to doubt whether or not it's going to turn up. Yet all of a sudden his finger flies off the page, then lands back down on it with emphasis as he exclaims, "Namatiti!"

"Yeah!" I exclaim. "It *does* exist!"

Based on the information provided in the binder, they know exactly where the village is. I thank them profusely for their help with the search, and within minutes I'm on the back of another *boda-boda*, heading off to finally reunite with this elusive family.

◆　◆　◆

I recognize those eyes, for sure. And as soon as he opens his mouth to say, "Hi, my goodness, you have come back!" I am certain this was the same guy that asked me to "save him" all those years ago. His name is Michael, and I'd guess he's in his forties. He's unmarried, unemployed, and living with his aging parents.

He leads me through the yard, past a laundry line and some chickens, to the front porch. As we pass through the door of the partially walled-in porch, I realize that this is where the photo was taken. But the telltale aqua paint has now been changed to a cream color, and the remnants of the old color can only be seen in the few places where the paint is peeling. As we enter the dark, gaudily decorated living room, the memories come flooding back. The concrete house looks nicer than I remember it, but it's still very basic. The living room is surrounded on all sides with a few well-worn sofas and chairs, with a couple of low tables in the middle covered in lace doilies. Down a dark hallway, there are four bedrooms, followed by an outdoor cooking area, a small enclosure for bucket bathing constructed of corrugated metal scraps and pieces of wood, and farther behind the house a pit latrine. Michael's parents, John and Agatha, age eighty and seventy-one respectively, live in separate rooms (which is apparently common for married couples around here), and Michael lives in a small hut behind the outdoor kitchen area that had been built to accommodate a Peace Corps volunteer a few years back.

I have doubts about whether or not Michael and his family really remember me, but they are delighted I've come back, and they urge me to stay with them for a few days.

As we sit down with a cup of tea and a piece of *chapati* bread to catch up, John reaches over to the nearby table and hands me an aging black book. "The guest book," he says. "You should be in there, I think." I carefully thumb through the delicate pages, whose entries started back in 1995, and soon my own handwriting jumps off the page. In blue ink it reads, "Oct. 2002, Tori Hogan, Virginia; Thanks for welcoming us into your home!" I usually dislike the formality of guest books. Everywhere I go in this part of the world I'm asked to sign one, and it can get rather tiring to think of what to write in the comments section, but now I have a newfound appreciation for them. It's surreal to see my entry again as proof that I, indeed, have found the correct place.

"So are you still hosting foreign visitors?" I ask John as I place the book back on the table.

"No, not since long time. We used to have connections with some universities and with the Peace Corps, but those have finished. People would come here and do their research and we let them stay. But no more," he says with a sad look on his face. Michael excuses himself from the room to boil more tea, and I'm left alone with John to chat.

"So," I say, quickly trying to decipher what sort of small talk is most appropriate when engaging with an eighty-year-old man, "how long have you been married?"

"Since '54," he says.

"Wow, that's fifty-six years!" I exclaim. "Tell me, what's your secret?"

He looks at me confused and he scratches his bald head. "Secret? I don't understand. There is no secret." I had been fishing for some sage words of advice from a wise old soul, but instead I'm informed that staying married that long apparently just requires one thing: staying married.

He looks at me and asks with a hopeful face, "Are you married?"

"No, I'm not married yet," I reply.

"How old are you?" he asks.

"Twenty-eight."

He looks at me and shakes his head quite seriously. "Ahh . . . I will pray for you."

I had no idea I had already reached the level of assumed spinsterhood! According to John's reaction, my love life is apparently so bleak it's going to take some prayers to the Almighty to set things straight. I thank him for his concern, and try not to laugh—or cry.

His eyebrows rise in hopeful expectation as he asks, "You have boyfriend?"

"Yes, I do," I say, avoiding the part about us technically being on a break at the moment, and trying not to think too hard about how much I miss him right now. "He's a very nice man, but I can't decide yet if I will marry him."

"Soon you will have to decide," John replies matter-of-factly. Yes, it's true. Soon I will have to decide.

◆ ◆ ◆

"*Muzungu! Muzungu! Muzungu! Muzungu!*" a handful of kids giddily chant as Michael and I walk past them en route to the local market. A little girl in a green dress who looks to be three years old runs to the roadside, then stops and yells, "*Muzungu*, where are you going?"

I smile and look over my shoulder as I yell back, "The market!" She looks delighted, and the entire group spends the next few minutes jumping up and down, likely plotting to catch me again on the return trip home.

As we pass by a particularly gorgeous stretch of lush green hills and a gently flowing river, I turn to Michael and say, "You are so lucky to live in such a beautiful place!"

"Beautiful?" he says as he looks at me in surprise. "Every day I see this hill," he says, pointing to the right, "and this hill," pointing to the left, "and this dirt road! For me, Kampala is the beautiful place, not here. I have lived in this village for over forty years—I prefer the city."

I can't believe he honestly thinks that crazy Kampala is beautiful compared to this. I guess in contrast to some other African capitals, Kampala isn't too bad, but I'd never choose it over this paradise of rural loveliness.

I'm easily captivated by outdoor markets, and I quickly find that this one is no exception. The animals for sale have already gone home for the day, but all the other vendors are still here, selling their wares with a mix of boredom and occasional persistence.

We pass by the butchers and the grain dealers and the produce ladies, who have all expertly displayed what they have to sell on small blankets or wooden tables. Farther in we come across the clothing vendors who are selling used clothes. The majority of these clothes were originally donated from abroad and have made their way onto the marketplace for sale. And while job creation and income generation are seemingly positive outcomes of this phenomenon, the used clothes tend to saturate the local clothing markets, putting local textile producers and tailors out of business. I still always find myself halfheartedly wondering if I'll run across my seventh-grade gym shirt in one of these piles of clothes one day.

We eventually leave the market and take a seat in a small snack shop with a television blaring music videos from the eighties as Michael orders a Coke and I get a Fanta Orange. We spend some time catching up on each other's lives and talking about the ways the village has changed since I last saw it. From what I can tell so far, life in this area is progressing well thanks to slow and steady self-initiated and government-supported development, the way it should be.

"Things are improving." Michael nods as he takes a sip of his Coke. "People here are simply living their lives, and little by little it gets better."

I smile brightly at him, relieved to hear this news about

the area's development. It gives me a warm feeling inside as I sit here absorbing the fact that even in a village like this, which on the surface might appear "poor" to any outsider, things are flowing and improving and there's no glaring sense of desperation or discontent. It was so easy on our last trip here for me and my classmates to come blazing in as naive college students with our ambitious ideas about the "improvements" this community allegedly needed. Now, returning only as a curious observer, I'm humbled by how wrong we were. It's embarrassing that I ever thought I had anything of value to offer this community, or that I feigned any hope that my textbook methods of approaching rural development would ever really "help them help themselves." They didn't need me then, and they still don't. They're developing fine on their own. And maybe even Michael has developed in certain ways since our last encounter, because so far I haven't received any "save me" vibes from him at all. I'm glad I came back. As I lean back into my chair and join Michael in watching Journey belt out "Don't Stop Believin'" on the fuzzy television set, I get a hopeful feeling that my jadedness about this place is starting to be resolved.

CHAPTER 11

"THERE ARE PROBABLY still bodies under here," Michael says as he points to the muddy ground we're standing on. "They haven't been able to find them all."

I look up to the hillside nearby as I try to comprehend the enormity of the tragedy that unfolded here only three months ago. A large chunk of the hill is missing, and a path of dirt runs all the way down to where we stand. Apparently it used to be even more shocking to see when the entire area was covered in mud, but now bits of green grass are starting to grow back, turning the landslide site into a slightly less disturbing scene. Yet knowing that hundreds of lives were washed away in a matter of seconds is eerie enough. Not to mention the fact that many of the bodies are still somewhere underneath us.

Michael had offered to take me here to the landslide site during our conversation about the tragedy over dinner last night, but I wasn't so sure I wanted to see it. I hate the idea of "disaster tourism," and I didn't feel it was appropriate to visit this place. But Michael assured me that it would be good to have context of the scope of the disaster if we wanted to visit the temporary camp where the displaced families are now living. I finally decided to go along, but as I stand here now, I'm starting to realize why I was so resistant. Initially I argued that the problem with visiting disaster sites is because it engages a rather sick part of the human psyche, the same voyeuristic part of us that is prone to slowing down to check out terrible car accidents. But now I'm thinking it might be something more. Standing on the site of a big disaster forces you to soak in the reality of devastation and the scary fragility of life, which, as happened here, can be over in an instant.

I take a few steps forward and notice part of a little girl's dress sticking out of the mud. Nearby I see some tiles from the health clinic, a jerry can for collecting water, and mangled pieces of what used to be someone's tin roof. Michael and I walk in somber silence, mostly looking down at our feet at the remains of a village of more than seven hundred people, and occasionally glancing up at the hill that caused all this mess. In the distance we can see three tractors that have been digging for bodies ever since the landslide happened. But apparently the thick claylike mud is hard to dig through, and all three tractors are inoperable at the moment.

"*Mulembe*," I say in greeting as a man passes by. He is walking slowly, wearing rubber boots and an open plaid shirt while following his two cows as they munch on the grass. Michael and the man strike up a conversation in the local language, Lumasaba, and I watch the man passionately explain something while pointing in various directions.

"What did he say?" I ask after the guy has walked on.

"He said his family just barely survived. As soon as they heard the loud sound, they started to run. Fortunately, all four of them are still alive. Most of his cows were killed, but these two survived. His home used to be over there," Michael says, pointing at the tractors.

"And why isn't he in the camp now?" I ask.

"Because he's not allowed to bring his cows to the camp. But they're all he has left when it comes to property, so he stays here with them for now," Michael explains. "He says he lost many friends and family. It's terrible, really terrible," he says, shaking his head.

I nod, unsure of what to say as I scan the scene from left to right. On all sides of me there are lush green hills towering over us, some farm plots covered with banana trees, and the rich reddish-orange color of the soil peeking out here and there.

"Look over there," Michael says as he points across the nearby valley to a row of large hills. "You see? There was another landslide recently."

"Oh yeah, I see it," I say as I stare out to what looks like veins of mud running down the hill.

"Less people were killed, but these problems continue. They say many more will happen until the people stop destroying the land with over-farming. There are no trees left on these hills, so the mud just falls away when the big rains come," he explains as he steps over a beam from what used to be someone's home.

We turn back toward the path that led us here, crossing over a small river that didn't exist before the landslide. Listening to the sound of the trickling water gives a sense of eerie serenity that feels out of place.

There are hardly any people around anymore. Most of them are living in the temporary camp several miles away. But as we begin the hour-and-a-half-long trek back to the bottom of the hill along a narrow mud path that provides the only access here, we pass by a blind man sitting alone next to a house that has been shabbily put back together next to the landslide site.

"Are you living here still?" Michael asks the man as we pause in front of the shack.

With closed eyes, he lifts his face in the direction of

Michael's voice and nods slowly. "I'm not leaving. Even if I die, at least I will die on my own land."

So much was taken from this community in a matter of seconds. It's not surprising to see this man holding on tight, refusing to admit defeat to the forces of nature.

◆ ◆ ◆

Her voice is almost a whisper, which stands out in stark contrast to the loudness of her hot-pink button-up shirt and bright blue long skirt. But other than her wardrobe, there's nothing loud about Edna. She stands timidly next to a beige tent with a baby in her arms, looking blankly off into the distance and then down to the ground as she recounts her experience the day of the landslide.

"My husband was at the trading center and he luckily managed to run away in time," she starts. "But my baby and I were back at the house, which was crushed by the landslide. We were trapped in the mud for three hours. And the only reason they found me was because my baby was crying. I was half-conscious when they discovered us because I couldn't breathe well under the mud, and I was taken to the hospital the next morning."

"And after you recovered they brought you here to the camp?" I ask.

"Yes, I came here with nothing. Just with my baby and my husband. Everything I have now was donated to me," she says, looking down at her mismatched wardrobe. "It's been three months now. They keep telling me that we will be resettled somewhere else, but we're still here. . . ." Her voice trails off.

"Will you go for resettlement to another part of the country when the time comes?" I ask.

"I'll go, but only because I have no other choice," she says with a dejected tone.

I thank her for sharing her story as I continue to follow Edson, one of the Red Cross workers, through the tent city that is now home to roughly ten thousand internally displaced persons. There are clusters of donated tents in every direction: the ones from the UN are large, white, rectangular structures (the penthouse suites of the tented camp), the Red Cross tents are small, shabby brown A-frames, and the Rotary International donations are hip, beige, dome-shaped tents, the type you'd see at campgrounds across America. According to Edson, there wasn't any rhyme or reason when it came to tent distribution. Some families were luckier than others, as the Red Cross tents seem to be showing the most problems with leaks and general wear and tear.

As we pass by another cluster of tents, I see kids playing in the hard clay mud, women washing clothes and dishes in tiny basins of dirty water, and others sitting idly under scavenged pieces of tarp, seemingly unsure if they're waiting for something or nothing. We pass through the communal cooking area that consists of a long line of small wood fires and a handful of cooking pots where a few women are hard at work preparing dishes for their families with the basic rations they've been allotted.

"It's over here," Edson informs me, as he points to the left and motions me to follow.

We round the corner and a large white banner greets us with a familiar name and logo that was part of the impetus for me becoming an aid critic in the first place: SAVE THE CHILDREN.

"This is the primary school," Edson explains as we enter the courtyard. The school consists of an L-shape set of permanent classrooms that used to serve the local community before the disaster struck, and an additional L-shape set of temporary classrooms made out of branches and plastic tarps. School isn't in session at the moment, but we pass by about forty children who are enthusiastically clamoring for a turn on the three swings and two climbing structures.

Edson leads us into a dark green tent where an older Ugandan man with a graying mustache is sitting behind a desk, surrounded by paperwork. He introduces himself as Ezra, the headmaster of the temporary school. As we start talking, I can tell he is a man of integrity who cares deeply about the children he's responsible for educating. But he also looks worn-out.

"Based on the banner outside, I'm guessing this is being run by Save the Children?" I ask.

"Well, it *was* being run by Save the Children. They helped with the construction and the school supplies and some of the teacher salaries," he says. "But they're gone now. They were only working on a three-month contract, and it has just finished. Now we feel like we're here stranded. We don't know what will come next."

"Why did Save the Children leave already when there is still so much work to be done?" I ask.

"It's not just Save the Children, actually. All of the NGOs have left now," he says. "We're on our own in the camp. The Ugandan government had signed contracts with the NGOs indicating they only needed their services for a three-month period, and when that time was up, the aid organizations just packed up and left. But with the government moving so slowly on resettlement, there is still a major need for aid here, though it's now finished. Maybe Save the Children has moved on to the next disaster. I'm not sure."

"So there are no other NGOs helping here?" I ask, with shock in my voice.

"Nothing," he says.

I turn to Edson. "Really? What about the Red Cross?"

"Our contract ended, too, but I didn't have the heart to

walk away, so I'm working for free now." He shrugs. I'm aware that most NGOs operate on short-term contracts, with budget resources allotted to only cover the specific contract period, but it still surprises me when I hear stuff like this happening.

"And what is the government's role now that the NGOs are gone?" I ask, turning to Ezra.

"The government is slow in their planning and decision-making. At the moment, they are only able to focus on giving food to the people. The school isn't a high priority for them," he explains. "And now that Save the Children has left, things are getting worse and worse here. For example, the teachers used to be getting a salary bonus from Save the Children to give them incentives to teach, and with that gone, they are losing their morale. Eight of the teachers have stopped working altogether because their salaries had been covered by Save the Children and now they are finished. Also the play structures are being destroyed by the kids, and nobody is here to fix or replace them."

"But while Save the Children was working here, was their assistance at least helpful?" I ask.

"To be truthful with you, it was only when they started going away that we realized they had been useful to us. But we expected more from them, really. We assumed they would have a school-feeding program for the children. And we also expected they would provide uniforms and water and sanitation facilities for the school. But they never did"—he pauses for a moment, shuffling some papers on his desk, then sighs. "The classroom tents will probably be taken soon. Now that their program is done, Save the Children will want them back."

I have pretty negative views about Save the Children for some of the ways they impose poor decisions on communities, waste money, and coddle donors, but I can't imagine they would be so heartless as to deconstruct the school while there is still such an obvious need for it here. I'm hoping that Ezra is only basing this comment on vague speculation but, then again, I've seen worse from Save the Children.

After our meeting with Ezra we follow Edson as he leads us over to the camp hospital. We enter the simple concrete building, which has little more than an examining table and a desk, and I hear the same story repeated. Paula, the young midwife attending to a long line of patients sitting on a wooden bench outside, looks utterly exhausted.

"We used to be twelve working here," she tells me as she grabs a patient's record book from the shelf and writes some notes from the examination in it. "The doctors and nurses were funded by the Indian Association and the World Health Organization for three months, but now it's only me and a volunteer or two every now and then."

She closes her eyes for a second and takes a deep breath, with one hand on her back, before she goes to the doorway to give some final advice to the patient she has just seen. As she returns, she comes closer to me and confesses, "It breaks you. I'm completely overloaded." She leans against the desk to give her feet a momentary rest as she continues, "I'm not even properly suited for this position. I'm a midwife, not a doctor. But I'm the only one that will agree to come, so I work long hours and I sometimes get ulcers working so hard on an empty stomach. Nobody in the government understands how hard I have to work," she says with exasperation and fatigue in her voice.

"So what keeps you coming back each day?" I ask.

"It's simple," she says with a tired smile. "I like to help people. I feel that I should do what I can to eliminate suffering."

◆　◆　◆

I walk down the main drag of Bududa town en route to one of the government offices, lost in thought about what I saw yesterday in the camp. I wish there was something I could do. But at this point it seems the only thing I can offer is my service as a "bridge." In fact, since a local person is infinitely more qualified to conduct fieldwork than I ever would be, I find that being a bridge is often my only option. For better or worse, my status as a foreigner allows me to walk between both worlds, and I'm probably a hundred times more likely to land a meeting with an influential official than one of the internally displaced people living in the camp.

So here I am at the office of Steven Wabusani, the commandant of the camp, to share what I've heard. I get the impression that Mr. Wabusani is filling a rather administrative role, and he doesn't spend nearly enough time in the camp getting the real stories on the ground. Not long into our conversation, I'm able to see how out of touch he is with the current situation.

"It's the government's mistake that all of the NGOs are withdrawing these days," he explains. "The NGOs only structured their budgets until May 30 because that's when the government told them the people would be resettled by. This has turned out to be false." But then he folds his hands on the desk and gives a reassuring look. "At least we still have Save the Children."

I am forced to break the bad news to him. "No, they are finished, too."

"They're finished?" he asks with disbelief.

"Yeah."

"No, they're . . . ahh . . ." He pauses while trying to soak in the information, information he clearly should have been aware of himself. "So that means we don't have any NGOs."

He looks bummed to hear the news, though he recovers quickly as he gets fired up complaining about the inadequacy of the government's response.

"We don't have a budget for that camp! When we tell the office of the prime minister we don't have food, they send food. But it means we are constantly begging, week after week. We can't plan. If we knew when the people were going to be resettled, then we could plan better," he says.

"Yeah, I can imagine that is difficult," I reply.

"We only planned for three months originally, and we're already past that," he explains. "Things like health and sanitation are going to be a big problem for us. The toilets will be filled up. Even as we speak, some of them are already full. The heavy rains in August will probably bring cholera, but the NGOs aren't there to provide more latrines. Not to mention the local host community. They are hampered. We have invaded them. Where our school is now, that used to be their marketplace. I don't think they will want to host these people for much longer. But for many of the displaced people it's too dangerous to go back to their communities because more landslides might happen, so rebuilding their homes isn't an option."

"So where will everyone go?" I ask.

"The government is looking for free land in other parts of the country. We are only praying every day that these people move away. We don't know where the government will take them, but there needs to be an immediate solution." His eyes widen and he gets a hopeful look on his face as he asks, "Or we can send them to the United States?" He's serious.

I shake my head. "Unfortunately, internally displaced persons don't qualify for asylum in the U.S. It's only for refugees who cross international borders based on a fear of persecution, not for people who are internally displaced by natural disaster."

"That's too bad," he says. "Refugees, they become posh people!" I don't bother correcting his sweeping, inaccurate assumption. I've volunteered for many years with resettled refugees in the United States, and I can guarantee that the life of a resettled refugee is far from "posh" and their path is not an easy road to travel. It's usually full of language challenges, crappy minimum-wage jobs, discrimination, isolation, and many other undesirable experiences.

He continues, "But actually, I think some of these displaced persons are feeling rather posh lately, too. When you look at the camp now and all the donations they have received, it is as if they are even better off than the local community!"

"Do you think some of the people are just living there to get free stuff?" I ask.

"Yes, those types are there. We originally wanted to use local leaders to write letters on behalf of families that were directly affected by the landslide, but then they started registering their friends and family, too, who were living far from there," he says.

"That happened?"

"Yes, from day one."

"There were only seven hundred people living in the original village where the landslide happened, a little more than three hundred died," I recount. "So how is the camp full of ten thousand people now? Are they all meant to be there?"

"No, of course not. But we didn't have good systems in place to verify who deserved assistance," he says with a resigned face. "People from a few neighboring villages were encouraged to come, too, because they were living in an at-risk location that could have a similar tragedy soon," he adds. "But many of the people came because they saw an opportunity for charity. But we are going to screen them when we transfer them. Not all of them will move. Probably only four thousand will go. It depends on how much land the government will buy for them."

It's hard to believe that approximately six thousand of the

displaced persons are actually just mooching off the largesse of the NGOs and government. Still, I know this is a common situation in disaster relief. I'm feeling jaded, for sure, but I'm not sure if it's mostly due to the failure of the aid response or the dishonesty of the majority of the recipients.

I use my remaining time with Steven to be as good of a "bridge" as I can be. I tell him the stories I heard from the people in the camp, the challenges I witnessed at the school and the health clinic, and the complaints from the Red Cross workers about insufficient supplies. He writes it all down and thanks me for sharing the information with him so he can follow up with the appropriate parties. It's unlikely my discussion with the commandant will translate into real changes for the displaced people, but I feel like I did what I could.

CHAPTER 12

My backpack is already packed and I'm nearly ready to leave, but Michael has insisted I stay for lunch before I catch a minibus to Mbale. I'm perched on the edge of a sagging couch, journaling about the aid efforts I saw in the camp and the slow and steady development here in Namatiti. My eyes are straining as I write in the dark living room, despite the sun shining outside, because all the shutters are closed and the only bit of light breaking through is coming from the open door on my left. As I write, it feels as if I'm being watched. Eventually the feeling becomes too strong, so I glance out the door, and sitting on the ledge of the concrete veranda is Michael's elderly father, John, staring at me.

"Oh John, I didn't see you there," I say with a startled expression. "Do you need something?"

I start to close my journal, but he puts his palm toward me and shakes his wrist as he insists, "No, no, whenever you are finished, I want to talk to you."

Oh man, I knew this was going to happen. I was *so* close to getting out of here without any "ask," but I can already feel it coming. It has felt awkward for a while, actually. All morning I half-expected Michael was going to ask me to "save" them again. It wasn't a specific thing I could put my finger on, but something about our interactions felt uncomfortable today.

John shifts his posture and gestures with his hand as he explains, "It's just that, as you know, life here is not easy." Here it comes. I knew it, I knew it, I knew it. "Our life, it is difficult. Very, very difficult. If only we could get an American sponsor like you to help us, to send us money regularly, life would be better." He drops his head for emphasis, and then looks up in hopeful expectation.

"John, I understand that things can be difficult, but I'm really not comfortable with the idea of sponsorship."

He persists, "Or if you have a friend outside there that can support us through you. I give the address and bank account in Mbale. I would be very grateful." His eyes look like a pleading puppy, and then he takes it even further as he adds, "Jesus would bless you." It's totally not fair to bring Jesus into this. I was honest and up front with him in my original response, but apparently he doesn't want to take no for an answer.

He continues, "Right now we live hand to mouth, just small, small things. We are poor, very poor. We have no source of income, only the *matoke* that we grow. It's not enough if you get sick," he says, with the most pathetically sad face I've ever seen from an old man.

My bullshit detector is on high alert, though. I already know that none of this is true. For starters, their compound is larger than any other home nearby, and their main house is made of concrete, not of mud like their neighbors. By local standards, they're affluent. Plus, Michael has already told me about the several plots of land they own throughout the area, many of which they rent out for additional income and the rest they use for growing crops. I even walked by their massive sugarcane fields on our way to the market the other day, which provide a reliable source of income for them. They also obtain additional money by renting their extra rooms in the house to visitors who pay a small amount to cover food and accommodation, as I have during both my visits here. And John has several daughters living in Kampala who are very well-educated and gainfully employed who send money home. This is hardly a family that would be described as living "hand to mouth."

Without a response from me, he presses on, "We will write each month as a report. We tell you how we spent the money." I can tell he's familiar with the NGO scene, as he already knows the value of regular reporting to foreign donors. "Michael is unable to support us because he is not married." I'm not sure what Michael's marital status has to do with his ability to earn a living.

"John, I hear what you are saying, but I'm not able to sponsor you. Not only do I not have the money for this right now, I don't think that sponsorship will help at all in the long run." I wait to let the answer sink in.

"It depends on you. We shall be praying to God for you. Every chance we pray for you. We shall be sending you a bank account. We are not forcing you, only if you are kindly or if you know someone who is kindly, I would be very grateful. If I receive it, you will receive a telephone call in two or three days," he says in a hopeful flurry.

"But, John, I already told you, I can't sponsor you," I remind him. "And to be honest, I doubt that it would change your life much."

"Change wife?" he asks with a confused look.

"No, change your *life*."

"With my wife?" We're clearly not getting anywhere here.

Fortunately, Michael walks in with a small bowl of rice and beans for lunch, interrupting my conversation with John. As we all sit there eating in silence, I am at a loss for words. In a way it feels depressing to see an old man stooping to that level, and essentially putting his hand out to be "saved" by a foreigner. I expected it from Michael, since he did it the last time I was here, but I never saw it coming from John. Maybe I can't blame him for trying. Once again, at the final moment of my time here in Namatiti, my hopes that things have changed have been dashed. After eight years, and despite all the positive developments here, the "save us" mentality remains, the hands are still out, and I am leaving this place feeling more disheartened than I had hoped.

◆ ◆ ◆

As the minibus gets closer and closer to town, I anxiously stare down at my cell phone, eager for a signal to return after all these days. I'm praying for a text from Mark, as I'm wondering where his heart is after all this silence. Before venturing out to Bududa I sent him an email describing some of my recent revelations about our relationship, and I'm curious what his response will be. In the email I told him how much I love him and the importance of finding my authentic self again *with* him, not *without* him. I don't want to be on a break. I asked him if he might be interested in spending the weekend in Uganda with me.

Though it might seem unexpected to have had a change of heart so quickly, the revelations I've had lately about Mark and me have been eye opening. While on my way to Bududa I stopped for a brief respite at one of my favorite spots on the planet, Sipi Falls. Sipi is a small Ugandan village on the slopes of Mount Elgon in an area known primarily for its excellent coffee farms and its magnificent waterfalls. When I was twenty, I stayed there with my study-abroad group in a place called The Crow's Nest, a simple lodge that was started by two Peace Corps volunteers years ago. The small, basic cabins overlook a truly impressive valley with expanses of bright green farms creating a mosaic below and enormous waterfalls cascading from cliffs off to the right. But the real gem of the place is the wooden swing that hangs from an old tree at the edge of the property. I don't remember which of us discovered it back when we stayed there, but it was one heck of a find. When you swing out it feels as if you're flying over the valley. It was there that I had some insightful revelations about life eight years ago. As I sat there on that swing one morning in the fall of 2002, staring out at the valley and the endless flow of the mesmerizing waterfall, I wrote the following in my journal:

Life isn't about jobs or money or status. It's about loving and being loved. It's about finding your own inner beauty. It's about acceptance, understanding, and compassion. It's about stepping outside of your comfort zone in order to learn more about others and the world. It's about breathing . . . and sensing. It's not about how people see you, it's about how you see yourself. And it's a determination to wake up each morning with the intention of living the day to the fullest. Yet even when we have grasped these truths it is so easy to get pulled back into the negative vortex of a superficial life. It becomes easy to forget the waterfalls and the people we love. Perhaps it requires conditioning to maintain your focus on such things in order to never forget what's important now. I have a feeling that if happiness and inner beauty are my primary goals, everything else in my life will work itself out. So here I go . . . making the most of this beautiful day.

I decided to return to Sipi again last week in hopes of having some new insights there.

What I gained from my many hours sitting quietly on that swing this time around was that I'm *way* too much of a perfectionist. Somehow along my life's path I learned to expect and demand perfection from myself and others. "Good enough" was never good enough. I ended up living a life of endless striving for best and then better than best, without even knowing what exactly would be waiting for me at the end of all my effort. Having such standards was not only hurting my ability to fully love myself—because no matter how hard I tried or how close I came, I was *never* quite "perfect"—but it has also hurt my ability to love others, Mark included. For much of our relationship I've been holding Mark under a microscope. Every little bothersome thing he does invokes the question, "Can I live with that?" The more I focus on the negatives, the more I seem to find.

Returning to that swing last week, I replayed our time together almost day by day, and what I discovered is that we actually make a pretty good couple 90 percent of the time. In fact, we aren't just "pretty good"; we're *great*. It finally became obvious to me that, in fact, Mark's quirks make him real and human, and they are undeniably part of what makes him so lovable. It's likely he feels the same way about mine. While I'm still not sure if Mark is necessarily "the one," I know that as soon as you drop judgment of another person, magical things can happen and relationships can be transformed overnight. I'm not ready to give up on our love.

Suddenly, I hear the telltale loud double beep, boldly signaling the arrival of a text message. I have two messages. I can hardly push the button fast enough. The first one reads:

I have tears in my eyes after reading your email—it means so much to me to know that you feel the same as I do. I love you, M

A wave of relief rushes over me. His response could have easily gone the other way, of course. He might have finally been tired of the long distances, and the language differences, and the complications of putting two stubborn, passionate people together in one relationship. But instead he feels the same as I do. He doesn't want to give up, either. How incredible.

I open the next message which he sent yesterday:

I booked a flight to Uganda, arriving Friday night. I can't wait to see you, my love.

◆　◆　◆

Everything feels right in the world at this moment. We're waiting for our dinner to be served at a cute thatched restaurant on the shore of Lake Victoria following a heartfelt reunion at the Entebbe Airport. Mark looks at me across the table with an adorable, innocent smile. It's a look that requires no words, but simply expresses the message, "I know you, I get you, and I love you." He reaches across the table and puts his hand gently on top of mine. "So now what?" he asks.

"Yeah, good question," I say with a smile. "Where do we go from here?"

"Well, we could just *be*," he says as he grins and looks down while stroking my hand gently with his thumb. "A lot of our troubles seem to come from being too future-focused, wondering if we will still be able to tolerate each other when we're seventy instead of enjoying what we have with each other in the present. We never seem to have any problems when we're present."

"That's true. It's the bullshit of the past and the future that messes us up. And, of course, our propensity to judge."

He laughs. "Yeah, that, too."

"Mark, I think I owe you an apology," I say as I take his other hand in mine and look into his eyes.

"Oh?"

"I've been so judgmental. I've held you up to impossible

standards, and then I'd internally blame you when my expectations weren't met. It hasn't been fair to you. I'm really sorry."

"Sweetie, I understand. I do it, too, sometimes. And I know about your high expectations and your fairy tale dreams. In a way, I like that about you. But there's a difference between shooting for the stars in a good way and having unrealistic expectations about life. You need to cut yourself some slack first, and then the people around you."

"Yeah, you're so right. I feel like I've wasted a lot of years buried in ridiculous expectations." He nods in understanding. "But, I mean, you didn't exactly come in the package I was expecting," I say as I raise my eyebrows and make a subtle smirk. "In all my years of fantasizing about the guy I'd spend my life with, never once did I ask for a tall, redheaded, Dutch guy who is eight years older than me, and who is bringing a considerable amount of past baggage into the relationship. Those things weren't exactly on my checklist."

"Yeah, I know." He laughs. "You were looking for, what was his name? Oh yeah, Prince Charming."

"Right, the nonexistent Prince Charming who would somehow match all the ideal criteria and then sweep me off my feet in a magical and uncomplicated love affair and cherish me forever."

"Other than the uncomplicated part and matching the ideal criteria, I think I can manage it," he jokes.

"Yeah, you're good at the magical love affair and cherishing me parts . . . maybe even forever?"

"There we go again getting future-focused." He laughs.

I laugh, too. "Oh, right." We pause a moment and look at each other, as I return to a more sincere tone. "Mark, I might not have specifically asked for a guy like you in all my years of dreaming and scheming, but you're better than I imagined possible. I didn't know that guys like you even existed."

He looks at me with deep admiration and pulls my hand toward his face as he kisses it softly. "Tori, I love you. That's what I know for sure. And I will never say that being with you is easy, or that things just magically flow effortlessly, but to me there's something like an inevitability to our love." He kisses my hand again and then sets it down on top of his.

"You said something like that in your second letter to me after we met in Chile."

"I did?"

"Yeah, you wrote something like, 'If I could formulate why I've fallen in love with you, I wouldn't have fallen in love with you. Love isn't about checking the boxes, assessing whether someone fits your criteria. It's something magical, and it should stay magical.'"

"Good memory," he says with a grin.

"I've reread those letters a lot," I confess.

"I think I also wrote something about my ideas on ultimate love, didn't I?" he adds.

"Yeah, the unconditionality of it, and the importance of freedom. And being able to see each other as they are, and loving that in every sense—even the dark sides . . ." I trail off as I start to consider this.

We pull our hands back and I fold my arms on the table leaning forward. "Maybe that's also where we've gone wrong?"

"Yeah, we've staked too many claims on each other." He leans back in his chair and glances out to the lake, which is shimmering from the moon's reflection. He then looks back to me. "Instead of loving each other without conditions, we started judging the other too much. And in sensing those judgments, we probably felt pressured to change ourselves to match what the other wanted." He pauses to think about this for a moment before adding, "That might explain why you haven't been feeling like yourself lately."

"I think you're right. You once wrote to me that ultimate love is about letting each other 'go, grow, and glow,'" I say, lovingly remembering those wise words. "We need to loosen our grip on each other, and just create the space where we allow each other to be who they are while continuing to grow into an even more beautiful version of our true selves."

"Exactly," he says, nodding slowly. "We've been there before, do you think we can get back?"

"Yeah, I think we've just taken a slight detour. At a soul level, I know we're capable of so much more," I say, moving back as the waiter sets the food down. "Thanks."

"We've gotten pretty far off track from where we used to be," Mark says as he picks up his fork. "It won't be easy to turn it around."

"If it's worth it to us, we'll make it work."

◆　◆　◆

The wind is whipping through my hair and I have that classic sense of unbridled freedom that is impossible to avoid when riding on a motorcycle. Mark's arm is holding me around my waist with his other hand grabbing tightly onto the back of the bike. Since I'm currently sandwiched between him and the driver on a bike that wasn't meant for three people, I'm trusting in Mark's grasp to keep me in place.

It doesn't take long before the paved streets give way to dusty and bumpy back roads lined with banana trees and small mud and concrete houses. We've decided to spend our weekend together in the laid-back town of Jinja, which is roughly two hours from Kampala and famous for being the place where the Nile River begins its long journey north, emptying out from Lake Victoria. Everything about this getaway has been glorious. I'm starting to feel almost bipolar in the way I can go from being uncertain about the relationship one minute, to feeling completely sure of things the next (now being one of those times). The dynamic that is capable of creating such hot and cold emotions is still unclear to me, but I decide to embrace the beauty of this moment and not overthink things.

"Bujugali?" the driver turns to ask us.

"Yeah, Bujugali Falls," I reconfirm as he turns down a dusty path. Mark and I are heading to some of the most impressive falls on the Nile River for a quiet day together.

The river doesn't disappoint. The falls are absolutely magnificent, though I would describe them more as rapids than waterfalls. Mark and I walk out onto the rocks for a better view, stopping just short of the sign painted with two skull and crossbones that clearly states "Danger! Do not go beyond this point."

We sit there side-by-side on the rocks in silence for a few moments, breathing it all in until Mark eventually breaks the silence with a cute sigh. "I love rivers."

"Yeah, I know." I smile.

He puts one arm around me while stroking my hair with his other hand. "For me, rivers are one of the ultimate sources of inspiration," he says. "They're an inevitable process caused by forces of nature. There's no choice in it, nothing manipulated."

I nod, thinking it's cute how philosophical he can get sometimes, just out of the blue. "It's a metaphor for how life should be," I say.

"Yeah. A river simply just *is* at every stage in the process. There's no final goal or destination for the water. When it arrives at the sea, the water will evaporate again and make its way to a cloud and then rain, to become flowing water again for a while." He looks down at me with a smile. "It reminds me every time I'm surrounded by rivers that most things in life are about the process, not about the final destination or goal."

I look into his deep brown eyes. "Like love," I say.

"Yeah, like love," he echoes softly, as he leans over to kiss me.

CHAPTER 13

"I came all this way in hopes of helping some orphans, but it wasn't what I expected," a twentysomething American girl named Laura explains to me. She takes another sip of beer. "Like, you know, they made the volunteer program sound so enticing, but really they had no use for me there."

It appears the youth hostel I've chose to stay at doubles as a mecca for jaded ex-volunteers, Laura being one of them. Mark left for Western Kenya yesterday for some work meetings, and I decided to spend some time in Kampala to see where my quest for answers about aid might take me next.

"How long were you supposed to stay?" I ask her, leaning forward to pick up my own beer off the table.

"Three months," she replies.

"And how long did you last?"

"Only three days." She takes another sip. "I couldn't take it anymore. The orphanage was so poorly run, and it was a zoo with way too many volunteers trying to help out, and I'm pretty sure there was some suspicious stuff going on behind the scenes."

"Really? Like what?" I probe.

"I don't know for sure, but there were rumors about embezzlement of funds and stuff like that. Something about the place just didn't feel right to me. I didn't want to be part of it." She scoots farther back into the sagging couch that graces the lounge area of our hostel. As she slips off her flip-flops and puts one foot up on the coffee table, she adds, "I wasn't even one of those people who was coming with grand visions of spending my time just holding cute African babies, you know? I wanted to be useful, to offer my skills in some way that was helpful to the organization."

"Do you feel like you were misled?" I ask.

"Yeah, in a way I do. I mean, the flashy 'volunteer abroad' websites that advertised the opportunity made it sound so great. But the reality is much different," she says. "I don't feel guilty about leaving, either. I probably did them a favor. Those kids don't need a bunch of altruistic young foreigners coming over pretending they're going to save them, you know?"

I fill Laura in on my background and my current journey to find answers about the truth of aid. Her eyes widen as she listens, then she quickly tears a corner of paper out of her notebook and scribbles down the address of the orphanage. "You should go check it out for yourself," she says. "Maybe I'm being overly cynical, but I have a feeling you'll feel the same as I do after seeing it with your own eyes."

"Thanks," I say as she hands me the address. "I'll go check it out tomorrow."

◆　◆　◆

As I walk up the hill toward the orphanage, I'm starting to have doubts about my decision to visit this train wreck of an aid project. My journey is supposed to be about finding answers, and ideally some *hope*, about aid effectiveness. But, based on Laura's comments, it's unlikely that this orphanage is going to provide me with any inspiration. So far on this trip I've had a few tiny glimmers of hope, but most of the projects I've seen in Kenya and Uganda have only reinforced my jadedness. Yet, despite my reservations, my feet continue to propel me forward, as if magnetized to the colorfully painted gate of the orphanage. *Maybe it's not as bad as she made it sound,* I think to myself, attempting to justify my curiosity.

"*Oli otya, ssebo?*" I say to the guard, greeting him in some Luganda I still remember from when I used to live here. He gives a nod and waves me through the gate. He doesn't ask my name or make me sign in. He doesn't even check my ID or ask what the purpose of my visit is. He just lets me in.

It's probably because I'm foreign, and young, and apparently nonthreatening, but it concerns me that there wouldn't be the slightest check before allowing a stranger to have access to fifty vulnerable children. The lack of security is already making me question the quality of this orphanage.

I head up the stairs of the outdoor area and poke my head into the first open door I find. Five volunteers, all young women who appear to be in their twenties, are glued to a television, immersed in a show.

One of them looks up and sees me in the doorway. "We're watching *House*, wanna join?"

"Actually, I was looking for the orphanage," I explain.

"Oh, the kids stay over there," she says, pointing vaguely to the left. "But it's their naptime now, so there's not much to see at the moment." She swings her legs out from under her and gets up from the couch. She comes closer and eagerly asks, "Are you a new volunteer?"

"No, I'm just a visitor," I reply. "I ran into an ex-volunteer yesterday who didn't have many nice things to say about the program.

And since my work is focused on the issue of aid effectiveness, I figured it might be worthwhile to follow up on the rumors."

Her eyebrows rise as she motions me to follow her. "Oh boy, do we have a lot to talk about! Come, take a seat." We enter the neighboring door, which appears to be a small sitting area where the volunteers staying in the on-site guesthouse can congregate. An older woman in her sixties with long gray hair and smile lines around her eyes is sitting at the table finishing a cup of tea.

"Lorraine, this is . . . sorry, what was your name?" she asks, turning back to me.

"Tori."

"This is Tori. She's here to investigate some of the problems at the orphanage," the girl explains, labeling me as some kind of an investigative reporter already. "Oh, and I'm Jenna. From Florida," she adds with a slight wave as she takes a seat on the couch across from us.

"It's nice to meet you both." I smile. "Though 'investigate' might be too strong of a word. But I have a strong interest in uncovering how aid can be more effective." I give them the abbreviated summary of my professional background, my encounter with Ahmed in 2002, and my current journey in search of answers on his behalf.

"I feel like there might be something to learn here," I add, hopefully.

"Ha! Welcome, welcome. *Bienvenue!*" Lorraine says heartily with a thick French accent as she shakes my hand.

"So, what have you heard? I'm curious!" Jenna eagerly asks.

"Well, I heard rumors about some shady dealings here, and some problems with the volunteer program. I'd be interested in hearing your take on things."

"I'm not surprised to hear it," Jenna replies as she pulls her curly brown hair up into a ponytail. "There are lots of problems. For starters, the standards of care are just so low in my opinion. We have clear ways to care for kids in the U.S. I don't want to say that they're doing it wrong here, but I can't necessarily say that they're doing it right."

Lorraine jumps in. "And besides, it's not clean enough or hygienic. And that should be improved."

"And what about the director, is she trying to improve the program?" I ask.

"Agatha? Ha!" Lorraine laughs. "In the three weeks I've been here, I've never seen her going over there to where the children are."

"Yeah, I only saw her when I first got here to welcome me and say, 'Here is where you stay, and here is where you pay,'" Jenna adds. "Each volunteer pays twenty dollars a night to stay here in the guesthouse next to the orphanage," she explains, "so they're definitely making money off the volunteer program."

"But aside from Agatha not being around much, do you think there might also be problems with corruption or mismanagement?" I ask.

"Yeah, for sure. The money and donations aren't being used right, as far as I can see," Jenna replies vehemently. "Clothes get donated and the rumor is they first go to the administrators to pick what they want for their own kids, then to the staff members, and finally to the orphans."

"I brought two full suitcases of baby clothes with me," Lorraine adds, "and for myself I only brought three outfits to wear. But I haven't seen the clothes I gave ever since I arrived. We can't trust them. When I go back to my French colleagues and show them pictures and they ask about the clothes they donated, what do I tell them?"

"I was going to bring a ton of donated clothes, but now I'm

glad I didn't since it seems they don't actually make it to the orphans," Jenna says.

"What else is being taken by the administration?" I ask.

"The money," Jenna says bluntly. "A friend's parents in Michigan donated a lot of money for the orphanage. The money was supposed to pay a large debt the orphanage owes the hospital, but instead it was spent on repainting the front sign, and who knows where the rest went." She rolls her eyes.

Jenna looks up as another volunteer who appears to be my age enters the doorway. "Oh, Emily could give you a much better answer on this one. She's been here longer."

I greet Emily and she takes a seat next to Jenna on the couch. "We were just having a chat about whether or not money might be going missing from this place. Any thoughts?" I ask.

"Oh my," she says, drawing out the words in a soothing British accent. "Well, I heard the administration before Agatha had transparency and accountability issues. They had to fire the accountant because she was pocketing money."

"Wow, that's terrible," I say.

Emily quickly adds, "But this is all behind the scenes, so I really can't be sure." She pauses for a moment, then says in a rather unconfident voice, "In my gut I think Agatha is trying to do her best. . . ." She hesitates. "I'd like to trust her completely, but the reality is that because we don't know one hundred percent where the money goes, some people are now reluctant to give it."

Jenna looks over to Emily as she says, "I don't see how the children are benefiting from all the donations."

Emily nods in agreement. "A load of shoes was given and someone wanted to write the initials of the orphanage on them so they wouldn't go missing, but staff members were acting funny and claimed that Agatha had to look over them first."

"That sounds a bit shady," I say.

"Yeah, when it comes to donations, that's where we all question whether it goes to the kids or if it goes out," Emily says.

Lorraine laughs and adds, "Yes, perhaps I will see my clothes donations at the market soon!"

The three of them let out hesitant laughs together. Her comment probably isn't far from the truth.

◆ ◆ ◆

The moment the volunteers descend on the outdoor play area, a frantic rush ensues as the kids scramble for prime real estate on their laps. Although I had hoped to fade into the background and just observe the volunteers today, it seems my lap is fair game, too, as a little boy expertly scales his way up my leg, beating out his competitor. I know it's only natural for young children to crave affection and attention, especially in an orphanage where fifty kids have to share their caregivers' time, but it feels more exaggerated than the attention-seeking behavior I normally see among young children. It's almost as if the steady stream of volunteers here at the orphanage has turned them into *professional* attention seekers. Some get attention by being super cute and playful, while others cry and cling on to legs, hoping to be picked up. Then there's the third group who I watch getting attention from the volunteers by constantly stirring up trouble. Just as I'm noticing this, I feel two hands on my hair as a three-year-old mischief maker who discovered a tube of diaper cream in the office smears some of the white gook down the length of my ponytail.

"They can be pretty cheeky sometimes." Emily laughs as she passes by with a little boy in her arms, pulling two fighting girls away from each other. She sits next to me on the outdoor bench as I try to wipe my hair with a tissue and she positions the little boy on her lap. "This one is my reason for coming back to volunteer here again. I'd adopt him if I could. I've started an education fund for him, though, and I'm sure he'll be part of my life forever, somehow."

"I guess it's easy to get attached, huh?" I ask.

"Yeah, definitely. All the volunteers have their favorites. I guess that's inevitable," Emily says with a shrug.

I look over to a college student from Canada playing lovingly with a little boy with cerebral palsy. Lorraine is focused on an eleven-month-old boy whom she refers to as her "fiancé."

There are eleven volunteers helping out today, including six foreigners and five students from a local university who are fulfilling their mandatory service requirements for their social work degree. But it appears as if the real work of changing the diapers, wiping the tears, and bottle-feeding the babies is mostly being done by four Ugandan women, who are referred to as the "mothers" here. Their faces are apathetic and tired, and they seem to avoid contact with the volunteers as much as possible.

As I sit on the floor playing cars with a few of the boys, including the one who finally descended from my lap, I overhear Jenna mumble, "I hate when they do that." I look over to see what she is referring to as she points to one of the mothers lifting a kid by the arm to move him from the stairs. "I've told them it's not good to pick them up like that, but they still do it," she sighs.

Jenna gets up to go inside with one of the kids and Emily leans over to me. "You see, people judge this place based on their expectations of what it should be like. But you can't do that. T.I.A. This is Africa. Accept it. You have to respect how it's done. You can't just come in here telling the locals how to do things. You're just another white person who thinks you know better."

Emily rustles her fingers through one of the boys' hair as he holds up a toy car to show her. "Of course, there are things that could improve," she continues, "but change needs to come from within. The staff themselves need to demand the changes. If someone came into my life and told me, 'You're wrong,' I'd be defensive, too! They don't necessarily want here what we have back home. We can't come in and judge our way of life as the way everyone should live. But volunteers are doing it all the time. They belittle the local expertise."

"I can see there seems to be a strained relationship between the staff and volunteers," I say.

"Yeah, the volunteers are not their favorite people. But most of the volunteers don't even talk to them or try to learn the staff members' names. So it doesn't surprise me that there might be some animosity," she says.

Jenna joins us again on the playground and we start talking about the root causes that lead to the kids being abandoned in the first place, and about the fact that the orphanage only serves as a band-aid solution to a much deeper problem. After a brief silence Emily says, "You sometimes look at things at such a large scale and think, 'What could little me possibly do to change it?' But if you think like that, you're defeated."

"Yeah, it's true." Jenna nods in agreement. "We just help moment by moment. It's overwhelming and discouraging to think of all of them and wonder, 'What if they're not adopted?' But you can't think like that. You're not going to change the system. I'm just here to hold babies for a month, and then I'll go home, and that's enough."

❖ ❖ ❖

I'm not entirely sure what compelled me to ask for a meeting with Agatha. I guess I didn't feel comfortable leaving this place having only heard one side of the story. I've already explained my background and told her the reason for my visit, and she was surprisingly open to my request for a meeting. But as my questions start to dig a little deeper for the truth, this impromptu interview is feeling like a rather audacious move.

Agatha's BlackBerry rings and she stops midsentence to answer it. I try to busy myself as she talks to her friend, but it's hard not to look awkward as you wait for the person you're supposed to be meeting with to hang up the phone. I can't help but notice that with her painted nails and perfect hair and fancy dress this thirtysomething Ugandan woman looks rather extravagant for an orphanage director. She finally hangs up, and her lingering smile from the phone conversation turns flat as she returns to meeting mode and asks, "What were we talking about?"

"I was asking you about the funding for the orphanage. Where does it come from?" I remind her.

"Oh right. Well, as I said, it's very, very hard. We get no donations from the Ugandan government, and we don't have regular funders. We just get sporadic donations as they come. And it's hard, you know, drawing up a budget when you don't know where the next penny will come from," she says.

"I guess the volunteers help bring in some income, though?" I ask.

"Yes, we charge them to stay in the guesthouse here, and we rely on that income to help run the program," she says.

"And do you feel like the money you receive is used well here?" I ask, digging deeper.

"It's never enough but, I . . . why? What are you referring to?" Agatha asks, suddenly looking defensive.

"I heard from a source that there might have been a problem with funds being embezzled, which is why the accountant was fired recently," I explain.

"No, that's not true," she says, violently shaking her head. Then, squinting her eyes and wrinkling her forehead, she asks,

"Where did you get that from?" She mumbles something about how comments can get misinterpreted as her eyes roll upward and she attempts to find her words. "I mean, the accountant, well, there were some problems . . . like being rude to the volunteers, but nothing like embezzling funds."

"I promise, I'm not meaning to sound accusatory, I just want to clear up some rumors and give you a chance to correct them. But while we're on the subject of clearing up things, I heard some speculation that you require the clothes donations to come to you first so that you can pick out the best pieces for your own children. Is there any truth to that?" I probe.

"Why would they first come to me for me to take what I want when they are meant for the orphans?" she says, cleverly avoiding actually answering the question.

"Some of the volunteers said they brought suitcases full of clothes donations, but they never saw where they ended up," I explain. "And apparently past volunteers have expressed the same concern."

"These people fail to understand the way this works. Because there are clothes here that we already have. Yet people expect to see the clothes they donate on the child tomorrow." She stumbles on her words. Then she adds, "Even if I'm to take clothes for my children, how many clothes do they really need?" I'm not sure if that was a partial admission or not. She continues, "Okay, sometimes we get clothes that are very old and so we ask the staff if they know of someone who could use it." She looks flustered and irritated.

"As I said, I just wanted to make sure I was getting the correct story," I tell her.

Her frustration seems to soften as she says, "At least you had the courage to come and ask me yourself. If the volunteers are thinking these things, they should come talk to me." She pauses for a moment, still fixating on my claims, then adds, "You know, we don't even need clothes donations. Everyone brings clothes and toys, but we already have enough of those. We need money to feed the kids, to pay the salaries, and to cover bills. These volunteers feel like they're doing us a favor by bringing all of this stuff. But it just ends up cluttering our storage closets while the bills go unpaid!"

I totally agree with her on this point. Volunteers seem to make this mistake all the time, myself included. I remember proudly collecting eight boxes of toys to take with me to an orphanage in Togo when I was seventeen, but I quickly discovered that toys were low on the staff's wish list.

"Do you think that the volunteers are adding something positive to the orphanage by being here?" I ask.

I can tell by her face she wants to blurt out, "No!" but she opts for a more underhanded response. "Well, the truth is that even twenty volunteers can't replace the work of the staff. That's because the volunteers only want to do the clean jobs. Often whites don't want to wash . . . I mean . . ." She's now trying to backtrack after having made a racial dig. "They don't know how to do it locally. Basically, the challenge with the volunteers is they don't want to do the hard work. They just want to cuddle the babies, sing to them, feed them, and that's all."

"So the staff don't find their presence helpful?" I ask.

"Honestly, the volunteers aren't helping much, in my opinion," Agatha concedes. "The staff would agree with me. Now they don't even bother asking the volunteers for help. We took volunteers to the laundry recently, but the ladies said, 'Take them to the classroom because they're not going to help us, they're just going to create more work.' Even the men want to cuddle the babies! Go cut firewood or sweep or do something useful!" She's really agitated now.

"So if the volunteers are more of a burden than a help, why keep them around?" I ask.

"Whether we like it or not, the volunteers are necessary because of the funding situation," she admits. "What can we do? They're paying to be here, so we want them to stay around because that money goes to help the children. Basically, we just have to appreciate whatever little help they're willing to give, even if it's not what we need most."

"Would you say the volunteers are actually doing more harm than good by being here?" I ask.

"It's a difficult situation. We, of course, need the funds they bring in, but is it good for you to come here and cuddle a child for a few days and have that child become attached to you and then you leave? It isn't fair," she says.

"Yeah, I've seen that happen many times before," I say. "It isn't right."

"And always the volunteers have their favorites, and they ignore the other children, which also isn't fair." Agatha pauses for a moment and then looks me squarely in the face as she says, "We may not be doing everything perfectly well, but the volunteers come in and they question our traditional ways of raising children and they criticize our work and they undermine our staff, and then they're gone. They take their photos and their good feelings from cuddling African babies, and they leave. If it weren't for the money, I'm not sure if it would be worth having them here in the first place."

CHAPTER 14

I'M HOPING THAT a stroll around town will help get me out of my funk. After all that I saw in Bududa, and then adding on the chaos of my visit to the orphanage yesterday, I seem to be caught in one of those "the world is screwed" days. I need a strong dose of hope and positivity.

Unfortunately, the streets of Kampala aren't helping to lift my spirits. This city has changed, and not in a good way. I feel cheated by my old hometown, which seems to have been sabotaged by misguided development. Though, technically, development should be a good thing, right? Isn't it what I'm trying to help along through all my work? But this type of dirty, haphazard, and rushed development never breeds the outcome you would hope for.

As I swerve in and out of the masses of people walking along Bombo Road, it's obvious that the city is now packed beyond capacity. Since I was last here, the population of Kampala has soared from 1.1 million to 1.7 million. Yep, rural-urban migration is in full swing. With this many people on the sidewalk I could almost swear some parade or festival has just ended, but it's just another regular day of people going about their business.

And what used to be a thrilling sport for us *muzungus* of attempting to cross the street without getting hit by speeding minibuses and *boda-bodas* (which I was successful at all but once—and had a fractured foot as a souvenir) has now turned into a boring game of squeezing in between the rows of cars stuck in bumper-to-bumper traffic.

There's also a certain energy here that I don't recognize from before. I used to get a sense of vibrancy and joy in this city, and now the primary thing I feel is *striving*. There seems to be a desperate clawing for upward mobility. The advertisements for the latest flat-screen televisions and flashy new cars are bombarding me everywhere. Western status symbols have become all the rage. But at what cost? So much of this "development" is probably just copycat behavior spurred on in large part by Western media. Even many of the aid organizations come into countries like Uganda either blatantly or discreetly heralding the message, "You should be like us!" And instead of asking themselves what would make them happy, given their own culture and needs, Ugandans appear to be embracing the cookie-cutter approach to "progress."

I take a right onto Kyagwe Road, heading toward the brilliant new mosque, a gift from Libya, perched on the top of the Old Kampala Hill that now serves Uganda's Muslim population and beautifully redraws the city's skyline. But as I reach the end of the street, I look right and can't believe what I'm seeing: The office of the Uganda Change Agent Association. I don't know if you can technically have a crush on an organization, but back when I was studying abroad here in 2002, all thirteen girls who were part of my study abroad group (the only year the program happened to be all-female) were enamored with the idea of helping people help themselves.

It doesn't surprise me that we latched on to the Uganda

Change Agent Association as our beacon of hope back then. We were all jaded beyond recognition. We were so annoyed with aid, in fact, that we had bright yellow T-shirts printed that said, DEVELOP THIS. However, the irony of the T-shirt ordeal was that the printer accidentally thought *develop* was spelled with an *e* on the end, which only reinforced our pessimism in the failures of development.

But the change agents gave us hope when little else did. The organization was all about equipping local people with the tools they needed to be able to identify the roots of their own problems, find their own solutions, and spread the methodology by training others. The method involved an eight-week residential training, with intensive modules centered around the idea of self-reliance and grassroots change. And even though I feared that the "participatory development" methodology could border on being patronizing, the founder assured us that the approach was working and the idea was sound.

Stan Burkey. That was his name. The guru and cult figure for us thirteen girls who were all amazed to see a foreign guy actually doing any good in the country. Stan had spent most of his career working in Africa, and helped found the Uganda Change Agent Association in 1992 after a couple of bad experiences in the aid world. I'm thrilled that the organization still exists. So on a whim I decide to go inside and am greeted by a friendly receptionist.

"Is Stan Burkey here, by any chance?" I ask hopefully.

"No, I'm sorry, but he has retired," she sweetly replies.

"Oh." I'm bummed, but not surprised.

"But he still lives in Kampala, and he sometimes stops by to pick up his mail," she adds. "I'll give you his number and maybe you can arrange to meet him."

"Thanks." I go outside with the number in hand to call him

from a public phone. He answers and informs me he's actually on his way to the office right now and he'd be happy to talk. What luck! He's not a celebrity or anything, but I still sit with nervous excitement as I wait for him to arrive. Does that make me a groupie?

◆　◆　◆

"When I look back at my career, I think I did my best, but it wasn't enough," Stan says as he sets down his tea and leans back in the chair.

Within minutes of sitting down to chat with the man I'd idealized for his vision and mission and dedication to helping people help themselves, he is blatantly admitting defeat. It shocks me to hear this. It all sounded so promising back in 2002, but now he doesn't waste any time conceding that in many ways the idea failed.

"It really didn't work?" I ask, still in shock.

"No, it didn't work. We made several mistakes along the way. We changed a lot of people's lives, but we didn't create a development movement," he says, looking down and shaking his head.

"But when we met you in 2002, it sounded like the Change Agent idea was such a success."

"We thought we were successful," he says, "but then looking at it when we stepped back, we realized we had made some bad assumptions. We were hoping to see the emergence of these people-led associations that would advocate for change in their own communities, and we didn't see that happen. But we did see a lot of personal improvement among the people we trained. We changed the lives of a lot of people, especially women. But we didn't manage to catalyze a larger growth process."

"What went wrong?" I ask.

"A lot of things," Stan replies. "Our first mistake was spreading ourselves too thin. We carried out training workshops all over Uganda instead of concentrating intensively on only a few districts." I nod in understanding, having seen the "quantity over quality" issue come up a lot in the aid sector.

"Second," he continues, "we didn't have any follow-up after the eight-week training was complete. We should have met with the trained change agents a few times per year to discuss their progress and provide additional support, but since we'd spread ourselves so thin, we didn't have the resources available to follow up with them."

"That might have made a noticeable difference," I concede.

"And there was one more big mistake we made," he adds. "We did the trainings in twenty different languages, which made it nearly impossible to have consistent quality control for each seminar. We should have concentrated on training a dedicated cadre of English-speaking participants who could then continue informal trainings with others in their local languages. But we didn't do that. . . ." He trails off.

"You should at least feel proud for the individual changes you've made," I say in a positive tone, attempting to point out the silver lining. He shrugs, indicating that that wasn't what they were aiming for. "What will happen to the organization now?" I ask.

"It will stop when the money runs out. And it will run out soon. From 1995 to 2005 we had fantastic funding, but now it's disappearing because you can't fund any one organization for more than seven years. Oxfam stopped funding us because of that cap. They say local NGOs are supposed to become self-sustaining . . . now when was Save the Children ever self-sustaining? When did they stop needing USAID funding? And that is just one of the many hypocrisies. Look at CARE—they get the majority of their funds from government agencies!"

I can tell he's getting riled up now as his distaste for the aid regime, which he was trying so hard to circumvent by stimulating people-led development, is coming out. And he brings up a good point about the problems with funding—most of the mid- to large-sized aid organizations aren't getting their money from individual donors or self-sufficient means; they're getting big grants from government entities like USAID. I'm not so sure the term *non-governmental* should even be used to describe aid organizations that fund their projects like this. There are clearly political agendas at work when it comes to where and how the money is spent.

"The waste in these agencies is unbelievable, too," he continues. "I was once asked by the World Bank to be part of their Ugandan advisory board for a thirty-four-million-dollar loan for a Nutrition and Early Child Development Project that was to include an income-generation component. They hosted an eight-day pre-proposal seminar where they brought in fifteen international experts. And I later found out that the money required for that eight-day seminar would have covered my organization's entire annual budget."

"Stuff like that irritates me so much," I concur.

He goes on, "And organizations like Save the Children have no collective memory. Most of them have too short a vision span. And while they talk about participation and self-reliance, they have no idea how to promote it. The 'participation' is usually 'participate and then agree to what we have decided to do for you.'"

"The problems are endless"—I nod—"and yet speaking out about the failures of aid still feels taboo."

"Because it's a racket!" he says emphatically, sitting up in his chair and gesturing with his hands. "Where else can you be so highly paid and get such good pensions? Especially in the UN!" I know the pension issue is a particularly sensitive subject to Stan, as he already informed me that he now has no choice but to live in Uganda until he dies because he can't afford to go anywhere else. He dedicated most of his life to working outside the United States with foreign aid organizations that didn't have fancy pension funds, and he's now only entitled to a mere $65 a month in Social Security from the U.S. government and a small "livable" pension from the Norwegian government, where he also holds citizenship.

He continues, "And you're not allowed to criticize aid because, well, do you criticize missionaries? No, of course you don't. In most people's eyes, aid is always assumed to be a good thing."

"Yeah, and most people don't want to hear any differently," I add. I know exactly what he's talking about. In many ways, I feel like I've been either ignored or demonized by most people in the past few years because I've had the audacity to question the so-called "good" industry. Most people haven't been so eager to listen to my claims that many of our good intentions to help others through international aid just aren't working. They want to keep on believing they can sign their checks and feel like they've done their part to help the world. Most of all, people don't want someone like me coming around telling them that not only did their donation probably get squandered on useless expenditures but that the little that did make it to the ground likely didn't change any lives in a meaningful way. I probably should add the title "Party Pooper" to my business card.

Stan's face softens and he says more quietly, "The NGOs mean well, and they try hard, but they don't get the root causes. They work according to fads. We're starting in the decline of microfinance as the development fad, now infrastructure is making a comeback. To me, one of the major root causes is a lack of critical consciousness. People are not always aware of their situation, why they're in that situation, and how they can change it themselves. And beyond that, a major root cause of all these problems is education. Uganda needs to revamp its entire education system. It's a joke right now. And it's part of the reason our method didn't work."

"How so?" I ask.

"I naively thought, 'Give people the training and they'll carry the bucket themselves.'"

"But it doesn't work?"

"It doesn't work. The education levels are too low," he explains. "In Africa it's a downward spiral where poorly educated and poorly paid teachers produce even more poorly educated and poorly paid students."

We sit there in silence for a few seconds as I let the essence of all he's said soak in before I ask meekly, "But, Stan, surely there had to be *some* success stories from all your hard work, right?"

"There was *one*."

"Oh?"

"Yeah, I hope to be buried in Kyarumba at the Bukonzo Joint Savings and Credit Cooperative because that's my greatest success in life. It's the only community that developed in accordance with the theory. And, other than the initial training, they did it with no external support from us," he says. "We trained a man named Paineto Baluku in the Change Agent methodology, and he went back to his community and made amazing changes. He trained several others, and soon after formed an independent savings and credit cooperative that now consists of over thirty self-help groups who are making enormous progress."

"That sounds great."

"You should go check it out, Tori. It might restore some hope in you."

That's definitely what I need right now. The wave of positivity doesn't last long, though, as Stan's cynicism returns. "I was so glad to retire. I couldn't take coming to this office anymore."

"But when you look back at your career, was it all worth it?"
I ask.

"I don't know. Yeah, I think so," he says, somewhat unsure.
"I had a lot of excitement, a lot of fascinating experiences, and
a lot of interesting frustrations. It's not everyone who can say
they've gone to Moroto and almost got shot at by two Karamo-
jong warriors." he says, laughing. "I also realized I didn't have
the charismatic personality that you need to start and maintain
this type of thing. Honestly, how many of the successful NGO
leaders could have also been successful evangelical preachers?
Most of them, I think. It's amazing how far you can get in the
world of aid with a silver tongue."

"So would you say you're jaded?"

"Yeah, I guess I am. Because I've become so pessimistic.
I hope I'm wrong but"—he takes a long breath—"but I'm still
curious. I like to sit back and watch what's happening. But I don't
see any radical changes in the wind in terms of aid programs."

"Any advice for me?" I ask.

"Keep fighting the good fight. If you're criticizing, then
that's one of the best things you can do right now."

◆　◆　◆

The Indian curry tastes as good as I remember. I'm actually
amazed that Sam's is still around. This restaurant used to be the
place where the other twelve girls in my study-abroad group and
I would come in extreme emergencies—when we couldn't go
another day eating *matoke* and "sauce." I guess it's not surprising that it has stuck around because the restaurant has some of
the best foreigner-friendly dishes in Kampala, and it caters to
an ever-expanding expat market of do-gooders and people-who-
think-they're-doing-good. But back when we studied here we

were living on a Ugandan budget, and Sam's, at about $7 to $10 a plate, was a big splurge. I think we only came here two or three times, but we always talked about it for weeks afterward.

Today I feel like I deserve the splurge. The chicken curry and the cold mango juice is helping to raise my spirits, though I'm still dumbfounded by my encounter with Stan. I have so few examples of successful approaches to development, and I feel let down that yet another seemingly promising idea has actually failed.

People ask me all the time, "Okay, so you've told us what doesn't work, but what *does* work?" That's basically what Ahmed was asking me, too, all those years ago. Do I have any *solutions*? My inability to properly answer that question is the whole reason I'm on this mini-quest right now. In the past, I always felt awkward in my feeble attempts to give an answer. Sometimes I opt for the "start with yourself" and "be the change" Gandhi-inspired conversation. And other times I talk about innovation and for-profit approaches to development. But even those have questionable results. Stan's approach of giving people the tools they needed to catalyze change in their own communities seemed like a good idea. Until now.

Then again, I'm starting to wonder if Stan's work was really as much of a failure as he claims. He admits that the trainings undoubtedly helped a lot of people on an individual level. Some went back to their communities and had the newfound confidence to start their own businesses or run for office. Isn't that something to be proud of? Do we perhaps get too bogged down by our grand schemes to "save the world," or, in his case, "create a movement," instead of celebrating the few individual lives that are better off because of whatever we did to help? I run into this problem all the time myself. And, like Stan, I am rarely satisfied with my small successes—like when students come up to me after a screening of my film series and tell me how affected they are, or when I spark a particularly enlightening dialogue about aid effectiveness over dinner with NGO fieldworkers and they walk away with a changed vision of their work. To me, that stuff barely makes it onto my radar screen because I haven't transformed the entire system.

I think Stan needs to cut himself some slack. Maybe I do, too.

CHAPTER 15

THIS CRAZY DETOUR to the very edge of Western Uganda in response to Stan's suggestion shows how desperate I am for inspiration. It seems I'll go almost to the ends of the earth to find it. Or at least this feels like the end of the earth. I really hope Stan was right about the success of the Change Agent's methodology in Kyarumba because getting here has been more difficult than I anticipated. One bus, two minibuses, two cars, three motorcycles, and seventy-two hours later, and I'm finally approaching the village. I'm hanging on tightly to the back of the motorcycle as we fly along the red dirt road.

Perhaps my obsession with finding something that works isn't so abnormal, though. And it's not just linked to my desire to be able to give Ahmed a real answer when I find him. I think humans in general crave positivity, even if most of what we produce and witness is anything but. And while Stan encouraged me to keep fighting the fight, I'm starting to think my days as an aid critic might be numbered. I'm tired of standing on mountaintops proclaiming, "See how crappy all this is?" when such a message does little more than bring attention to what doesn't work. Turning out hoards of jaded people isn't exactly the legacy I was hoping for. But it's so much easier to be a critic, especially in this field, than to seek out the glimmers of hope. Though I'm starting to realize that the world has a lot more to gain from my stories of inspiration and possibility than my tales of failure and woe.

It dawned on me as I contemplated this epiphany last night that my career doesn't match my personality. I'm actually a very positive, optimistic person. So how the hell did I end up on this path? It seems my deep belief that the recipients of aid deserved better than what they were being given ignited a fire in me years ago that trumped my optimistic spirit. I saw an injustice and felt compelled to respond. But I sense the tides are changing, thanks in large part to this trip and my recent reflections. I'm ready to use my life to offer inspiration instead of my "see, I told you it sucks!" wisdom to the world. I hope that my time in Kyarumba can be a step in the right direction, because I still don't have an answer for Ahmed.

"We're nearly there," the driver, Andrew, says loudly over the hum of the engine.

I don't want this motorcycle ride to end. It has been the best part of my arduous journey to get here. And the scenery, with its big green rolling hills and meandering rivers, has left me with a permanent smile on my face for the bulk of this forty-five-minute ride. We take a left after the bridge and slowly make our way up a slight hill, passing by what appears to be a small market area and local grain mill, before pulling through the metal gate of a modest compound with a white concrete L-shaped building and small courtyard.

"Here we are. The Bukonzo Joint Cooperative Micro Finance Society," Andrew says as he puts the kickstand down and I shimmy off the back of the bike.

I already heard rumors yesterday in Kasese that I'd missed

Paineto by a day or two. He's apparently on his way to Europe for a conference or something. So I'm not surprised to have this confirmed by Teddy, a short, feisty thirtysomething Ugandan woman who works as a trainer for the organization. I explain to her that Stan encouraged me to come here to meet Paineto and to learn about the organization's success.

"Yes, unfortunately Paineto is not here. But you are most welcome to visit our program," she says with a smile. She pauses for a moment and then adds, "for a fee."

"There's a fee for visiting?" I ask.

"Yes, we have so many requests from people interested in seeing how successful our model is that we started losing too much time in showing people around. You see all these people in there?" she asks, pointing to a small, dark room in the corner of the compound where a group of forty people are listening to a presentation.

"Yeah."

"They are from another district nearby. They heard about the success of our model, and they have come here to learn how to do it themselves. They each pay a small participation fee to learn about the program. The demand is high, so this is one way we can protect our time and resources," she explains.

"I've never heard of an organization charging visitors, but it's a great idea," I admit. I've often thought other organizations I've engaged with in the past should have done the same. Hosting curious visitors like myself takes up a considerable amount of staff time and energy. So, in exchange for two nights in their simple guesthouse and being able to tag along with Teddy in the field, I hand over the equivalent of $35 to the organization's financial manager. Some of it will serve as a donation for their work, some will go to the cooks, and Teddy will get a portion of it, as well. I appreciate how transparent they are regarding how the money is spent, especially in light of what I saw at the orphanage a few days ago.

"Come," Teddy says, motioning me to follow her to a nearby office, "I'll give you some background on our work."

She leads me into what usually serves as Paineto's office. It's a simple white room with a few bookshelves lined with carefully labeled binders. We sit down at the desk and she starts drawing a model to explain how the organization works.

"Let's start with the groups. This is the heart of our program." She points to the bottom box on her diagram. "This all began with only three self-help groups, started by Paineto after being trained by Stan as a change agent in 1992. Then a few more of us were trained a couple years later. We started having branch Change Agent meetings with all the people who had been trained, and Paineto suggested in 1999 that we bring our self-help groups together so we could form an organization focused on village savings and loans programs. Back then we didn't have a building or anything formal, we just used to sit on stones behind the church," she says, pointing outside.

"And what were the groups doing?" I ask.

"The same thing they are still doing—meeting regularly and supporting each other, saving money each time, and taking loans from the pool of savings when it's their turn."

"How many groups do you have?" I ask. "I think Stan told me there are more than thirty."

Teddy smiles. "No, that was a while ago. We now have ninety-six groups and five thousand and sixteen individual members."

Wow, that's a lot of self-help going on. What Teddy is explaining sounds like a traditional "table banking" scheme where groups come together, mostly women, to save their money and offer credit as needed to each other using the pooled resources. It's been around for a long time. I've seen it work beautifully in India and elsewhere, but a lot of these groups are now being wooed toward individual microfinance loans instead, which isn't turning out to be as successful as most people expected. There's obviously some positive social pressure involved when engaged in a group setting, and individual micro-lending eliminates that component.

Micro-lending, though, has seen an enormous surge in popularity in recent years with both private and nonprofit microfinance institutions (MFIs) cropping up all over the world. But the criticism of some of these organizations has been substantial. Average interest rates apparently range between 35 and 55 percent per year (even for the *nonprofit* lenders), many of the MFIs don't question or help build the business acumen of the loan recipients, and due to a lack of capital within poor communities, many people who have taken on loans are still only making ends meet, not pulling themselves out of poverty. Bukonzo Joint, in contrast, seems to be addressing all these issues by focusing mostly on group lending, offering business training programs, and even linking farmers to export markets to bring in new capital.

Teddy explains that 85 percent of the group members are women, and most of them are coffee farmers. That's why they started the Bukonzo Farmers Marketing Association, which provides larger loans to farmers for production and connects them directly to local buyers and international exporters so they can get the best price for their harvest. It's a brilliant idea, and it has increased their production levels from thirteen tons in 2005 to over *three hundred* tons today, helping the farmers bring in more income than ever before.

The final part of the organization's core services includes a training component, serviced by the Bukonzo East Training

Team, where trainers like Teddy go up into the hills on foot to train group members on issues ranging from business development and financial planning to women's empowerment.

"Most of the trainers are change agents, actually," Teddy adds. "They were trained by Paineto and a few others."

"That's great," I reply. "And how much money are we talking about in terms of savings and shares among group members?"

"Last year we had 248 million shillings in shares, and 290 million shillings in savings. Oh, and 182 million shillings in outstanding loans." That's over $200,000 in shares and savings, which might not sound like much but is actually impressive for such a poor village.

I try to piece it all together in my head: Stan trained Paineto, who later trained others, who started self-help groups, who then came together as one cohesive group, and are now a force to be reckoned with when it comes to coffee export, training, and savings and loans.

"And since the start, you've done it all on your own?" I ask.

"Yes, we've continued for ten years without assistance from anyone," Teddy says proudly.

"Would you say it's been a success?"

"As we look at the vision of Bukonzo Joint as a model within our district, indeed we have made it. After ten years we've seen so many major changes. Less people are now living in grass huts, conflicts in homes have reduced, women and men are working side by side, female children are starting to go to school, and the members are producing much higher quality coffee lately. This is all thanks to the self-help groups and the training we pass on," Teddy explains.

She stands up and pulls a photo album off one of Paineto's shelves behind me. She puts it sideways on the desk so we can both see, and starts flipping through it slowly. It shows pictures

of the groups and the celebrations and Paineto conducting trainings. She stops for a second and looks up at me. "It's hard to
believe Bukonzo Joint started under a tree, and now look how
far we've come." She looks down at a group picture of the trained
change agents and smiles.

◆　◆　◆

We step into the office of the Bwethe Cooperative, trying hard
not to distract the twelve women who have gathered for their
group meeting. A handful of babies are quietly attending the
meeting, too, either tied snugly on their mothers' backs or enter-
taining themselves on laps.

"This group is new," Teddy whispers to me as we take a seat
near the back of the dark mud-brick room. "They have only been
meeting for two or three months so far. I trained them myself."

"And who's that guy?" I ask, discreetly pointing to the man
sitting behind a small red desk at the front of the room, surrounded by the women who are seated on wooden benches in
two semicircles.

"He's not part of this group, actually, but the woman who
counts the money is absent today, so he agreed to fill in for
her. We have some men in a few of the groups, but most of
them are all women. Today this one has already had their
group discussion, and now it's time for the savings collection,"
she explains.

The man calls one of the women up and she presents a
small paper notebook that Teddy refers to as a "savings book,"
along with a handful of coins that she has saved up since the
last meeting. He carefully counts the change and marks the
amount in her book using rubber stamps.

"Is that a stamp in the shape of a goat leg?"

"Yes, that's a goat leg stamp," Teddy confirms. "It represents three hundred shillings. Most of the women are not familiar with numeracy, so the different stamps help keep it simple."

There are other shapes, too, but I can't quite make out what they are at this distance. I'm amused that there are even goat leg rubber stamps on the market. I kind of want one. It looks like the woman has saved much less than the expected minimum of 1,500 shillings, as she only received two goat leg stamps this week.

He calls the next woman up, she has 1,500 shillings saved. She gets three stamps of what appears to be a fish.

After all the women have presented their money and received their stamps in their savings books, the guy in charge gathers up the coins and small bills and begins counting out loud.

"He does this so the whole group knows how much they have collected," Teddy explains as we wait for the final count. "Six thousand, one hundred shillings in total today," she reports. She looks a little disappointed. "They're still a young group, and they aren't saving as much as they should yet."

A lively conversation breaks out among the women. "What are they saying?" I ask Teddy.

"Well, they're discussing the options. One woman is interested in possibly taking the loan to do some reconstruction on her small house, and another is considering taking it for school fees for her son." She waits as she listens in, then continues. "No, it seems they have all agreed that the woman here is going to take it to buy coffee seedlings." The woman presents her savings book to the man at the desk and he helps count up all the stamps. She has saved 4,200 shillings so far.

"They just give one to two," Teddy explains. "When one saves one thousand, they loan two thousand. So she can get eight thousand, four hundred shillings. But they only saved six thousand, one hundred shillings today, so she'll have to collect the rest at the next meeting. And she pays an interest of five hundred shillings, which goes toward the group's account." We watch as the coins and bills are handed over to the woman. "It's a challenge for the group because they aren't saving enough yet so there isn't much money available for loans. But at least this new group is starting to learn about the dynamic of savings and repaying loans. It's an important aspect of Bukonzo Joint, to train people to not be in deficit with loans."

"When does she have to repay the loan by?" I ask Teddy.

"She has two months to repay it, and then they can loan that money to someone else. That's how it works. It's a constantly revolving fund to help people get ahead."

We get up as the meeting comes to a close and shake hands with the women, thanking them for allowing us to sit in. The woman who has received the loan this week carefully ties the money into the upper corner of her sarong and heads back up the hill, a little richer, for now.

CHAPTER 16

It's early on a Sunday morning, and I don't have any plans before I have to meet up with Teddy at noon. I leave the guesthouse and start wandering into the village. The peacefulness of the now-silent market area, a place that is usually bustling with activity, is wonderful. Even the goats have taken the morning off and are lazily lying on the side of the path. As I'm enjoying the serenity, a little girl dressed in her Sunday best runs by me, yelling, "Hello, *muzungu!*" as she speeds by. Her frilly yellow party dress no longer fits, but a safety pin holds the back together to prolong the dress' lifespan since the zipper can no longer be used. As I watch her skipping off to her fancy-dress occasion, it dawns on me that while this serenity is nice, there's really only one place to be on a Sunday morning in a Ugandan village: church.

It's been a while since I last attended church. I was raised Catholic, but got tired of the hypocrisy and rigidity of the church by my late teens. I ended up finding my own deep spirituality that is Christian-esque with a dash of Buddhist meditation and a lot of "do unto others" universal Golden Rule ideology thrown in. And while I certainly don't feel you need the four walls of a church to worship, I can't think of a better place to be at the moment. I follow the little girl up the path, behind the grain mill, past the Bukonzo office, and eventually to the front door of the church.

An old man who is serving as an usher looks up at me in shock and excitedly says, "Yes! You are welcome!" His friends nearby nod in agreement, all smiling. I can sense them thinking, *Wow, so* muzungus *aren't devil-worshiping heathens after all!*

Curious eyes follow me as I make my way down the center aisle, passing by rows of long wooden benches, eventually picking a seat halfway back on the far right side. The yellow interior paint offers a cheery mood in what is otherwise a rather dark building, tented with a tin roof and surrounded by concrete walls with small windows. A scrawny Ugandan man energetically plays a battery-powered keyboard at the front of the church as people slowly file in. The service was supposed to start twenty minutes ago, but it seems things are rather flexible here.

What does not appear to be flexible, however, are the gazes of the thirty-plus kids who have gathered around me, all eyes fixated on my every move. Some are hiding behind pews, with only their little eyes showing, stealing glances from afar, while others are more courageous, clamoring to sit next to me.

Things are finally underway as a jubilant choir wearing purple and white robes starts coming down the aisle, singing a song in the local language with high energy. Despite the fact that I can't understand the lyrics, I feel like I'm in a traditional Baptist church in Alabama or something. You can't fake this kind of praise-to-the-glory-of-God enthusiasm.

Following the choir down the aisle is a sharp-looking preacher, also wearing a white robe and a purple stole. His smile beams as he reaches the altar and welcomes the congregation in the local language. He then shifts to English, turns in my

direction, and says, "And we must also welcome our distinguished visitor from abroad who has joined us this morning." All
two hundred sets of eyes are now on me. Urged by a few men
nearby, I stand up and awkwardly nod in appreciation, adamant
that my particular mix of skin color genes doesn't qualify me in
any way as "distinguished." So much for blending in.

There's some quiet chattering between the priest and a man
sitting eight or nine rows in front of me, and the next thing I
know, the man comes and sits down next to me, scooting the eager
kids over, on high orders from the priest to act as my translator for
the service. As he shakes my hand, introducing himself as Samuel,
the priest nods in delight, and continues the service in the local
language. Samuel pulls out his tattered Bible, with his Certificate
of Confirmation serving as the bookmark. "Psalm one hundred
five, verse five," he whispers to me as he thumbs through it.

The pastor's voice booms from the pulpit. "All the time,
remember what God does for you," Samuel roughly translates
in a whisper. He then adds, "Remember to give thanks all the
time." He listens to the explanation about gratitude and remembering God's blessings, forgetting to translate the bulk of it.

"*Amina?*" the pastor calls out after his sermon.

"*AMINA!*" they all yell back. *Amen.*

Samuel finally turns to me and says, "As the people came to
Canaan, God provided food and water to them and then parted
the Red Sea so they could flee Egypt. God will provide, and you
need to be grateful." He thinks for a second, then matter-of-
factly summarizes, "So the theme is really remember what God
has done for you." I find his paraphrasing endearing.

The heat gets turned up as the pastor says loudly, hands
raised in the air, "Testify to others what God has done for you!"
A rumble of "*Aminas*" goes through the crowd with passion.

The pastor then looks my way. "I was in a village not long

ago and they invited many Europeans to come and to pray for them and their situation." I have a sudden flashback to the hoards of missionaries I've met along my travels in recent years—some nice, some terrible. Some honestly doing their part to be, as they put it, "the hands and feet of Jesus," helping in loving and practical ways. Others using fire-and-brimstone rhetoric to "save souls" or conning villagers to accept Jesus as their Lord and Savior in exchange for a water well. Not cool.

My wandering thoughts are brought back to the present as the pastor boldly proclaims, by way of Samuel's translation, "It does not require you get people from Europe to come pray for you!" The congregation laughs, most looking over at me. He raises one hand, holding the Bible as he exalts, "Just obey the Lord and testify to the Lord all that he has done for you. God will provide!" I really like this guy. This village is even preaching self-sufficiency in church!

As the ceremony continues, I stand there clapping with the other parishioners, attempting to sing along in a language I don't know (something about "Jesus is my friend" and "we're going to heaven," according to Samuel), and a wave of joy overcomes me. It's this very spirit of gratitude that has brought me all this way in search of Ahmed, and it seems to be working wonders in this village, as well.

❖ ❖ ❖

Teddy has invited me for lunch at her new house, and as we weave along the dirt trail past some papaya trees and mud houses, she has the same giddy expression on her face that I used to have when it was my day for "show and tell" in kindergarten. For years she has diligently started new entrepreneurial endeavors and saved like crazy so that her dream of owning her own house could finally come true. She stops suddenly and we both fix our gaze on her trophy of self-reliance. There it is, standing out among the coffee trees with its brand-new tin roof, smooth concrete finish, and newly painted bright blue shutters.

"It's beautiful, Teddy," I say as she shines with delight.

"I have only lived here for six months, but I've been so happy ever since I built this," she says as she ducks under the laundry line, leading me into a small room on the left. "I'll be right back," she says from the doorway. "Please sit and make yourself comfortable."

There's nothing in this concrete room but a table covered in a turquoise cloth, two stools, and a radio with a super-tall antenna. But there's a simplistic beauty about it. The next thing I know every inch of the table is covered by an array of colorful dishes that Teddy has spent all morning cooking. There's rice, potatoes, groundnut paste, spinach, avocados, beans, bananas, mangos, and, of course, the Ugandan staple of *matoke*, which is made from mashed-up plantains.

"Oh my gosh, Teddy, you've outdone yourself," I say, as I eye the dishes, unsure of where to start.

"No, it's nothing," she says as she motions me to take a plate and start serving myself. Luckily we don't have to eat all of this wonderful food on our own, as we're soon joined by Joseph, a fortysomething Ugandan man who was also trained as a change agent many years ago.

"I saw you in church today," Joseph says as he pours beans over his *matoke*.

"Oh yeah?" I ask, not surprised that he noticed my presence after all the attention the pastor insisted on directing my way. "It was an experience," I say with a laugh. "I was a bit of a spectacle. But I appreciated the message of self-reliance and gratitude from the pastor. It seems like the theme of this entire district must be self-reliance, huh?"

He laughs. "Yeah, I guess that is true. We've come a long way since the war."

I ask them to tell me more about that period, and they spare no details as they explain the terror of the civil war that was started in 1996 by the Allied Democratic Forces as they surged across the border from their bases in Congo, devastating communities, raping and abducting women, and killing countless people in their wake. The fighting was so bad, Teddy recounts, that the majority of the people from this area, themselves included, had to live in camps for internally displaced persons.

"During the war people suffered a lot," Joseph says, shaking his head. "Everyone moved from their land, the houses were burned or destroyed, they left their farms, they left their coffee, everything. You'd hear the guns and you'd start running without taking anything with you."

"The five years we spent in the camp were terrible," Teddy says.

"It was a bad situation," Joseph agrees. "We were overpopulated, there were so many diseases like malaria, cholera. . . ."

"Even the children were not going to school!" Teddy jumps in.

"And we had no money during that time," Joseph adds. "But that's when Bukonzo Joint started," he says with a smile.

"During the war?" I ask.

"Yes, during the war." He nods. "Paineto could see that relying on the aid we were receiving in the camp was not enough. We needed to start working in small ways and saving little by little in order to be able to support ourselves and rebuild our lives when the war was over," he explains.

The two of them go on to explain that Stan and Paineto put out an advertisement for people to apply for the change agent course. Teddy and Joseph were selected for the few spots in the training program among over one hundred applicants. During the intensive training period they learned about a range of topics from poverty analysis to bookkeeping.

"As I completed the course, I was eager to share it because I realized that most people had resources, they just didn't know how to use them," Teddy says. "So I wanted to help them figure out ways to use the resources they had. They should be self-reliant, I thought. I told them, 'Let us at least save one hundred shillings per month to start saving.' Then we started a revolving fund, and the members would use the loans to start small businesses in the camp like selling *matoke* or pans like this," she says, tapping her dish.

"And you saw improvements by focusing on savings instead of handouts?" I ask.

"Yes, we were really moving forward," she replies. "And the change agents we kept meeting monthly, monthly—me, Erik, Paineto, and others—until we came up with the vision of making Bukonzo Joint. And since the war ended, our efforts with starting these self-help groups have grown and grown," Teddy adds. "People were realizing that the aid organizations were not going to stick around to help us rebuild, that we needed to do that on our own."

"This seems like a special place," I say, impressed by what I'm hearing.

"It is a special place because of the spirit of self-reliance here," Joseph says. "Like, for example, if I can give an example like Teddy, using her salary from the government and income from other sources, she purchased this land and she managed to build her own house. She's managing to pay the school fees of her children." His praise for her is touching, but she insists she just does what she has to do.

"You have no choice but to feel responsible," she explains matter-of-factly, "because there is no one else that is going to take care of things for you. You just say this is my situation, and you do A, B, C, and D to change it by yourself."

But Teddy's ambition and success in being self-reliant is extraordinary to anyone who knows her story. I've gotten her background in bits and pieces during my time here, and what I know so far is that she was only sixteen when she was forced into marriage as the second wife of a man she hated. As the youngest of eighteen brothers and twenty-five sisters (spread over her father's three wives), she was lucky that one of her older brothers was able to pay her school fees for several years. But when he died of AIDS, she had no choice but to drop out in her first year of high school. Before long, her crappy husband had taken on a fourth wife and decided to leave the area, abandoning her and their four children. Fortunately, this was around the time that she was trained as a change agent, which inspired her to go back to school with the help of a loan from her self-help group. She not only finished school but she also went on to complete teachers' college and now teaches third grade in the village. The rest of her income comes from coffee trading, farming, a few smart business investments, and the occasional small fees she gets as a volunteer trainer at Bukonzo Joint. At only thirty-five years old, she already has a nineteen-year-old daughter who has just entered nursing school, she owns seven acres of land, and has just built her own house, which she plans to turn into an investment property one day. The three self-help groups she started, including one that is specifically for women who were abducted by rebels during the war, are thriving, each with millions of shillings in savings and shares. In short, she kicks ass.

We finish up the delicious meal, and Joseph excuses himself to meet up with a member of one of his groups. Teddy insists we leave the dishes where they are for now, as she eagerly says, "Come follow me."

She takes me past the house and down a narrow mud path surrounded by tall grasses and skinny trees. We arrive at the river behind her house and she effortlessly walks across a few stones to get to the water and balances on a rock as she bends from the waist, washing her hands in the water. She smiles bigger than I've ever seen her smile, looking radiant in an orange headpiece tied loosely on the side, a bright yellow shirt, and a patterned sarong tied around her waist. She stands up, looks downriver, and pauses for a moment. "You like it?" she asks.

"Are you kidding? I love it, Teddy. Your house and your land are beautiful."

As we head back up the bank from the river, Teddy grabs my hand to help me over the slippery part. She then stops suddenly as she looks down lovingly at a small field of tree seedlings she recently planted that are starting to take root.

"When these eucalyptus trees grow up big, I'm going to sell them to send my children to university." We both stand there for a moment, reflecting on that remarkable fact.

We continue walking, but before we reach the house she stops again and looks back toward the river, then around to all her fields as she says, "The term self-reliance has real meaning for me." She smiles warmly as she looks off into the distance. "I'm so proud."

◆ ◆ ◆

It's five thirty in the morning and I can barely see a thing as I softly walk through the still streets of Kyarumba. The fact that the village still doesn't have electricity, despite persistent advocacy from Paineto and others, means I only have a tiny flashlight that Mark gave me and the light of the full moon above to guide me. I can hear the sound of a vehicle starting up in the distance, as a handful of passenger cars and big trucks get ready for the early morning commute to Kasese and elsewhere. I was informed last night that the only reliable transport out of the village is by way of one of these special "taxis" that leave before the crack of dawn, hence the reason I'm up this early.

As I get closer to the taxi area, I can't help but feel bummed that I didn't have a chance to meet the famous Paineto during my visit to Kyarumba. After all, he's the one responsible for sparking much of the moving-and-shaking that has been going on around here in recent years. But, then again, from what I've seen it's not really about Paineto at all. This village might have needed his vision and help to get things started, but it's clear from what I've heard that he has a habit of simply sharing whatever knowledge he can and then backing off to let others lead their own way. I remember asking Stan back in Kampala whether or not the success of Bukonzo Joint was specifically because of Paineto's influence, and he told me, "He is certainly the rock on which it stands, but he's unassuming and he pushes everyone else forward."

Instead of the credit going solely to the founder (a mistake that happens more often than not), or to Stan, who trained Paineto in the change agent methodology, the real kudos should go to all five thousand plus members of the cooperative who diligently save their money, soak up new knowledge from the various training initiatives, and invest wisely in their futures. I can see why Stan wants to be buried here—this is self-reliance at its finest. The rest of the change agent initiatives might have failed from Stan's perspective, but he unquestionably has this single success story to hold on to.

"Yes, okay, taxi?" A man in a heavy winter coat says as he motions me to follow him to an old, gray, five-seater Toyota. I'm placed in the front near the door, which ends up being quite lucky because by some absolute miracle they manage to squeeze a total of ten people into the car—four up front and six in the back. I'm pressed up against the door with my backpack on my lap, but the open window helps keeps any claustrophobia at bay.

We take off with a lurch and head down the bumpy dirt road. The front of the car is so packed that the driver, too, is wedged up against his door and has to shift gears in between another guy's legs. This early morning clown car experience only makes me laugh.

An hour later I can finally stretch out as I emerge from the car and wait on the side of the main road for a bus to Kabale. I feel like I just emerged from something special—not the clown car, the village. It was a moving experience to see the concept of self-reliance in action. But I also feel protective of Kyarumba. I want to put up a massive gate right about here and not let any outsiders go down that crazy dirt road, for fear that they might mess up such a good thing. Success stories seem to be rare in these parts, and I hope Bukonzo Joint can continue like this for a long, long time. I watch the sun rise up over the grasslands on the other side of the road as I savor the feeling of hope that has found its way back into my system.

RWANDA

CHAPTER 17

THE BENCH IN the last row of this worn-out minibus isn't bolted down, so me and the three others who are crammed together back here have to carefully balance our weight to prevent the seat from tipping forward whenever the driver slows down to go around the hairpin curves. Ignoring the awkwardness of the wobbling bench, I gaze out the window to watch the scenery go by. I remember this road. Anyone who has ever had the chance to drive from Uganda to Rwanda wouldn't forget it, either. I came along this road at the same time of day eight years ago, as a matter of fact, and the way the late afternoon sun illuminates the majestic hills with golden light mesmerized me then as much as it does today. I remember thinking at twenty years old, within minutes of entering this country, that Rwanda was one of the most beautiful places I'd ever seen. Since then I've been all over the world, but Rwanda remains high on my list of most stunning countries.

But there's another feeling I got eight years ago when entering Rwanda that I still feel today, and that's the blatant eeriness of this place. The history of a genocide that killed nearly a million people is simply too fresh. In 2002, I remember looking into people's eyes as we passed them along this road and thinking that it was impossible to know whether they had perpetrated the brutal violence or if their loved ones were victims. Everyone was affected by the 1994 genocide in one way or another. But even those who committed some of the most atrocious massacres are still around today. And the scars are going to take a long time to heal. Mass graves are still being discovered, and sixteen years later, the reality of what happened is still being processed by a grieving nation and a guilt-ridden international community that didn't act faster to help stop it.

But just when the gravity of the genocide starts to feel overwhelming, we come around another hairpin turn and get a spectacular view of the most impressive hills I've ever seen, momentarily clearing my head of the pain and sadness of this place. They call Rwanda "The Land of a Thousand Hills," and I wouldn't be surprised if there are even more than that. For as far as I can see there are gently rolling hills, one after the other, that are covered in an intricate patchwork pattern of dark green trees, the reddish orange mud of cleared land, and terraced farms in every shade of green you can imagine. There are even some hints of yellow thrown in there and, of course, a perfectly blue sky with fluffy white clouds.

I look out the window as we come around another curve, with a sheer cliff face on the right and an expanse of golden, sun-kissed hills on the left. How could a place so breathtaking have something so terrible happen to it? Clearly the beauty of a country has no correlation to the brutality of its history.

◆ ◆ ◆

Returning to Rwanda feels right. Not only to reconnect with the memories from my last trip here in 2002, but also because I've heard rumors that Rwanda has lately become a beacon of hope in Africa due to the country's deliberate and effective approach to development. Last night, while having dinner with my friend Kate, who has been working here for a few years on various development projects, she confirmed the rumors. Her stories made me even more curious to explore what's going on here in greater depth. Hence the reason I currently find myself being escorted through the swanky U.S. Embassy to visit the USAID offices in an attempt to get the lowdown on what's happening these days with Rwanda's development.

A program officer named Sam enthusiastically welcomes me to his office, and we both settle into our chairs for an impromptu meeting. I look across the desk at this thirtysomething guy with deep red hair and large brown eyes, and I can't help but be reminded of Mark. I've been thinking about him more than usual lately. But the momentary feeling of longing I have for my love back in Kenya is interrupted by the sound of Sam's thick Southern accent as he starts to explain USAID's various programs in Rwanda. Listening to him talk, I can't help but notice that despite having been with the Agency for several years, Sam still exudes a sense of naivete about the realities of development. He's gushing as he talks about their health programs. It's almost cute.

"The programs sound interesting, Sam," I say as he wraps up the overview. "But I recently heard rumors that it's getting harder and harder for foreign aid organizations like USAID to operate in Rwanda. Have you felt that lately?"

"Yes, definitely," he replies. "We're constantly butting heads with the Rwandan government. They have their own vision of how things should go and what kind of help we should be providing."

"But isn't that a good thing?" I ask, slightly puzzled.

"Sure, of course. But it doesn't align with our mandate. Our funding is allocated by Congress for extremely specific purposes—we aren't allowed to stray from what they have ear-marked the money for. And it's frustrating because we keep get-ting push back from the Rwandan government," Sam says.

"What sort of push back do they give?"

"Well, they believe that donors should concentrate on only a few development sectors to maximize their impact. USAID believes in a more holistic approach and typically engages in a wide range of categories, along with our implementing partners, and usually these areas are dictated by Congress. But the Rwan-dan government is now introducing guidelines where they ask each country to only specialize in a maximum of three catego-ries. I don't think USAID is used to being told by the host gov-ernment how to use the funds."

"It sounds like following Rwanda's requests might be a bet-ter approach than the 'take whatever we give you' methodology I often see with USAID field projects," I say, aware that I might not have chosen the nicest way to put it.

He knits his brow as he thinks about it. "Well, I'm not sure how it is in other places. All I know is that I am in constant email communication with the people over at the Ministry of Finance who are essentially the gatekeepers of aid in this country. They make it hard to fulfill the mandate set by Congress."

"Hmm, that must be tough," I say.

He continues, "A new NGO law has been pushed through here. They want Rwandans to lead these development initiatives instead of expats. And if they can find a way for Rwandans to run these projects, they're going to do it." He taps his pen on the desk. "But who's going to train these people to take the lead? I'm skeptical that Rwandans will be able to do it themselves in the near future because it takes time to build the necessary capacity," he confesses.

I can't tell if he's worried about the security of his job given this new trend or if he's actually part of the minority of enlightened individuals within the development sector who believe that real success in this field means working yourself *out* of a job. But whichever side he's on, I can't help but feel celebratory at the news that a country is actually taking its development into their own hands and not just accepting whatever the Western world feels like giving them.

"So who are these gatekeepers?" I ask. "I'm curious to meet with them."

Sam turns to his computer and searches his email for the name "Vincent Kananga." A bunch of emails pop up as he turns back to me and emphatically says, "You see?" referring to the amount of correspondence he has to deal with as a result of all the push back, as he jots down the email address for me.

With Vincent's email in hand, I make my way out of the heavily guarded embassy gates in deep anticipation to finally meet a guy who can give a development behemoth like USAID a run for its money.

◆　◆　◆

Emmanuel and Vincent both look sharp in their suits and ties as we settle into some chairs around a table in the far corner of the office. And it's not just what they're wearing that gives them a particular "sharpness." After only a few lines of introduction, both of these Rwandan officials already give me the impression of being very intelligent and perceptive, as well.

"Thanks for agreeing to meet with me," I say.

Vincent smiles. "It's our pleasure. From your email it sounds like you are sympathetic to Rwanda's new approach in dealing with foreign donors."

"Yes, absolutely," I reply. "When I met with Sam at USAID I was surprised to hear about all the new guidelines. It sounds like you're really taking control of your own development processes."

"We found a long time ago that the donors were coming in and imposing their aid," Emmanuel says, "and we found it wasn't good for the country's development."

"Right," I concur.

"Now we have well-structured mechanisms here," he continues. "We have regular meetings with the development partners, like USAID and others, and we even have assessment tools to help us evaluate their work. On a yearly basis the development partners have to meet and state whether or not they've achieved their goals in front of everyone. It has increased accountability and effectiveness in measurable ways."

"And I heard the partners are only supposed to focus on three major thematic areas instead of doing a bunch of small projects in many areas, right?" I ask.

"Yes, exactly. You can see it here," Emmanuel says as he hands me a copy of the chart. "We want to avoid duplication of efforts and we hope to encourage specialization through this approach," he explains.

"And what about USAID?" I ask, looking down at the grid. "It looks like they're still focusing on too many sectors."

"Yes, they are, but we're working to change that. But they keep telling us that the U.S. Congress decides how the money is spent and apparently they have allocated money for ten different sectors. So if they're limited to only three areas, then they might start giving less they say," Emmanuel explains. He then adds, "In 2008 USAID had sixty-two projects in Rwanda. That is just too much, which is why we are encouraging them to organize themselves."

"And this method ensures that the donors get spread out to all the priority areas?" I ask.

"Yes, precisely. There is too much focus on health. So much duplication of efforts. Everyone wants to come and do health projects here. We need donors to focus on productive sectors, especially areas like agriculture. If Rwandan people are making money, they can pay for health later. But donors are reluctant to invest in agriculture," he says.

Vincent jumps in. "For some reason the development partners like to appear in all sectors. They resist specialization. Like in the Australia example," he suggests.

"Yes, like with Australia," Emmanuel echoes. "They came in with fixed ideas to do something in the health sector. But when we assigned them a different sector to work in, they didn't like that."

"We're still waiting to hear back from them about whether they will agree," Vincent adds.

"If they are coming to help us here in Rwanda, we are the ones who know what we need and what we want," Emmanuel asserts with passion in his voice. "They should come here and align their work with our priorities!"

Amen.

I've long known that the international development world has a history of operating from a "we know better than you do" perspective. Whether well-intentioned or not, foreign governments and NGOs have typically felt confident that they had the answers for the developing world, regardless of whether they were asked to provide them or not. The imposition of aid projects is something that has bothered me ever since I started this work.

Whenever I get people to consider this issue, I encourage them to turn the tables: how would you feel if someone came traipsing into your community telling you what to do and imposing projects that directly affected you and your family without them understanding your real needs and priorities? For example, what if a Rwandan guy showed up to a school board meeting in Topeka, Kansas, and explained all of the changes he intended to make in the education system through his various donations. It wouldn't be tolerated, of course. People would say, "You're not from here, you don't know what our kids need," or "You don't even speak English, so how can you design our school programs?" or simply, "Who do you think you are?" But the reverse happens all the time across the developing world. Donors build schools and design curriculums and start health centers and dig wells without ever asking the people, "What do you actually want and need?"

I love that the Rwandan government has identified their development priorities in such clear terms and are brave enough to say to foreign donors: "Here's what we need from you—are you in or out?"

I look to them both hopefully. "So, is it working?"

"Yes, I'd say so. The development partners are now very well coordinated. And almost all of them are clearly following our priorities," Emmanuel replies. "The donors used to be the ones driving development in this country, but now it's the government that does that. It's actually a big change."

"It's still not perfect, of course," Vincent adds. "Rwanda would prefer that the development partners just provide budget support in the future so we can do these projects ourselves."

"Yes, our preference is definitely general budget support," Emmanuel agrees. "But some donors don't yet have the confidence to just come and give money because they fear corruption. But we now have a strong institution for accountability with clear feedback loops to donors."

"And what about the international non-governmental organizations that are typically the implementing partners for big donors like USAID? My friend told me it's getting harder and harder to be accepted to work here as an NGO. Apparently you've really raised the bar?" I ask.

"Yes, we are becoming much more selective about who we allow to operate here," Emmanuel replies. "For a while, anyone was allowed to come here and work. But we found the organizations to be uncoordinated and hard to track. Having so many small projects wasn't helping us make progress toward achieving our priorities. And, also, the country is starting to move away from aid projects in favor of for-profit initiatives that bring jobs and profit to this country. It's probably easier to start a company here than an aid organization," he adds, laughing.

As we wrap up the meeting and Vincent leads me back to the elevator, he adds, "Development is step by step. We aren't expecting changes overnight. We are practical and strategic about the improvements we want for ourselves here in Rwanda and how we can achieve them. But they have to be *our* priorities, not someone else's."

I hope other countries are taking notice.

◆　◆　◆

It's easier to start a business than an NGO, huh? I think to myself as I walk down the street away from the ministry. I'm tempted to put this to the test for the sake of my current research.

I don't have any plans this afternoon, so I decide to head over to the Ministry of Local Government to see what it would take to start my own NGO. After arriving at the ministry building, the first five people I ask have no idea what I'm looking for. And I'm pretty sure it's not my mediocre French that's the problem; it's that the bulk of the work here is actually focused on *important* things like improving local governance, not coddling international do-gooders. Eventually a man insists he knows the way and he'll take me there himself. But after a few minutes of winding along this dark dingy hallway in the basement of the ministry building, I'm starting to wonder if it really exists. This office couldn't be more hidden in the bowels of this building if it tried.

"*Ici!*" he finally says cheerfully, as he points to the office I'm looking for.

"*Merci, beaucoup,*" I say as I shake his hand.

I'm able to meet briefly with the director after he wraps up another meeting and he invites me into his small, dimly lit office. "So you would like to start an aid organization here?" he asks with a suspicious look. I'm not feeling so welcomed.

"Yes, and I am curious what the steps might be," I reply.

"We have new laws in place that make it illegal to be unregistered as an NGO in the country. We don't want international organizations operating without our knowledge, because we believe all development work needs to be in line with the country's priorities," he explains, echoing some of what Emmanuel and Vincent told me.

"Yes, I understand that," I say.

"And to register your organization we will need several things from you."

"Like what?" I ask.

"We will need a detailed action plan for the upcoming year, and, if you have been operating elsewhere, we would like to see your annual report from the previous year." I nod as I start writing down the requirements. "We also need proof that you have already secured funding for your work. And we need statements that outline how your work will align with the Rwandan government's 'Vision 2020,' as we won't approve organizations that are not in line with the national priorities, as I mentioned before." He stops and thinks for a moment. "We'll also need a very detailed budget for your work and for the activities you plan to do here. And we may also require a recommendation letter from the relevant ministry that aligns with your work."

"Right, okay," I say, jotting down the last few bits.

"So perhaps we can meet in two weeks and discuss the details of the process further," he suggests. He scribbles down his email address and stands up, indicating that the meeting is over.

"Well . . . I, okay, I will email you," I stutter. "Thanks."

I start making my way back down the dark hallway, and I smile as I look at the long list in my hand. To be honest, it makes me feel good that the ministry has so many hoops that need to be jumped through to start an NGO here. It shows responsibility and attention to what the country needs most. I have a feeling they weed out a lot of less-than-motivated international NGOs through all the required paperwork and waiting.

Now it's time to test out the opposite: I head over to the Rwanda Development Board to see what it would take to start a company instead.

◆　◆　◆

"Is anyone sitting here?" I ask an old Rwandan man who is waiting for his turn at the business registry office. He has smiley eyes hidden behind thick glasses and a head full of gray hair.

"No, feel free," he says, motioning to the seat. He introduces himself as Eugene, and he explains that he's here to register his first business.

The room reminds me a little of the DMV in the States, minus the stressful vibe and disgruntled workers. Okay, on second thought, it doesn't feel like the DMV at all. It's clean and organized and there is a sense of efficiency in the air with short wait times since there are multiple desks processing applications at once. There are only two rows of chairs in this room, and everyone is waiting patiently for their number to be called.

I look over to Eugene and in his left hand he holds an

application form, 25,000 Rwandan francs (the equivalent of about $40), an ID, and his ticket number.

"Is that all you need?" I ask him.

"Yes, it is very easy. There were only five pages, and I didn't even need to fill in every section," he says as he lifts the application for me to see. He smiles. "And they will process my business within twenty-four hours."

"What kind of business are you registering?" I ask.

"A consultancy company," he says with pride in his face. "I used to work as a customs official, but now I'm retired and I will start my own consultancy that specializes in legal consulting and English, French, and Kinyarwanda translation." He puts the application form on his lap and transfers his cane to the other hand. "This is my daughter," he says, pointing to a woman on his right. She nods at me and smiles. "She wanted to come to help me, but I think it will be so easy that I won't need any assistance."

"It sounds like this process is quite simple. They must really be encouraging business development here," I say, stating the obvious.

"Yes, very much so," he replies.

"And would it be as easy for me to start a business, even though I'm a foreigner?" I ask.

"Yes, yes, of course. They are encouraging foreign investment, and they have made it just as easy for outsiders to start companies, as well. You fill in the same form that I did, and the process only will take you one day to get approval. The international investors are coming much more lately thanks to the new laws and procedures."

It's intriguing that there's such a higher degree of trust in foreigners wanting to *make* money here rather than for those who want to *give it away*. Emmanuel and Vincent were right, it really is easier to start a company than an NGO in this country. In many parts of Africa, that's not the case. It sometimes feels like in most developing countries almost *anyone* can start an NGO, regardless of whether they have a solid idea, an invitation from the community, or a real plan for long-term sustainability. The barriers to entry are usually quite low for international NGOs, which is why so many countries are inundated with ineffective organizations that are operating with hardly any oversight.

Eugene looks over to me and smiles as he adds, "The difference is clear. Things here in Rwanda are much better lately. Life has improved in the last few years." He pauses and shakes his head as he repeats with a sigh, "It's so much better."

"That's great to hear. Best of luck to you and your new company, Eugene," I say.

"Thanks." He smiles. As I get up to walk away, his number is called and I watch as he approaches the desk slowly with a look of excitement and intense pride.

CHAPTER 18

"Do you stop in Nyamasheke?" I ask, pointing to a spot on the map near the Rwanda/Congo border while butchering the pronunciation of its name. The bus driver cocks his head to the left as he squints at the map, then slowly nods as he says, "Yes, no problem. Nyamasheke, we go." He doesn't sound very convincing, and I'm a little worried that my spur-of-the-moment decision to head west might end up backfiring on me. Nobody is expecting me in this mysterious village of Nyamasheke, and I'm actually not even sure this is the right place. All I know is that a social enterprise I once gave some advice to a few years ago is allegedly operating in the area, and I'm curious to see how things are going for them these days. This snap decision was made over breakfast this morning after I was informed that my room would no longer be available at Saint Paul's guesthouse thanks to a weeklong World Vision conference.

As the bus weaves its way out of Kigali and into the countryside, the soundtrack from the bus radio blasts a steady stream of Kelly Clarkson and what sounds like American country music from the seventies. Dolly Parton at her prime. It doesn't match the landscape. However, misfit music aside, what is striking me most about the scenery passing us by is not the beauty of the hills with vibrant greens and reds and browns and yellows that mesmerized me when I entered the country last week. Instead, it's the constant stream of USAID signs that keep catching my eye. Every few miles there's another sign from either the European Union or USAID touting their investment in a particular village. Schools, health clinics, and agricultural projects are all advertised on big metal or wood signposts for everyone to notice.

If you ask somebody like Sam why there is such a focus on putting signs around the project sites, he'll probably tell you it's intended for accountability reasons, so that it's clear where the money is going. But sometimes I think it's a covert political campaign, trying to win over the hearts and minds of the developing world or something. Okay, maybe that's a bit over the top, but I wouldn't be surprised if there are ulterior motives for such blatant signage.

It also doesn't surprise me to see so many signs along the nicely paved main road. The majority of development projects tend to follow the paved roads. If you ever tried to map out where international development is done, you'll notice that most of the projects take place within a comfortable one-hour drive of the capital city or other large towns. The expats and donors in charge of such projects seem to like staying within reach of their creature comforts. A small percentage will take place farther away, but will remain relatively close to the paved roads. And only a handful of the projects will be led by the real adventurous international organizations that are willing and able to rough it in the bush where the needs are most dire. USAID seems to be following the paved roads a lot in Rwanda.

After two hours on the road we make a brief pit stop in a small village. I buy a slightly dirty piece of *chapati* bread from a local vendor (which tastes great as long as you don't look at it too closely) while other passengers find a place to pee. As I get back on the bus, I notice a remarkably old woman with a face full of wrinkles and sad-looking eyes begging for money at the window of another passenger. She looks desperate as she reaches out her frail, shaking hand. A Rwandan man carefully places a few coins in her palm as he reaches out the window. It has never failed to impress me that it's often the people who have the least to give who are the most generous. I've been brainwashed by a particular belief structure that it's not okay to give to beggars—you only encourage the behavior. Maybe that's true, but how do you make the call in a case like this? I am always torn about it. A part of me desperately wants to help this woman, to give her whatever money I happen to have on me, to buy her a damn *chapati* or something. But the other side of me feels like it wouldn't solve the problem, it would only perpetuate it.

Before I have a chance to make a decision about my moral stance on this issue, the bus starts to pull away and my eyes meet with the old woman as we drive off. For that brief second that our eyes are locked on each other, I try to imagine what her story must be; why her family would allow her, or possibly even *encourage* her, to roam the streets begging for money at such a frail age. What had she seen in her lifetime? What were her hopes for the future when she was my age? And how does it make her feel, as she nears the end of her life, to be standing out in the hot sun as her bony hands reach out to ask passing strangers for help?

The only thing this encounter has confirmed for me is that decisions about who to help and how to do it are not as black and white as I try to make them out to be.

◆　◆　◆

The green trees of the National Park stretch out as far as I can see, and there's little else in sight other than the occasional passing vehicle and a handful of black and white monkeys who like to hang out on the side of the road. The soundtrack has now shifted from Dolly Parton to a cassette tape of local music that includes several women singing in high-pitched shrill tones. The driver has the volume pumped up as if he was playing the latest hip-hop single, but this is not the kind of music you want to be listening to at full blast. I'm praying for everyone's poor eardrums.

As the road twists and turns around the side of the hills, I try to block out the music and just enjoy the magnificence of the landscape. It's great that the main road to the west happens to cut through the National Park, allowing for wonderful free sightseeing. But the serenity of seeing nothing but trees is suddenly broken by a handful of people lining the road with metal picks in hand. They are standing inside a ditch that they're in the process of digging, and they look up at us as we pass. But as we round the corner, I'm surprised to see that it's not just a couple of people who are digging the ditch, but a long line of almost one hundred Rwandan men and women lining the road with picks and shovels.

It's unexpected to see them here, as we're so far from any village. I lean over to the guy sitting next to me and ask, "What are they digging? Is it for water lines?"

He smiles and shakes his head. "No. For fiber optic cable."

"What?" I ask in shock. "We're in the middle of nowhere, why would they be laying fiber optic cables?"

"Rwanda is planning to be the technology hub of Africa. We are landlocked and we have a small country with limited resources, so this is something we can do well that doesn't require a port for exporting. We will soon have the fastest communications system around," he says proudly.

"So there will be high-speed Internet even all the way out here?" I ask, still in disbelief.

"Yes, eventually," he says. "We will be connected to the East African Submarine Cable System once Uganda and Tanzania do their part to get the lines dug farther west," he explains.

"Unbelievable," I say softly, shaking my head.

Talk about forward thinking! The fiber optic cables haven't even reached all the way across the neighboring countries yet, but Rwanda is primed and ready once the cables make their way here. And in the meantime, they're giving rural villagers work opportunities to lay the cables, even if they've likely never heard of the term *fiber optic* in their life. In a few years, they might know it well, even all the way out here in the middle of nowhere.

Some might say, "How can you focus on fiber optic networks when the people digging the trenches for it are so poor?" But Rwanda is thinking strategically. Unlike some of their neighbors, Rwanda isn't just dealing with the symptoms that are in front of their faces. It's not only about feeding someone today; it's about figuring out the nuts and bolts of job creation so those people can feed themselves in the future. And given Rwanda's limitations as a small, landlocked country, it seems they've found a great solution for long-term job creation and knowledge transfer in the twenty-first century. And, granted, the people digging on this road might not even learn how to use a computer for another few years, if ever, but when their kids are exposed to computer technology in school and they start to excel in these areas, noticeable improvements could take place in these communities. It's a long-term outlook.

We come around another curve and pass the end of the line of diggers. The last guy looks up out of the trench at the bus, with only his head and the top of his torso visible from the ditch, and gives a slight wave with his shovel.

Farther down the road we encounter another group of workers, only this time they're not digging trenches, they're laying new roads. And standing at the front of the Rwandan road crew, carefully supervising their work, is a Chinese man in a wide-brimmed hat. Apparently fiber optic cables aren't the only new arrival in Rwanda these days. The Chinese have come, too. Much of the infrastructure development here is being done by Chinese firms as they lay the necessary pathways throughout Africa to ensure the success of future business opportunities in one of the most untapped markets on the planet. I must admit that the way the Chinese seem to have covertly slipped in and infiltrated an entire continent is rather impressive, though the long-term impact of their presence in Africa has yet to be seen, and it might not be pretty.

◆　◆　◆

It has taken more effort than expected to get here, but hopefully it will be worth it. As predicted, the bus didn't stop *exactly* in Nyamasheke, but I didn't mind because the view of the sunset over Lake Kivu from the back of the motorcycle on the hour-long drive to the village was mesmerizing. I spent the night in a convent next to a genocide memorial and was woken up early this morning by the sounds of the nuns singing. It was better than the annoying beep of my alarm clock, for sure.

As I started asking around about the One Acre Fund last night, a Peace Corps volunteer I ran into informed me that it's actually in a village called Tyazo, not Nyamasheke. So this morning I found myself on a minibus to Tyazo and nearly got a concussion on the way from hitting my head so many times on the roof thanks to the bad roads and the driver's lead foot. (Where are the Chinese roads when you need them?) But, thankfully, I'm now in Tyazo standing in front of the Rwandan headquarters for the much-loved One Acre Fund, a social entrepreneurship organization that is trying to help subsistence farmers by providing them with agricultural training, access to fertilizer, and linkages to markets where they can sell their harvests in bulk. I came here with the intention of proving myself wrong about this organization. I want to believe that they actually live up to all the hype.

I first encountered the One Acre Fund folks in 2007 when I was asked to provide some feedback on their project at a conference for Echoing Green Fellows. At that time I was fully immersed in the world of social entrepreneurship, having recently interviewed more than thirty social entrepreneurs around the world during my travels, including countless Ashoka Fellows, and was serving that year as a Reynolds Fellow in Social Entrepreneurship at Harvard University. By that point the definition of social entrepreneurship, which had long been debated, was more or less agreed to be organizations or individuals that use innovative and/or entrepreneurial practices to tackle social problems. Based on how the One Acre Fund had been pitched to me, it sounded like they probably fit the description.

When I first encountered the organization, the One Acre Fund had only been operating for a year, working at that time with 600 farmers in Kenya and another 40 in Rwanda. However, they had already run into problems, and their allegedly innovative idea to get farmers to grow passion fruit for export wasn't working out the way they had hoped. They eventually realized that focusing on staple crops like corn and beans would likely be a better move. However, it was more than just the passion fruit missteps that raised red flags for me. I remember listening to one of the founders complaining about having a hard time getting the poor rural farmers to take the international staff seriously. When I pressed him on why they needed expats in the first place, he told me that he didn't think there were Kenyans who could do the job. I was under the impression at the time that perhaps he just needed to look harder.

I also remember while talking to him that there was a general lack of respect for the local knowledge and approaches. The separateness between him and the people his group was trying to help seemed like a large chasm. I got the impression there were a lot of assumptions about what was actually needed, and his inability to speak the local language didn't help the process. It seemed like a recipe for disaster. And as he explained the limited impact they had in the pilot stage of the project, it didn't sound like the idea was succeeding. When my friend Jan wrote me to ask if I'd heard of the organization and would I recommend that she donate to them, I emailed her back saying, "The organization might not have a very long shelf life."

But since their initial launch, the One Acre Fund has become a superstar on the social entrepreneurship circuit, winning all sorts of grants and accolades for their work, including the prestigious Skoll Award for Social Entrepreneurship. However, it's also the case that lately a few of the most promising social entrepreneurship organizations are turning out to be outstanding on paper and unimpressive in the field. I'm hoping that's not the case here.

I enter the large two-story house that serves as both their office and living space and I'm told by the receptionist that I can speak with the director, Eric, upstairs. Once I get to the charming loft, I'm surprised to see an American guy in his late twenties with blond hair sitting behind a giant flat-screen Mac monitor. He looks up, clearly surprised to see a random white person in the middle of nowhere. As I explain why I've come, he seems genuinely pleased to have me here.

"It's always nice to have visitors," Eric says with a smile. "And you should definitely go and check out some of the field projects while you're here. In fact, I'll text JB now to see if you can join him this afternoon." Within minutes he has a text back from the local field director, Jean-Baptiste, confirming that he'd be glad to have me tag along on his afternoon field visits.

After talking for a while with Eric about his life here in rural Rwanda, he brings me downstairs to meet some of the other staff members. But, much to my surprise, other than the three Rwandan women at the front desks, all five people he introduces me to are young, bright Americans. I don't know why I was so hopeful and expectant, but I assumed they would have transitioned to a Rwandan-directed program by now. One of the American guys I meet tells me he's responsible for agricultural training, and so before I can stop myself I ask, "Oh, are you a farmer?"

He blushes and shakes his head no. "My mom has a small farm in upstate New York. But, no, I'm not a farmer." He pauses and then adds, "I'd love to be a farmer!"

I'm obviously not going to push the issue because I've only been here a few minutes and I don't want to be questioning his relevance as an agricultural trainer with no agricultural experience. That wouldn't be so courteous—though I'm already feeling concerned about having so many twentysomething foreigners running this project. Hopefully whatever I see in the field will reverse my doubts about this organization.

◆　◆　◆

JB and I dismount from the motorcycle following one of the most beautiful, but bumpy, hour-long rides of my life. By the time I have my helmet off, a small crowd has already gathered around us here in the village of Karengera, as they warmly welcome JB and me, while also eyeing me with curiosity. We're guided through the village by Betty, the local coordinator for the One Acre Fund whom JB has come to touch base with, and I'm struck by a feeling that this is a community that's on its way up. Piles of drying mud bricks litter both sides of the path waiting to be used, and several of the homes have already had face-lifts. The kids surrounding me appear to be relatively healthy, even if their clothes look old and dirty.

JB and Betty catch up on business for a few minutes as we walk through the village with a small group of onlookers in tow. She then turns to me and says with a bright smile, "You should meet some of our group members!" She guides us down a path away from the village to the surrounding fields, where I'm introduced to Francine, a sixty-year-old widow who has recently started planting sweet potatoes.

"Your sweet potatoes look beautiful," I say to Francine as JB and I overlook her field in the valley below. She beams with pride. She certainly has a lot to be proud of, as she has overcome enormous challenges to get where she is today. With only two small fields she has somehow managed to provide, not only for her six biological children but also for four adopted children who she took in after the genocide. As she stands there in a light blue T-shirt, patterned sarong, and beige cloth tied around her head, I can see the signs of her hard work in her calloused hands.

"Francine is part of one of the Tubura groups," Betty explains to me.

"'Tubura' is the local name for the One Acre Fund, meaning 'multiply' in Kinyarwanda," JB leans in to tell me.

"And what's your role, Betty?" I ask.

"I have two main roles. The first is to form the groups, and the second is to bring them the trainings. Tubura's model is the first to bring together and empower local farmer groups. Sometimes these groups already are operating for other purposes, and sometimes they are newly formed. Then the local trainers, like myself, we come and we train them regularly on farming practices that will help them increase their yield."

"And there's also a loan program?" I ask.

"Yes, we have a program where we provide a loan to the farmers in the form of seeds and fertilizer, which they repay over time. Tubura buys the fertilizer and seeds and brings them to a local storage building here in the community, so it is convenient. Now these farmers are using higher quality seeds than before, and many of them are using fertilizer for the first time."

"And the fertilizer is helpful?" I ask.

"Oh yes, very much. Before there was over-farming and the nutrients are gone from the soil, so having fertilizer is helpful," she explains.

"But isn't it damaging to the environment to be using a lot of fertilizer?" I ask.

"We are careful to train them to use only a small amount— you only need a pinch of fertilizer per hole, you know—many people used to think more is better, but the research shows that idea is wrong. So a single sack of fertilizer can go very far in a field like this," she says, pointing to Francine's land.

A male farmer in a blue and green sweater who has been standing nearby listening to the conversation jumps in as JB translates for me. "And it makes a difference. After Tubura came, the harvest increased."

"By how much?" I ask.

"It tripled," he replies.

"And what do you think was the cause of the increase?"

He thinks for a second, then responds, "First, the weekly education sessions, and second, receiving the fertilizers and learning the techniques for using them. Before we only used compost, and it wasn't enough."

Another guy next to him adds, "And before Tubura it was impossible to find fertilizer locally. The government provides cheaper fertilizer for sale, but it's only stored at the sector level, not in the villages. So the transport is a problem. Tubura is some more expensive, but we can pay back over time and they cover the transport costs to get it here."

"Do you want to go see the field?" Betty asks, gesturing toward Francine's sweet potatoes.

"Sure," I say as I follow them down the narrow path.

It's good to hear encouraging anecdotes from the farmers about the success of Tubura's model, but as JB and I chat about it on the way down, it becomes clear that the organization is also quite serious about verifying these claims with extensive monitoring and evaluation of their programs. In fact, based on what Eric was telling me earlier today, Tubura has one of the most rigorous approaches to measuring impact I've ever seen in a nonprofit. They currently have nine full-time staff members solely dedicated to measuring their success in the core areas of scale, impact, and sustainability. JB informs me that according to their most recent metrics, Tubura is now serving approximately twelve thousand farmers in three districts; doubling farm income per planted acre; and operating at 60 percent financial sustainability, having collected 100 percent repayment from farmers in the last planting season. That sounds impressive for such a young organization.

We carefully step in between the plants in Francine's field, trying hard not to squash any of them. The field looks good—not extraordinary by any means, but good. Stuff is growing, and it all looks relatively healthy. If this is triple the growth, though, I can't imagine they ever tolerated a third of this harvest. Francine squats down and demonstrates for me how Betty taught her to plant the seeds and how to add the fertilizer. Betty looks on with a delighted expression.

Francine looks up at me. "I used to plant aubergines and cabbages. This is the first season I'm planting sweet potatoes because I saw from the others what a good harvest they got last season." She digs around a little, picking up a weed or two, and then adds, "I also have a cornfield over there"—she points beyond the hill—"but it has got a disease so it's not good."

"Will you still get enough with this harvest?" I ask.

"Yes," she assures me. "I should be able to get twenty thousand francs from this field of sweet potatoes, which should be enough for my family to live. And I can still have money to pay back the loan for the fertilizer, little by little."

As we walk back toward the village, Francine confides in me that the sweet potatoes are great, but her real dream is to get some livestock and eventually open up a store in town to trade. Tubura's help is appreciated, but it doesn't seem to be revolutionizing this community.

CHAPTER 19

The fourteen group members circle around Yvette and stare intently at the ground as they watch her dig up the soil with a hoe. They just finished their weekly Tuesday morning meeting where they make their loan repayments, learn about new concepts in effective farming practices from their group leader, and strategize with each other on how they'll approach the next planting season. Some of the people in the meeting looked bored, but now, at this week's practical demonstration on soil testing, they've all perked up.

I can tell Yvette is a smart lady, but to have been chosen as a field officer in Tubura's rigorous selection process, she also had to pass what Eric refers to as the "mud test," where they spend time observing the candidates in the field to make sure they aren't overly chic. The field officers are the heart and soul of Tubura's success, and while it's rather prestigious to be selected as one, they need to be willing to get dirty. Walking long distances along muddy paths and doing trainings like this one on soil sampling are part of the job. I wish that this type of double-check for intense humility was more the norm when hiring field workers, but sadly it's rarely done in other organizations. As Eric put it perfectly to me, "There's a certain group of people who think they're hot shit because they work for an NGO."

Tubura has an incentive, as they see it, to first select the very best people, and then to train them well. But an intense focus on building and supporting a strong, dedicated staff is not the norm in the aid world. Most aid organizations, unlike in the corporate world, see their staff as easily replaceable—often within a short time period. And since there's such high turnover in aid work (from jadedness, burnout, low pay, lack of quality management, etc.), there's little incentive to invest in high quality training for the employees, which, of course, only worsens the cycle. And for those who do just see an NGO job as a way to be "hot shit," very little meaningful work ever ends up getting accomplished.

I lean back against a banana tree and start to think about what I'm seeing. This training isn't perfect, despite Yvette's obvious passion for her work. But the point is that by the end of this meeting, these fourteen farmers will know the basics of soil testing—something that has never been taught to them before, but that might have a positive impact on the upcoming planting season. Tubura has provided the group facilitators with the testing equipment, and once each farmer has collected their soil samples as demonstrated, Yvette can come around to their farms to do the test easily for them.

As I watch the question-and-answer period continue amidst the banana trees, I feel a softening of the subtle feeling of disappointment that has been surging inside me lately. This project isn't revolutionary. It's probably not bringing people out of poverty. It's just giving them a little extra food and income each season with rather simplistic inputs of training and fertilizer. Which is a good thing, for sure, but before it didn't seem like enough for me. I wanted it to be a dream project that totally changed lives. I wanted the One Acre Fund to be the social enterprise that lived up to the hype and totally changed the way agriculture is done. But as I stand here in full awareness that it doesn't do that, I find myself smiling at the realization that *that's okay*. They're playing their part.

I can't deny that at my core I'm a total idealist and perfectionist. I've spent much of the past eight years searching for a silver bullet, even when the rational part of me knew that such a thing doesn't exist. This journey has woken me up to the fact that it's really about all the tiny changes that come from many different directions and all add up to a larger social shift. I guess I should finally admit to myself that there's really no one-stop-shop for economic progress or social change. I mull over that reality in my mind for a moment, unsure of whether it makes me relieved or bummed.

◆　◆　◆

We crouch down on the ground as Jean-Pierre, a local farmer who belongs to one of Tubura's groups, starts digging with his hands in the dirt. JB has brought me to this farm on his motorcycle so I can see one of the group members' plots. I'm not entirely sure what we're looking for under there, but his five-year-old daughter excitedly gets in on it, too, as she drags over a hoe that is twice her size and tries to dig with it. Before long they uncover the treasure they've been searching for: huge red sweet potatoes. As he holds them in his hands, he looks as proud as Francine did yesterday about her own sweet potatoes. It seems to be the hippest thing to plant these days.

"I used to plant cane sugar," Jean-Pierre explains via JB as we stand up, "but I decided to grow sweet potatoes instead because they're more productive here. Now I only have a few rows of cane sugar over there," he says, pointing down the hill.

"It's better to have sweet potatoes because they sell for fifty to one hundred francs per kilo." He looks over his one and a half hectares of land from left to right and then adds, "I'm going to get rid of those banana plants to plant more sweet potatoes. And maybe I'll add beans, too."

"Only that?" I ask, alarmed that he's not growing more variety to feed his family. "Don't you need more nutrients?"

He picks up his two-year-old son, who hasn't gotten used to my presence yet and still eyes me with uncertainty. "We used to plant for eating, but now we plant for selling," Jean-Pierre explains.

It strikes me as strange that all the people I've been meeting yesterday and today have recently shifted to planting sweet potatoes. I'm assuming it's based on Tubura's recommendation, but I hope it isn't a fad they'll soon regret. If everybody is planting the same thing, the market will be saturated in no time. And as good as they taste, man can't live on sweet potatoes alone. It worries me to see such a lack of crop diversity here. I'll have to ask Eric about this later.

"So what have you implemented from the trainings, Jean-Pierre?" I ask.

"I've learned many things. I've learned how to make the compost from the grasses and dung, and how to mix the soil and the compost, and also how to use the fertilizer," he says. "I actually started the program just out of curiosity because I heard it would improve my harvest. And now my harvest has increased by four times." He smiles. "And that helps a lot because I have eight children—five in primary, two in secondary, and my baby," he says, touching the head of the little boy in his arms.

We start climbing the hill back up to his house as we talk about the ins and outs of composting. I credit Mark for the fact that I know anything about compost at all because he has recently become obsessed with his composting worm bin on his balcony in Amsterdam. At the top of the hill, just next to the cow shed, we stand in what used to be an open area that is now dotted with large wooden posts.

"You are building a new house?" I ask, as we weave through the posts on the way to his home.

"Yes, but it will take some time. We're now waiting for a metal roof," he says, as he pats one of the posts. "I don't have any other work except the harvest, though. And the harvest isn't enough because I took credit to buy all this land so I'm repaying the bank credit. And I also have to pay the school fees for my kids."

"So I guess you don't know when you'll get the roof?" I ask, looking up to the cross beams above us.

"No, there's no fixed time because I won't finish it before paying the school fees or the bank credit, so I don't know when it will be done," he says, shrugging.

We enter his house nearby, which is small and dark and is, surprisingly, made of wood. That's not a common sight around here, but apparently the clay nearby isn't good enough for making bricks, so he had to build with wood planks instead. JB and I are asked to take a seat in two wooden chairs in the dark living room, and Jean-Pierre's wife, who has one of the sweetest smiles I've seen lately, comes in with bowls of pineapple to share with us. As we sit and talk with him, I begin to get a better sense about Jean-Pierre. He's clearly a guy who cares a lot about his family and their future, but he has resigned to the pace of change. He has grand visions for his land and his house, but he takes it all season by season. Yet he's also a bit of a risk taker, and in many ways I'm fearful he might be taking too big a risk on these sweet potato dreams. But that's not for me to decide.

As we later start heading back to the motorcycle, I shake

Jean-Pierre's hand and say goodbye. I then turn around, pointing to the maze of wooden posts, and add, "Next time I come back I hope your new house will be finished."

He smiles and replies, "Then you'll need to pray to God."

◆　◆　◆

"It's usually like this," Eric says, positioning our water glasses a foot apart from each other on the wooden table for a demonstration as we sit on the upstairs veranda of Tubura's headquarters. "The NGO provides a product or service, but they're not dependent on the recipient liking what's being offered."

He moves my glass to the edge of the table, and then positions his next to it, tipping it over the edge at a forty-five-degree angle. "Now, imagine there is a string between our glasses that's preventing me from falling off the table," he says.

"Uh-huh," I say, trying to focus on the business analogy instead of the sudden realization that I'm thirsty.

"This is the relationship I want. If for any reason I do something to make you, the client, dissatisfied with what I'm offering or how I'm offering it, then the string will be severed and I will fall off the table. The business won't survive." He pushes my glass of water back to me and then adds, "Essentially, with our model, we're dependent on *them*."

I smile. "That's quite a role reversal from the norm in this field."

"Yes, absolutely. And it's why my favorite metric that we collect is client retention," he says. "Each client has to pay a five percent service fee, ten percent interest on their loans for the fertilizer, and a one-dollar membership fee to be part of our program. This is intended to cover the cost of our field operations, and so we are totally beholden to our clients for our success. A sign of success and validation is whether or not they want to pay us for the services we're providing," he explains.

"That must give them more clout, being clients instead of beneficiaries," I say.

"Of course," he replies, "because if you don't pay for it, then I have all the power in the relationship. I, the *muzungu*, can decide how it comes, or if it's late or on time. But when you pay, you become the boss. We need to deliver on time and provide the services you want or else we'll lose our clients and fall apart as an organization."

"But it must be hard to change the expectations of the farmers after so many decades of aid," I say, taking a sip of water.

"We're living in the wake of *cadeauxs*," he says, using the French word for "gifts" that is used locally when talking about aid. "It's going to take a while to break that. But agriculture is one of the best places to start fixing that because there's money to be made."

"But is there *really*?" I ask, raising my eyebrows, probing Eric for proof about the real nature of agricultural profitability. I explain to him some of what I heard and saw in the field, and my uncertainties about the lack of crop diversity and the challenges of finding realistic export markets. Not to mention the fact that just adding a pinch of fertilizer doesn't seem like it's going to pull people out of poverty.

"In a way, you're right. Because there's no accumulation of wealth or capital happening at the moment. New money has to come from somewhere. And export options are limited since food prices in this region are higher than the neighboring regions." He pauses for a moment. "When we look at our results and when we're honest with ourselves, nobody is getting out of poverty in one or two seasons. Even in one or two years."

"But you are essentially setting yourself up as the buyer, right?" I ask, remembering back to what JB explained to me on our first day in the field.

"Yes, we have initiated a buy-back service to ensure there's a market for the farmers to sell their crops. Essentially we tell them, 'We're going to buy beans at this price this season,' it's usually ten to twenty percent above market level. We pay them all at once for the beans at harvest time, and then we store them in our warehouses and sell them after the harvest at a higher price once the supplies have diminished. And since we're able to sell them in bulk to local schools and prisons, we minimize the transaction costs."

"So by guaranteeing the farmers a market, you can ensure their profitability," I say, nodding in understanding.

"There are obviously a lot of questions about how we're going to scale it up, though, because we're only breaking even at this point. It's not making us any money." He leans back in his chair and adds, "It's a really poppy idea to create market linkages, especially in the developing world. It's so 'buzzy' right now"—he laughs—"but it's not exactly easy to do. So here we've had to get our hands dirty."

"I think the idea is right, though. I hope it can scale," I say. I look out over my right shoulder at the village below, which is perfectly framed by the arched opening of the veranda wall. I turn back to Eric. "But if the wealth accumulation is relatively small, as you said, what changes *do* you see?" I ask.

"The impact that's not appreciable is the food that wouldn't have been consumed."

"That's at least a good first step," I say.

"Yeah, and more changes will be evident in the long term. We're approaching it from a business perspective where we'll grow the project over time instead of just leaving it in two years. It's hard to get fellow NGO colleagues to wrap their heads around that."

"Yeah, I can imagine." I nod.

We're told that lunch is ready, so we head downstairs and join the other expat staff members whom I met the other day. We're all seated around a small outdoor table near the kitchen, enjoying freshly made soft tacos. It still strikes me as puzzling that this organization, based in the middle of nowhere, is run predominantly by a handful of twentysomething Americans. It's not the formula for success I would ever advocate. So as we wrap up lunch and Eric and I stroll over to sit on the concrete steps in the back of the villa, I can't help but bring the issue up.

"Eric, tell me honestly, what's up with having all these *muzungu* staffers?"

"Being here at the house gives the wrong impression," he says. "Because in actuality we employ two hundred people in Rwanda, and only seven of them are expats. But the reasons for *muzungus*? . . . That's a good question." He thinks about it for a moment while shuffling his feet on the concrete. "I think, one, you can get amazing people with high professionalism and dedication who are able to push out very high quality work."

I nod, still not convinced that such high quality expertise doesn't exist in this country.

He continues, "And, two, we want the best people for the positions that we have because the goal is making farmers richer. And there are cases where the best people we can find for the salary range we are able to offer are young expats who are looking for a couple years of interesting work experience in an adventurous location. The really excellent Rwandan brains are working in the president's office or at high-end businesses in Kigali. There's unfortunately a lack of talent who would be willing to work so far from a major city. But we invest a lot in building leadership and management skills internally, so hopefully we'll be able to grow a group of local professional managers to take over in due time."

"I can see your points," I say.

"And working here as an expat is no vacation." He grins. "We work them almost like investment bankers . . . hopefully with more redeeming value." We both laugh.

We continue sitting on the steps, talking about all sorts of things from the origin of the idea to how they align their work with the government's agenda. And by the end of it, as we both sit there in silence looking out at the breathtaking scenery beyond the villa walls, I realize that I'd been wrong about them. The One Acre Fund is not perfect, and they're not exactly "changing the world" per se, but they're doing very good work and they care about the people they're serving. I'm glad I took the time to come out here and give them a second chance.

I turn back to Eric. "So you think social entrepreneurship has a promising future?"

He nods. "I think everyone is realizing that there's more than just profit out there. It's a very motivating incentive, but it isn't creating a world we want to live in." He looks back out to the hills and adds, "I think social entrepreneurship, and its idea of sacrificing profit for impact, will gain much more traction over time . . . and it should."

CHAPTER 20

Iᴛ ᴛᴀᴋᴇꜱ ᴍᴇ longer than usual to swing my leg over to get off the motorcycle as I'm feeling pretty tired this morning. I'm back in the capital of Kigali after the long trip back from Tyazo, and somehow I managed to get a room at Saint Paul's again, despite the World Vision conference still going on there. Last night, however, the participants decided it would be fun to hang out near my door and talk loudly for hours, despite my kind plea for them to move. It was pretty frustrating.

Mark's fieldwork is nearly done, so I'm looking forward to getting back to Nairobi soon. We've been staying in touch via text messages and occasional emails, and it's clear we're both missing each other a lot. But there's one more thing I want to see before I leave Rwanda: a true social business. Not social entrepreneurship, which is often a different thing altogether, but a legitimate large-scale social business that not only turns a profit but also helps the world along the way. Clear examples of social businesses are hard to come by, though, because the sad truth is that many companies who maintain what is known as a "double bottom line" (focusing on both social and economic returns) have a hard time successfully going to scale. When I heard about the socially minded work of Rwanda's largest textile manufacturer, UTEXRWA, I felt compelled to check it out.

So here I am at the gate of UTEXRWA on the outskirts of Kigali in what appears to be the growing industrial zone of the capital city. From the outside it doesn't look so special. The company name stands out in big bold red letters on top of the two-story main office, which has been painted light blue. Around it there are a handful of warehouses and work buildings where I'm guessing the magic happens. I make my way along the carefully landscaped path that boasts a manicured lawn and a handful of small shrubs, and I'm eventually directed upstairs to find the deputy general manager, Prem. The meeting has been set up by the company's CEO, who is currently away on business, but who seemed eager over our email exchange to share UTEXRWA's new projects with me. I'm surprised that this is Rwanda's second largest company, as I sort of expected it to be swankier than this. But the executive offices are far from lavish.

"Are you Tori?" an Indian man asks from the doorway of one of the offices.

I stand up and approach him to shake his hand. "Yes, hi. Prem?"

"Yes, nice to meet you. Please, come and have a seat in the conference room."

He appears to be young, in his early thirties or something, and despite being here for only a year, he is very knowledgeable about the company. I explain my background in aid effectiveness to him and he gives a look that indicates we're on the same page.

"The main keyword these days in Africa is *aid*," he says, "but our strategy isn't aid because that's just a one-time investment of money. Our point of view is that we need to invest to build industry, bring jobs here, and increase the GDP for the benefit of the country."

"I couldn't agree more," I enthuse. "So, tell me, how are you doing it?"

"There are three main social projects we're focused on at the moment, in addition to our regular textile work, which includes bed net production and distribution, silkworm production, and banana fiber processing," he explains. "I'll start with the bed nets. Usually, as you know, bed nets are provided by big organizations. And the money is all given to the Asians—the Chinese—because they are producing them from abroad and then they sell them here to aid agencies or on the streets."

I nod in understanding as he continues, "But as we see it, Rwanda should be doing it themselves. Doing this creates wealth, gives taxes to the government, and employment for the people. So we have begun a program in which we import only the netting fabric from abroad, but we do the rest of the work ourselves. Eventually we hope to produce the fabric locally, too. This program is currently producing two thousand nets per day, and soon we should be able to produce twelve million nets per year, employing three thousand people."

"Wow, that's terrific," I say. "And I heard it's being done as a joint venture, is that right?" I ask.

"Yes, it's a joint venture with the Heineken Africa Foundation," he replies.

"Heineken? The Dutch beer company?" I ask, confused.

"Yes, exactly. There were a few reasons for the partnership. First, they had a set amount of money that they wanted to donate to provide mosquito nets here, and we encouraged them to promote local production instead of sourcing the nets from abroad. So instead of buying nets, they provided the funding for us to set up the necessary infrastructure here at UTEXRWA so we could make them ourselves."

He continues, "There was a second important reason that

we believed strongly in the Heineken partnership: A problem we identified in the bed net industry was not that they were too difficult to produce here, but that they were too difficult to distribute. The aid organizations only reach so far. We wanted to find a way to get the nets farther to the places that need them most. And the only thing we could see reaching to every corner of the country was the beer trucks," he explains.

"Yes, the beer gets everywhere." I laugh, trying not to get mired in the sadness of this reality for the moment.

"So the beer distribution trucks will take a certain number of nets with them when they go," he says.

"And will these be sold or given away?" I ask.

"For now we're giving them away." He can tell by my face that I don't approve of the methodology. "I know, I don't believe in this approach, either," he assures me. "But it's what the foundation wanted for now. We're just waiting for the packaging to arrive and we should be able to deliver the first nets starting in a week or so."

I'm impressed by the innovative nature of this endeavor. It's a creative way to solve the distribution problem. And, sure, I wish the nets weren't being given away for free, because countless studies have shown that paying a small amount for nets increases the perceived value and the chance that they'll actually be used properly, but I think it's a worthwhile start.

Prem continues, "The next thing we're working on is silk production. Here silk is a one hundred percent value addition to the country. We import the silkworms, create self-employment among people who rear the worms and cocoons, produce the silk here in the factory, and then market it abroad. This helps at a lot of levels in a social way, especially because it can bring employment to the village level."

"Yeah, I can imagine."

"Our director actually decided to partner with the Ministry of Defense on this particular project. At first I thought it was strange not to partner with the Ministry of Agriculture, but he explained that the idea was actually to do the silkworm production with retired military people in order to give them employment. It's an innovative approach, I think. So far we have educated sixty people and given them certificates in silk extraction. We can process three tons of silk at this facility, but we don't have enough silkworms producing yet," he explains.

"Are you already processing any silk?" I ask.

"Yes, we've already started on a small scale," he says proudly. "In the future we'll be doing more trainings, setting up cooperatives, and also we will try to increase the number of mulberry farms in Rwanda for silkworm rearing and cocoon production."

As he goes on to explain the details of the banana fiber project (which is cool, but not nearly as promising as the other two ventures), he emphasizes the importance of their approach. "We want to stop the dependency cycle," he explains, "by creating employment, enabling knowledge transfer, and providing technology to this country." He pauses for a moment and then adds, "Handouts just don't work."

"It all sounds great to me. Are we able to visit the production facility?" I ask.

"Sure, of course. I'll take you now."

◆ ◆ ◆

"Where is everybody?" I ask as we walk through the first two large rooms of the factory that are used for fabric dying and printing.

"We're unfortunately lacking in raw materials lately," Prem explains as we walk. "We get most of our raw materials like cotton from nearby countries—Burundi, Tanzania, Congo, and Uganda. But sometimes, like now, there are delays in the import process and we have to shut down operations," he says. After a few more steps he suddenly stops and turns to me, adding with emphasis, "But I still pay my employees."

"That's good," I say, "but it must be hard on the company's finances."

"Yes, it's not easy. But it's the right thing to do," he says as we continue walking.

He shows me the area of the factory that is being dedicated to producing the new mosquito nets, with tables full of finished nets waiting patiently for the packaging to arrive any day now. In an upstairs loft there are forty or fifty sewing machines, ready and waiting to take the mosquito net business by force.

As we exit into the sunshine and cross over to the next large warehouse-style building, I'm unaware that I should have savored those last few breaths of fresh air. The air quality in the cutting and sewing building is stifling. On the first floor a couple dozen men and women stand around long tables using a jigsaw-style tool to cut patterns from large reams of cloth that are layered several inches thick. Each shape is drawn onto the top layer with chalk, traced from pre-drawn patterns printed on thin paper. I stand with Prem next to a table surrounded by six people who are involved in cutting the various parts of an army uniform. The camouflage pattern cloth is being cut into several different shapes, which will all eventually be assembled into a military jacket by the sewing team upstairs.

I'm immersed in watching them work until Prem interrupts my attention. "Tori, I'd like you to meet Clarisse." I turn and see a middle-aged Rwandan woman wearing a yellow traditional patterned dress. "She has worked here for ten years. I'm going to let her take you around to see the rest, and then you can meet me back in the office when you're finished."

"Great, thanks, Prem," I say as he turns to leave. "Clarisse, thanks for taking time to show me around," I say with a smile.

"It is my pleasure."

She walks me through the process of the pattern cutting, showing me the various bolts of fabric they're currently working with and the racks with the patterns hanging from them. She gives good explanations, but it's quite apparent that Clarisse doesn't seem to be particularly enthusiastic.

"Do you like working here?" I ask as we walk down an aisle between two rows of fabric.

She thinks for a second and then replies, "These textile companies, they don't pay very much, they give the lowest, I think. Private companies they"—she gives a *tsk* sound as she shakes her head—"they don't give much, the salaries are low. Here twenty-seven thousand is the lowest."

That's only $45 a month.

"It's not so much," she continues. "But permanent workers get four percent added to their salary each year, because of Rwandan law, and they also get a small bonus." She smoothes her hand over a layer of fabric sitting on the nearby table. "Most of the workers, they try to get some other jobs in government because they're paid well and you can get some medical coverage. But here, not like that. They are strict somehow."

She takes a look around the factory floor and continues, "Air conditions and sanitation are not that good in textiles. So many, when they get a chance, they just go."

"Why not you?" I ask. "You've been here ten years."

"I'm trying also!" she says, with a big smile and eyebrows raised. Her face then turns serious. "But it's timing. I'm trying, I'm trying. . . ." She trails off, shaking her head. "When you don't get a chance to continue your studies, you can go for tailoring or something else. But if you have an education, you look for work elsewhere."

"So most of the people here weren't able to finish school?" I ask.

"Yes, they're here because of the war and all those problems. Some people never got the chance to go to school because of what happened," she explains.

Her face starts to light up as we approach another row of fabric. She again touches it with care as she boasts, "But this is our fabric. It's not imported. All this is manufactured here!"

We walk over to meet with some of the screen printers, who all enthusiastically concur that the salaries are, indeed, too low. One guy, a new employee, says he's currently only paid 21,000 francs. But they dream of being able to earn something closer to 60,000 so they can take care of their families better.

"Are you happy to work here?" I ask the new guy, already knowing the answer.

"In Rwanda, no job. We continue here because no other job," he says with a shrug.

◆　◆　◆

Some of the workers were complaining to me downstairs about the air quality, but as I get to the top step of the second floor of the factory, I get a better picture of what they were talking about. In front of me are two hundred and forty sewing machines, whirring at full speed. There are a handful of fans scattered throughout the room, but none of them are turned on. There are few windows in this place, and all the machines, bodies, and fabric bits make it hard to breathe up here. It's not a toxic smell or anything, it's just stifling. Like there's not enough oxygen to go around. The floor is a little dirty and there isn't much space to move. I don't think this is at the level of a sweatshop (though I can't say I've ever been in one before). I guess my best assessment is that the conditions aren't great, but they're also not over-the-top horrible.

Clarisse takes me from one station to the next. We watch a woman sewing buttons. Another one working the fusing machine to make the collars. Guys with irons, and a man using the embroidery machine to print all the soldiers' names on the jackets they're currently making. They apparently have a huge order from the military, and they only have four months to finish it all. All two hundred and forty machines are hard at work with camouflage fabric.

Clarisse introduces me to Claudine, the supervisor for the garments section, who has worked here for over twenty years. She's wearing a pretty pink silk suit and has an air of kind authority here on the second floor. The hum of the machines makes it nearly impossible to hear what she is saying to me, though, so she invites me into her office to talk after I say goodbye to Clarisse.

She looks out through the glass of her interior office at the rows of workers as she proudly says, "Every worker that comes here, I train them. I train people two weeks on a machine. After that you train on how to stitch. Most people, they come here with tailoring skills, but I still need to train them further for an additional month."

"Why do you like to work here?" I ask. Her answer is hardly the stuff of the "find meaning in your work" gurus back in the West.

"I like it here because I get money," she replies, and then adds, "And there are no other jobs."

"Is the money enough?" I ask.

"Nah, ahh . . ." She rolls her eyes and laughs. "It's not enough. It's not enough for anyone. The salary is low here. But at least they offer free lunch and medical leave and some annual leave . . . small things. And a uniform," she adds. "You can see all the permanent employees—they have a uniform."

"And how does it compare to other companies?"

"Other companies are better than this, I think. Our big bosses, they're here to sell, they're not here to help the Rwandese." She goes on, aiming right for the jugular. "The Indians, they just like more money. I see they like money more than people. Because everything here is low—transport, salary, everything. If you want to know this, check another factory, see the salary. I think all of India is like that, it won't change."

It surprises me to hear such distaste for the company coming from one of their longest-serving employees. This isn't the first time I've heard racist undercurrents from the Rwandan people chastising the local Indian businessmen. I'm not sure how far back it goes, but the relations seem strained.

Claudine leans forward in her chair. "The Indians, they come here one year and then they go back. They change every year." She thinks for a second before adding, "But our director, he has maybe ten years here, and I have no problem with him."

So far I've heard nothing but overwhelming praise for the company's CEO, who apparently has an enormous heart, a keen business sense, and a passion for using his company to make a difference. Apparently it's the general managers like Prem, who come in and out for short stints, that aren't so well tolerated.

"For me, it's no problem," she says. "Because I come here, I work, and I go home."

Claudine tells me about her three children, ages sixteen, eighteen, and twenty, all of whom are still in school. She works so she can afford the high cost of tuition for them, along with six orphans whom she still supports after the genocide with school fees, clothes, shoes, and other things.

She gets a sad look on her face as she reveals to me, "In the genocide I lost all my family—my mother, my husband, my father, my sister, all my cousins. . . . I don't even want to tell you. All died. I keep working for my children and for the orphans I support."

"And where's your hope?" I ask.

"I get hope from my children, that their lives will be good. And me now, I start to study. Now I am in Senior 6. I study at night and on Saturday. I try to finish my secondary degree. I came here to work because I knew how to stitch. And I worked my way all the way to this position. But now I want to continue to study. To get a better job one day and, if I get the money, to go to university."

"Would you say you're happy, Claudine?"

She smiles and nods. "Yes, I'm happy. I don't want to continue thinking about the problems behind me, the genocide and the other problems. I want to see in front of me for my future. This job, slowly, slowly, can help me get there."

❖　❖　❖

"What did you think?" Prem asks me with wide eyes as we sit back down at the conference room table.

"Well . . ." I take a long pause, attempting to figure out a way to be polite about what I just heard and saw. "The employees had a few complaints."

"Like what?" he asks, sounding surprised.

"They said the salaries were too low," I say.

He looks a little peeved. "When you compare what we pay, which is about seventy thousand, to what other companies pay, we are extremely fair."

"I heard twenty-seven thousand."

"No, that's not right. I can show you the financial statements," he says defensively. He then amends his comment, "We do have *some* casual laborers and they get paid less, but most get paid more. The workers whom you talked with, many of them used to clean toilets for a living. But now they are excellently trained and they have a stable income." He then pauses and takes a breath to calm himself before adding, "We are trying to do the best we can given our constraints. We're not one hundred percent perfect, but we're trying to be perfect."

"So would you say business is the answer to Rwanda's development?" I ask.

He ponders the question for a moment, and then answers by saying, "As an employee of UTEXRWA, I'd have to say yes." I can tell there's more to this answer, but I don't press it. "Our director has brought a lot of innovation to UTEXRWA," he continues. "In the near future it will create a lot of changes in Rwanda. But you can't bring development in overnight. It comes gradually, step by step."

"A lot of people want to believe that business is the answer, though," I say.

"Yes, and Rwanda is doing a lot to scale up their business development lately. But if you want my honest opinion, when I look around at the common person, they aren't doing any better than what I saw five years ago."

"But you believe in UTEXRWA's contribution?" I ask.

"Yes, definitely. The company is one of the only consistent employers in the country, and, in my opinion, we pay our employees reasonably and we educate them to know the technology as part of our knowledge transfer process. The Rwandan government is one hundred percent supportive of us. That's the difference between us and other businesses, because we're not just a business, we want to create something good in the country."

"The social components of your work are impressive," I say.

"I agree," he says. "There's a lot of social innovation at this company and a heart for making positive change for Rwanda. But, for the workers, at the end of the day it's just about bread and butter. They don't necessarily care about the bigger picture."

CHAPTER 21

THE BUS PULLS out of the dilapidated gas station parking lot as the sun is starting to rise over a nearby hill. It's going to be a long day of driving all the way back to Kampala from Kigali, and then another full day on the road to get back to my love waiting for me in Nairobi. But I guess the endless overland journeys that we take in life to get back to where we started give us good opportunities for reflection.

As we wind back along the hairpin turns leading out of the country, I look out the window at the scenery, which looks completely different in the early morning light. Still spectacular, just different. I feel a twinge of sadness as I stare out the window. It's hard to believe that my quest for answers is finally coming to an end after nearly two months of overland travels. But ending up in Rwanda was definitely a good move, as it helped fuel my hope, if only a little, when it comes to promising alternatives to traditional aid. What I saw these past few weeks in Rwanda wasn't mind-blowing, but it seemed more effective than the majority of the projects I saw in Kenya and Uganda.

But, then again, that might be my bias talking. Ever since the concepts of social entrepreneurship and social business emerged,

I've been a huge supporter, shouting the idea of innovation and business mind-sets in the aid industry from the rooftops. I want to believe that it works. And in many cases it does. Some of the most inspiring people I've met around the world have been social entrepreneurs, and I've watched in awe as they've sparked massive social change movements in their communities, thanks in large part to their particular mix of passion, vision, and dogged determination. Their ability to inspire social change through entrepreneurial methods is nothing short of amazing. However, I've also started to notice lately that the concept might be getting diluted as many of the new organizations that are pitching themselves as social entrepreneurial endeavors are actually just slightly hipper-than-normal NGOs with marginal levels of innovation or entrepreneurial approaches in their work.

Perhaps what has been bothering me most lately is what seems to be the growing *imposition* of innovation on less developed countries. A number of new social enterprises tend to originate from the confines of business plan competitions at fancy U.S. universities (that's how the One Acre Fund got its start after winning competitions at both Stanford and Yale) or as a result of limited field experiences by super overachieving young people with a mission to save the world. So often it's the idea itself that holds the most weight (and how cool it can sound in a Power-Point presentation heavily laden with shots of smiling African children) and the actual usability or demand from the communities being served is of lesser importance. I guess for me the bottom line is that innovation is great, but only if it's being done in direct response to the expressed needs of the community, and only if there's no simpler, more logical approach that would generate the same results. More often than not, the projects that are most effective and most aligned with the needs of the people are those that originate from the community members themselves, not from well-intentioned outsiders. That's why I've always been so supportive of locally-based social entrepreneurs, like the Ashoka Fellows I've met abroad, who are finding creative ways to address social problems in their own communities. That being said, I'm glad I got to see the One Acre Fund in action because I think they're doing important work, and it feels nice that my critical opinion of their work was able to change.

And then there's UTEXRWA, the legitimate business with a moderately social aim. My feelings after spending some time at the factory the other day are mixed. They are essentially just a large textile company that employs a bunch of people and happens to do some socially minded projects on the side to keep things fresh. Fine enough. Their bed net distribution idea is cool, their silkworm project might help a few hundred people find a new source of income and introduce silk production to the country, and the banana fiber project is okay. But the main contribution I see them making is in giving people jobs. And for the majority of people on this planet, that's all they want.

With the rapid spread of microfinance organizations around the world, there's this assumption that everybody's an entrepreneur. I beg to differ. If you even take a random selection of ten people you know, I'll bet that only one out of ten would have what it takes to start and run their own successful small enterprise. Most people, it turns out, just want jobs. So if UTEXRWA wants to really make a social impact through their work, it should start by paying people high enough wages for them to be able to support their own families well, improve the working conditions to be as dignified as possible, and continue the knowledge transfer programs to build individual capacity. And hopefully other companies will follow their lead.

The bus approaches the border, and we're told we need to get our exit stamp here before walking across the road that separates the two countries to wait in line for the Ugandan entry stamp. As I am walking over the border past a small river, I start to realize that perhaps this mini-quest to find "the answer" for a better alternative to aid has only made me realize that there's no one perfect answer when it comes to which aid organizations are the best. There's no magic wand to cure all the world's ailments—just slow and steady approaches by a range of players, from the grassroots organizations and social businesses to traditional NGOs and international development agencies. Whether I like to admit it or not, they all have their role to play. At the end of the day it's going to be the combined efforts, not only of these groups but also of national governments and global policies that make the difference. Because in my heart, I know that tackling the root causes of poverty is going to require the tireless commitment of all these players as they work to ensure social, economic, legal, and political *justice* for the world's poor. It's not an easy road ahead. It never was (although some aid organizations have tried to make it seem so in their glossy brochures).

Though, even with this clarity, I still don't feel like I've found the answer I was looking for yet. But at the moment my thoughts are focused on only two things: (1) getting through this ridiculously long Ugandan immigration line, and (2) reuniting with Mark.

◆ ◆ ◆

Reunions appear to be our specialty. Airport reunions are a particular forte for us (and we've had *many* over the course of our international relationship), but today it appears Mark and I excel at street corner reunions, as well. I can already see him weaving in between the cars of the perpetually chaotic Westlands roundabout, parting the sea with Moses-like perfection to get to the other side where the bus just dropped me off. In his left hand he's holding a single red rose. We rush into each other's arms, and he holds me tight, then kisses my cheek, puts his forehead against mine, and looks deeply into my eyes as he says, "I've missed you." And then, though mildly inappropriate for local cultural norms, he kisses me, right there on the streets of Nairobi. As usual, it's not until after a few more minutes of hugging and laughing and smiling and kissing that he remembers to hand me the rose. He picks up my backpack, insisting with such adorable chivalry that he carry it, and we walk back to the apartment hand in hand, full of love for each other. *Why exactly have I been doubting this relationship?* I keep asking myself the whole way home.

◆　◆　◆

"So how was your trip?" Mark eagerly asks as we sit on the couch sipping tea. "What are you feeling now?"

"About us or about aid?" I jokingly ask, slipping my shoes off and repositioning myself on the couch so we're facing each other.

"Let's start with aid," he laughs.

"I don't know, I've been trying hard to make sense of what I've seen," I start out hesitantly, "but the answer that kept coming to my mind on my bus ride today seems too simplistic."

"What is it?" he asks.

"Well, all this time I've been focused on the 'system' and why it's so damn broken. You know, how the donors are misusing their power, the aid agencies aren't connected to the needs of the people, the projects usually don't address the root causes of poverty . . ." I trail off. "But when I think about it in terms of *individuals*, I have nothing but hope."

I tell Mark about Francine and Claudine, who both took in orphans after the genocide in Rwanda and who work tirelessly to make ends meet so both their biological and adopted children can have a better future. I tell him about how Osman has been working so hard as a teacher in the refugee camp, often without pay, because he believes deeply in preparing the next generation of Somali leaders. Then there's Stan, who may not have started a movement as he had hoped, but his efforts undoubtedly changed countless lives, including the people of Kyarumba. Not to mention Edson and Paula from the camp of landslide survivors who were continuing to work even after the NGOs pulled out, just because it was the right thing to do. Or Benson, the AIDS orphan who had his school fees sponsored and decided to return as a teacher so he could "pay it forward." Then there's Dr. Jane and her compassionate approach to healing, and Teddy's devotion to promoting self-sufficiency, and even people like Fatima or Edna, who weren't involved in any major project but who were so kind and open with me.

I stop myself. "The list could go on and on," I say. I sit there in silence for a moment, soaking up this realization that I hadn't articulated until now. Mark doesn't say anything, he just watches me with a smile and then reaches out for my hand as he sees my face light up with sudden clarity. "Individuals," I say, nodding. "That's it. It's all about the one-on-one. The way we are in the world. The kindness and compassion that each of us brings to the table. It's not about the organizations—they're probably always going to be screwed up in one way or another—it's about people."

"How true," Mark says with a proud smile.

"People," I repeat to myself out loud, mulling the word over for a moment. "People like *Ahmed*."

Two months of searching and it finally becomes clear: The solution Ahmed was asking me for eight years ago was easier than either of us thought. It was him, and it was me. Not Save the Children, not UNHCR, not some newfangled, allegedly innovative aid project. It's individuals, changing the lives of others in unknown ways, like he did for me.

Mark pulls me close and hugs me. "I hope you're able to share that with Ahmed eventually."

"Yeah, me, too," I reply, ignoring the fact that so far no leads have turned up.

"So it sounds like it was a good trip," Mark says, winking at me. "I'm glad you followed your gut and did it." He kisses my forehead. "Though I've missed you so much."

"I've missed you, too," I say as I kiss him tenderly.

"And so, what was the answer to the second question?" he asks, reaching out to gently touch my face.

"You mean how I'm feeling about *us*?" I smile. "Well . . . the things I know for sure are that I absolutely love you, that the bond we share is divine, and that I'm not willing to give up on us." Mark's face is beaming as he takes both of my hands in his. "What about you?" I ask.

"Tori, when you were away these past few weeks, it became even more clear to me that you are a precious part of my life. You are truly my soul mate. And the sad reality of the situation is that it seems we can't live *with* each other, and we can't live *without* each other." We laugh together. "We both still have some grow-ing to do. But if I had to take my pick, I'd opt for dealing with the challenges together, rather than being apart."

"I agree." I smile.

"I don't need you to decide now, but I want you to think about moving to Amsterdam this fall to live with me." The offer hangs in the silence of the air for a few seconds as he kisses the top of my head and holds me close.

I look up into his beautiful brown eyes and whisper, "Yes."

CHAPTER 22

It's NICE TO be back at home in Virginia, hanging out with family and getting things ready for my new life in the Netherlands, but a feeling of failure keeps wafting over me. I mean, come on, I went halfway around the world on a mission to find a boy who changed my life eight years ago so I could thank him face-to-face and I didn't find him. He just wasn't there. And, sure, the trip wasn't a total wash, because in the process of looking for Ahmed I managed to uncover a deeper perspective about aid. But my inner perfectionist refuses to let this search die. So the detective work continues. Osman gave me an email address for Ahmed and I wrote him long ago, more than once, but it's been weeks and I still don't have a response. Osman also informed me he heard Ahmed has been resettled to Chicago. I start calling around to some of the refugee resettlement agencies in Chicago to see if anyone has heard of an Ahmed Abdulahi Abdi. Nobody can give me any information on him.

So no leads in Chicago, no email response from him, no phone number to try. What am I supposed to do? Mark arrives next week to meet my family for the first time, and then we'll be moving to the Netherlands three weeks later. My window of opportunity to find Ahmed is closing fast. There's only one option that I actually hadn't thought to try yet: Facebook.

I type in "Ahmed Abdulahi Abdi" and I'm shocked by the number of variations of the three names. There's a ton of Abdulahi Ahmed Abdis and some Abdi Abdulahi Ahmeds, and, of course, Ahmed Abdi Abdulahi, but no Ahmed Abdulahi Abdi. I click on "see more results" and another slew of variations come up. There are even a handful of variations of Ahmed Abdulahi Abdi, but they're spelled differently than his with extra *a*'s and *l*'s and they don't look like anyone I know.

I'm about to call it quits. Maybe it's not meant to be. But before I close down my computer and resign to total failure, I click over to the unreturned emails I sent Ahmed and notice that his email address has a different name in it. So I click back over to Facebook and try one last time, this go-around with "Ahmed Kiranja" as my search term. One result pops up. It's him. I know it.

I immediately send him a "remember me?" message on Facebook, and another one via his email address, hoping that something will turn out.

Nine hours and two minutes later, I hear back from him. It's a two-line response. He's living in Minnesota, not Chicago. And I'm welcome to come and visit. Within minutes I book a $340 last-minute ticket from D.C. to Minneapolis departing in two days. I can't believe I actually found him.

◆　◆　◆

It's hard to contain my anticipation as I board the second leg of my flight to Minneapolis. I'm both nervous and excited to meet Ahmed again after all these years. A girl sits down in the seat next to me wearing a pink and black track suit with a girly black trucker-style hat adorned with sparkles. Her hair underneath is covered with a black scarf that ties behind her neck. I glance over to her more than once as she gets herself settled, and I swear she looks Somali.

"Are you heading home?" I ask, pulling out the most over-used starting line when trying to chat up the person sitting next to you on a plane.

"Yes, I am. It's a long way back from Rio de Janeiro, so I'm glad to be nearly finished with these flights," she says with a smile, buckling her seat belt.

"You were there for vacation?" I ask nosily.

"No, I was actually playing soccer," she informs me. "I'm part of a professional women's soccer team in Minnesota and a few of us were selected to go to Brazil for a tournament."

"Wow, what an opportunity!" I say. "Did you enjoy it?"

"Yeah, definitely. Brazil is a beautiful place," she says as she puts a magazine in the seat pocket.

"Are you originally from Minnesota?" I ask, hoping that the mystery will be solved.

"No, I'm from Cairo," she says.

"Oh really?" I say. "I used to live there for a year."

"Oh? Well, technically I'm from Somalia." I knew it. "But we fled when I was two years old due to the fighting, and we lived in Egypt for seven years. So, for me, I consider Egypt more my home than Somalia."

"Yeah, I can imagine you don't remember much from Somalia since you were so young. What was it like growing up in Egypt?" I ask.

"It was great. I had a lot of good friends there as a child. I went to Saint Andrew's school." She pauses and then adds, "I don't know if you ever heard of it."

"Saint Andrew's? Are you kidding? I used to be a kinder-garten teacher there! What a small world," I say, shaking my head in disbelief that my life is so closely overlapping with the stranger sitting next to me on the plane.

We hardly notice the plane take off as we're deep in conversation about her life since getting resettled to the United States and my upcoming reunion with Ahmed and our shared memories of Egypt. I find out her name is Hani. She's surprised to hear that I've been to Somalia myself, and she hopes one day she can see it, too, if things ever settle down. The serendipity is surprising.

"Can I get you something to drink?" the flight attendant asks us, interrupting our conversation. He's a tall African American guy who is radiating excitement at the moment, which is a nice change from the usual boredom or painfully faked sweetness you get from most flight attendants. We both order water and Hani and I continue our conversation. But a few minutes later the flight attendant comes back down the aisle, stops suddenly at our row, and asks, "How's the water?"

I take another sip as if it's a fine wine before reporting, "It's much better than United's and American's."

"Yeah, they serve diet water," he jokes, "but here at U.S. Airways we give our passengers the real stuff." The three of us laugh. He perches himself on the arm of the empty aisle seat across from us, apparently eager to join in the conversation, and asks me, "So, you going home?" He's stealing my line.

"No, I'm going to Minneapolis to track down a guy who changed my life eight years ago so I can thank him in person," I blurt out.

His eyes get wide and he looks astounded. As I hear the words coming out of my mouth, it dawns on me that what I'm doing isn't so normal after all. Everyone has people from their past who have touched their lives or changed them in some major way, but few of us ever take the time to tell that person about the impact they had. Even fewer would be willing to go to the lengths I've gone to find Ahmed. But it feels like something I need to do.

"Hang on, I'm coming right back. I need to hear this." He hurries down the aisle to put down the few cups he was holding and scurries back, perching himself back on the arm rest across the aisle and leaning in for the juicy details. "Okay, tell me, tell me!"

I try to opt for the abbreviated version of the story, as I realize he probably has more drinks to serve. I fill him in on my previous work with Save the Children, the boy's comment, the way my life's purpose changed as a result, and all the work I've done on behalf of aid effectiveness since then. Then I give the recap of my recent journey back to East Africa to find Ahmed.

"So did you find him?" the flight attendant eagerly asks, leaning forward.

"I discovered two days ago that he's living in Minneapolis. So I booked a ticket and here I am, en route to express my gratitude."

The flight attendant looks like he's about to cry. "And does the boy know why you're coming?" he asks.

"No, he has no clue," I reply.

"That is the most incredible thing I've heard in a long time. It's beautiful, just beautiful," he says as he shakes his head. "I hope the reunion goes well," he adds with a smile.

"Thanks, me too," I say as he walks back down the aisle to the galley.

◆　◆　◆

I pull my rental car into the parking lot of the local McDonald's as I try to collect my thoughts before the reunion. I just made the hour-and-fifteen-minute drive from Minneapolis to St. Cloud where Ahmed lives, but I'm still a few minutes early. I'm *so* eager to see him today, but it's also a bit awkward because, in reality, it's not like we actually know each other. We had one hour of contact eight years ago with forty-seven other students present. And even if he remembers me from back then, it's not like I'm reuniting with an old friend. To him I'm just some random *muzungu* aid worker who came into his classroom one day a long time ago. But to me he's much more than that. He just doesn't know it yet.

Last night I stayed with my dear friend Britt, whom I studied abroad with in Uganda in 2002, only two months after I met Ahmed. She and I were roommates back then during our field research in Mbarara, and it was great to catch up on life and love with her over some red wine and her mom's Tater Tot Hotdish (a perfect pairing). And as I opened up to her about my uncertainty about how exactly you're supposed to tell someone, "Hey, dude, you changed my life, *muchas gracias*," she assured me that it didn't matter how it was said, the message would convey. So I'm approaching today with a "go with the flow" attitude—I want to spend some time getting to know Ahmed and to be able to say what I came to say, which mostly just boils down to "thanks."

The phone rings and Ahmed's number pops up. He told me he'd call me at 11:45 to direct me to where he'd be waiting to meet me. I pick it up with a nervous "Hello?"

"Is this Tori?" he asks in a strong Somali accent.

"Ahmed! Yes, hi. How are you?" I ask, trying to contain my nervous excitement in hopes of sounding seminormal. I'm pretty much failing at that.

"I'm fine. I'm looking forward to seeing you today. Have you made it to St. Cloud?" he asks.

"Yes, I'm here. Where should I meet you?" I put the phone on speaker as he directs me down Roosevelt, right onto

University, left onto Washington Memorial Drive, and then, before I have any more time to get flustered or anxious about the rendezvous, I spot his black Ford Focus parked on the right side of the street. By now I've traveled eighteen thousand miles in search of Ahmed, and there are only a few more feet to go.

◆ ◆ ◆

The car doors close in unison and we start walking toward each other. I recognize him instantly. There's no doubt in my mind, I found the guy I was looking for. He's wearing a white long-sleeved dress shirt and beige pinstripe pants with a brown belt. He didn't have a goatee when he was a student, but it suits him.

He smiles as we get closer. "I can't believe it's Tori Hogan."

"Ahmed. Wow, it's been a long time!" I say. I kind of want to hug him as we approach, but he puts his hand out to shake instead. It strikes me as an overly formal way to greet the guy who changed my life, but I roll with it.

Another Somali guy emerges from the other side of the car. "You remember Mohamed?" Ahmed asks me, pointing to his friend. "He was in the class that day we met you, too."

"You were there?" I ask with surprise as we shake hands. "It's great to see you again, Mohamed."

Ahmed steps back and looks at me. "You are the same person as I remember. You haven't changed."

"I know." I laugh, used to people mistaking me for being much younger than I actually am. "You guys want to grab some lunch?" I ask.

"Sure, good idea," Ahmed says.

We decide to take just one car so they park Ahmed's car in the parking lot of the nearby Mogadishu grocery store. I had no idea St. Cloud, Minnesota, was such a Somali mecca. Ahmed gets in the front seat and Mohamed gets in the back.

"Okay, so where do we go?" I ask as I pull up to the light.

Mohamed leans between the seats and asks, "You ever eat Somali food?"

"Yeah, I tried Somali food when I was working for Save the Children in Hargeisa, Somaliland," I reply. "I liked it."

"Oh? Okay, so uh, go straight!" Mohamed exclaims.

"I think I even ate camel," I add.

Ahmed shakes his head solemnly. "Camel is not available here. . . ."

Mohamed interjects, "Well, *sometimes* they get camel meat here . . ." Then after thinking about it he adds, "I don't know how they get it . . ." I can only imagine.

As we head toward the Somali restaurant, it's already apparent that they Google-stalked the hell out of me. They've already seen all my films, they know where I'm from, they're curious about my masters degrees, they scoured all the pictures in my Facebook profile, and they can name off the places I've traveled to.

"You went all over the world, huh?" Ahmed says. "Where did you visit lately?"

"Actually, I was in Dadaab in May."

"To Hagadera?" Ahmed asks with shock in his voice.

"Yeah, Hagadera."

"Left here," Mohamed says, directing me from behind.

"Just last May you were there?" Ahmed asks, still in disbelief.

"Yeah, just recently," I reply. "And I was able to see six members of your class while I was there."

"Oh wow," Ahmed says. "Why did you return to Hagadera?"

I desperately want to tell him I was there searching for *him*, but I figure it's probably too soon. "I was there to see your class."

"Oh yeah?" Mohamed asks, equally surprised.

"Yeah, I wanted to talk to your class again to see how things were going, and to see if anything had changed."

"Take a right here," Mohamed says as we turn off into a side ally.

"Dadaab didn't change much, did it?" Ahmed asks, likely already knowing the answer since he apparently left the camp only three years ago.

"No, eight years later and not much has changed," I say as we pull into the restaurant parking lot.

◆ ◆ ◆

"You like it?" Ahmed asks pointing to the meat on my fork.

"It's good!" I exclaim. "It's really good. I forgot that I liked goat." I can't say that I've ever eaten goat in the United States before, but I've had it in East Africa. I'm impressed to see it gracing the menu of this tiny Somali restaurant that has the Real Madrid game blasting at high volume as a handful of Somali men sit nearby eating lunch with their eyes glued to the television. And while it's not my favorite meat on the planet, this restaurant knows how to cook up some damn good goat.

"So what are you guys doing here for work?" I ask.

Ahmed points to Mohamed. "This one, he goes to technical college."

"Yeah, I'm studying for accounting," Mohamed says. "To get an associate's degree and try to get some job, you know?" I nod. "I spent five years as a truck driver. I think I've seen the entire United States by now! They actually tested me when I came here and they wanted to send me to Utah because they said I was smart, I could get an education. But I told them, 'I need a job. I want to see the dollars,'" he jokes. "And now after five years, I finally decided to take that chance."

"Hey, it's never too late to go back to school," I say. "And what about you, Ahmed?" I ask.

He looks down at his food and says quietly, "I'm unemployed."

"Oh, I'm sorry to hear that. It's a rough time right now with the economy, isn't it?"

"Yeah." He looks down again, picking at his rice.

"But you were originally working in Chicago?" I ask.

He looks up. "I used to drive a cab there for one year. And then I spent another year working in a factory assembling disc drives, but then one day all one hundred and fifty employees were let go. And when I lost my job, Mohamed encouraged me to come here to St. Cloud where my family is living, so I just came. Now I'm looking for work again, but it's not easy."

"I'm sure," I say.

"My friends and family who are back in the camp, they don't believe you can be unemployed in America," Ahmed says. "They think you have a lot of money."

Mohamed adds, "Yeah, people in the camp, they think if you live in America you have it so easy. Like the money grows from the trees," he says with a laugh, pointing outside. "The reality is that it's not easy at all. Although we still do what we can, and we send them money regularly, because we remember how hard things are there."

"And who came with you to the U.S.?" I ask Ahmed.

"I came with my father, mom, brother, and sister," Ahmed says. "We left September 2007. But first we got settled in Las Vegas."

"They sent you to Las Vegas?" I ask, surprised.

"Yeah, the Sin City." He laughs.

"Gosh, sending refugees to Las Vegas sounds like a crazy idea. How long were you there?"

"I was there two months, and then Mohamed was able to sponsor us to come to Minnesota and so I came with my family here."

"And then you got married?" I ask, knowing this from his Facebook status.

"Yeah, less than a year ago. She used to live in Dagahaley camp," he says. He then shyly adds, "And I liked her then, so when we both were randomly resettled here, we decided to get married."

How cute. They ask me about my love life and I give the abridged version of where things stand with Mark and me at the moment. They're curious to know why I'm not already married to him, as I guess in Somali culture being with someone for a year and a half is more than enough time to decide on whether or not you're going to take the leap. Maybe overthinking and uncertainty when it comes to relationships are predominantly Western traits.

"When are you going to Amsterdam?" Ahmed asks.

"In three weeks, after he comes here to meet my family," I say.

"So you're going to stay there for a while?" Mohamed asks.

"Yeah, until we figure out whether we're supposed to be together."

They smile at me and then Mohamed asks, "How come you didn't get an American boyfriend?"

"You can't choose who you fall in love with, right?" I reply.

Ahmed nods his head. "Yeah, that's right. Love is like waves. It will take you to the shores you don't even think about."

"That's true," I nod.

We move on to talk about their new lives in the United States and their memories from the camp. Ahmed even reveals to me the story of how his family ended up in the camp to begin with. His dad had a stable position in the Ministry of Agriculture and his family lived a comfortable life thirty kilometers south of Mogadishu. But once the fighting broke out in 1991, everything changed. They had to flee to the border with whatever they could carry and they settled on the Somali side, hopeful that the fighting would subside and they could return home. But then the fighting intensified and one night they had to leave all their things behind and cross the border into Kenya quickly. While they were fleeing the gunfire, his three-year-old sister was struck by a stray bullet and died. They stayed in Liboi camp until 1994 and then were transferred to Hagadera, where they lived for thirteen years.

Ahmed adds, "Life in the camp was hard for us. Because we had come from a comfortable life, and then we suddenly found ourselves living in a refugee camp below the poverty line." His mom opened up a small tea shop in order to pay for his school uniforms and other expenses, but life was always challenging for them.

They ask me if there are security problems in the camps these days, and about the new Community Secondary School where, I inform them, Osman is now vice principal. I can tell that as much as they're glad to have been resettled, the camp will always feel like home to them. They seem happy to get updates on how things are going there.

"And what about Hagadera Secondary?" Ahmed asks. "How is it there? We still have good memories from those years."

Mohamed jumps in, pointing to Ahmed. "This guy here, he was our class leader. That's where he got his nickname, Kiranja. It's Swahili for 'class prefect.'"

Now it all makes sense. I couldn't figure out where the name Kiranja could have come from when I was searching for Ahmed online.

"So you were the leader of the class, huh?" I ask. Ahmed nods. "And you used to sit next to the girls, right?"

He smiles and Mohamed gives him a small punch on the arm. Ahmed sheepishly replies, "Yeah."

"You remember the class?" Mohamed asks. "You have a very good memory."

"The school is mostly the same these days, but they rebuilt some of the classrooms," I tell them. "Now they're made of brick."

"That's good." Ahmed laughs. "We used to learn inside the tins of USAID cans!"

"Yeah, I hated to see that," I say.

"When it was hot, you really felt it," he says.

"So are you glad you're here now?" I ask.

Ahmed thinks for a moment and then says, "I enjoy it, but I also miss some of my best friends."

"Life changes. . . ." Mohamed says softly.

"Yeah, life changes," Ahmed echoes.

"But it looks like we have more opportunities over here," Mohamed admits.

"But life changes," Ahmed repeats. "Because when we were in a refugee camp we don't have options for land or for work, we were just stranded."

"And as you get older in the camp, you're so idle. You have nothing to do," I add.

"Yeah, you feel useless," Ahmed says. "But here, at least you have opportunity, and if you have work, you have that inspiration and at least the chance for a bright future. Over there, there's no bright future."

We all nod in agreement, keeping our eyes down as we finish our last few morsels of goat in silence.

CHAPTER 23

"WE THOUGHT YOU might like this," Ahmed says as we all get out of the car and start walking toward St. Cloud's famous Munsinger and Clemens Gardens. It looks like an old English garden with perfectly planted beds of flowers in all colors and varieties and quaint brick paths leading to a series of fountains.

"We like to come here sometimes," Mohamed adds. "They don't have flowers back in Dadaab," he laughs.

We stroll around for a while, commenting on the flowers and talking about random things, and I can tell I'm stalling. I'm not sure why it's so hard to just come out and tell Ahmed "thanks." It's probably because the buildup of four months of searching for him has made my impending expression of gratitude feel like a really big moment.

We come down a hill to another level of gardens and paths and suddenly there it is, as majestic as it sounds: the mighty Mississippi. You couldn't ask for a more picturesque sight or a more perfectly sunny day. Everything about it is stunning. As we walk down the gravel path that runs alongside the river, I figure there's no better time than now.

I start cautiously, "So I have to tell you guys, there's obviously a reason that I came all this way to find you."

"Yeah," Ahmed says with a curious and expectant face.

"I traveled halfway around the world to find your class, but really I was looking for a specific person. Back in 2002, all I knew was that there was one student in that class who said something to me that changed everything. And while I was in Dadaab, I figured out that that student was *you*, Ahmed."

I stop walking and turn to face him.

"So I came all this way to say 'thank you' in person. Because you completely changed my life. Just one comment that you made, and nothing's been the same ever since." We smile at each other, and it's clear he's at a loss for words.

"Wow," he eventually says. "I can't believe it had such an impact. I'm trying to remember what I said."

I repeat to him the words I know so well: "A lot of aid workers come and go, but nothing changes. If the aid projects were effective we wouldn't still be living like this after all these years. Do you really think you have the answer to our problems?" I search his face. "Did you say that?"

He smiles while nodding. "Yeah, yeah, I did say that."

"And it was so critical and it was so honest, and nobody was that honest to me before. You called me out."

"Yeah. But the organizations, they come and they think that they're gonna change everything for better. But nothing changes. Still we are in the same place. That's why I said that."

"Did you think what you said might affect me the way it did?" I ask.

He shakes his head no.

I tell him about the feelings I grappled with that night after he made the comment and all the changes that took place in my life afterward as a result. A redefined purpose, thanks to him.

"You were the catalyst for all these changes," I tell him. "Originally I was going to become an aid worker, but you prevented me from that track. And instead I became an aid critic. Perhaps I would have ended up on this same path eventually, but not that young. It would have taken me a lot longer to admit how crappy this system is. I don't know where I'd be right now if it wasn't for that moment. So . . . thank you." I look at him and smile again.

"Oh, wow, okay. Thank you for telling me. Thanks a lot."

"Thank *you*. Seriously, thank you," I repeat.

"You're welcome." He smiles proudly.

"And it feels nice to be able to say it to you in person," I add as we continue walking along the river. "I know I could have just called you and said it, but I wanted to tell you . . ."

". . . face-to-face," he finishes for me. "It's better," he says, with a big smile.

❖   ❖   ❖

I follow Ahmed and Mohamed to a booth as I carefully hold my teacup that has been filled to the brim. We've stopped by a local café to hang out and continue catching up. As Ahmed stirs his coffee he looks at me and shakes his head. "I still can't believe you have come here. It really means a lot."

"I felt like I had to let you know what a difference you made in my life," I say.

"I never knew it," he says.

"You know, Ahmed, it always made me curious to know how you managed to be so brave that day to tell me the truth the way you did," I say.

He shrugs and says, "I'd been the class leader for years, and so in a way I felt it was my role to speak on their behalf. I had to tell you what I knew we were all feeling and what was going on in the camp. I didn't have anything to lose, I guess."

"You were tired of the ineffective aid?" I ask.

"Yeah, we were all tired of it. That was clear," he replies.

"And did you ever tell anyone else, any other aid worker or researcher, what you told me?" I ask.

"No, we never had another opportunity. No one else ever came to ask us," he replies. He then looks me in the eyes and says, "You know, Tori, you have come here to thank me for what I said, but I need to thank you, too."

"For what?" I ask.

"For listening to us. For taking the time to care about our problems and be curious about the truth. Even if nobody ever read that report you wrote. Even if nothing changed. We were all appreciative of your"—he glances up at the ceiling as he looks for the word—"your solidarity, your compassion."

I blush and look down for a moment, caught off guard by his comment. "I only wish I could have done more for you then," I finally say.

"Well, it is good to hear you have used that inspiration to make a difference in the aid world," he says. "There's so much that needs to change. The system isn't helping people at all. Things in the camp are the same as they used to be, and in some cases they're even worse."

"So what do you think still needs to change?" I ask, dipping my tea bag.

"To begin with, there's a lot of corruption," he says. "I'll give you an example. While we were students the supervisor for education at CARE in Hagadera decided to hire his brother as a teacher in our school. But the man had never even graduated from level six, and here he was teaching us in secondary school. How could he teach us when we already knew more than him? So our class protested, and luckily we eventually won. But that sort of corruption happens very often."

"Yeah, I hear about those problems a lot," I say.

"And there's really a need for more transparency and accountability," Ahmed adds. "Sometimes money comes in, but then it goes to somewhere you don't even know. Also, there is a tendency to hire outside people instead of the Somalis themselves, despite there being so many well-educated people in the camps."

"Like you both," I say.

"Yeah. And when Somalis work for their own people, they'll be honest and more effective, you know? They're not the same as these people who come from somewhere else." He takes a sip of coffee before continuing the rant. "And they need a lot of other changes. There aren't many business opportunities in the camp. And there are hardly any scholarships available. Even the medical is poor."

"MSF?" I ask.

"No, in Hagadera it was GTZ," he says, referring to a large German relief organization.

"Oh right. MSF is in Dagahaley."

"MSF is better than GTZ," Mohamed adds.

"That's another problem," I say. "There's no consistency."

"Yeah. And then one comes and the other one goes," Ahmed says. "But in the end it doesn't matter what we think or if the service isn't good. Nobody asks. Nobody listens. Even when we say, 'We want these things, we don't want these things,' nobody even responds."

"That's why nothing has changed, right?" I ask.

"Yeah, the few people who try to advocate are ignored," he says. "That's why it's my dream to go back to school for a degree in international relations. I want to be able to work abroad in the future as an aid worker helping Somali refugees," Ahmed says. He adds, "If you can help others, if you have that ability, then you must give them a hand. That's why I hope that some-day I can work to help my own people."

"But you would be more effective, I hope," I say.

"Yeah. I'd be able to fix the errors and bad things the aid organizations are doing now," he replies. "Because I know the problems from the inside."

"You can be the one to change the system," I say with a hopeful look in my eyes.

He smiles. "I wish I already had that power now. But even here are Somalis that I can help, and so I do what I can every day. Like, for example, yesterday I hoped to come to Minne-apolis to see you, but this old woman called and said, 'Please, I have a problem. Do you mind to come and help me?' And I said, 'Of course.' She was having a hard time with her rent, and the landlord had come to say that if she didn't pay, they would throw her out next month. So I went to translate and help with the situation, and then I was able to get in touch with the resettlement agency to get their help for temporary finances for her. So even if I'm not an aid worker yet, I can still help in small ways."

"Yeah, that's a good point. We all can help the people right around us." I smile, remembering my talk with Mark on this topic. It really is compassionate individuals, not complicated organizations, who are making the changes that matter. I fill Ahmed in on my recent search for answers about aid effective-ness that I embarked on in response to his original question to me. He seems pleased by my findings, and we both agree on the power of individuals to change the world. I smile at him and add, "And you never know when that one little thing you do might make a difference."

"Yeah," Ahmed nods.

"As you see," I smile, gesturing between us.

◆ ◆ ◆

I can still see Ahmed in my rearview mirror as he waves from the gas station parking lot where we just said goodbye. He insisted on having me follow his car to this point so he was sure I made my way back to the highway with no trouble. His kindness and concern is endearing. I roll down my window and give one last wave as I make the right turn toward the I-94 ramp.

I feel elated after my day with Ahmed and Mohamed. It couldn't have gone any better. And even though it took months to finally track him down, it was all worth it. I pass by rows of corn growing tall on either side of the highway. It's the Midwest in full bloom. And as I drive along in my little rental car with this goofy grin on my face, a feeling of peace is coming over me. I have been let off the hook, in a way, after all this journeying and searching to find the answers. And the truth I'm now faced with is that I don't have to save the world. I don't have to revolutionize the aid industry. All I have to do is be clear in my heart about what's fair and what's good, and then use my life, day by day, to stand up for and promote those things. To help people when they ask for help, but only in the way they want to be helped. To embrace every interaction with total humility and kindness. And, perhaps most important, to start with myself first; to be the best human being I can be before I start trying to help anyone else.

And I'm also realizing that perhaps my impact on the world is greater than I think. Ahmed had no clue that he'd helped me in any way. It never occurred to him that our brief encounter that day would be so catalytic for me. I can only imagine the small things I've done in my own life that might have had a similar effect on others.

On my way home from East Africa last month I had an extended stopover in England, and I used it as an opportunity to catch up with my old professor and pioneering aid critic, Barbara Harrell-Bond, whom I'd studied with in Cairo. I remember one moment in particular as we walked back from the grocery store together in Oxford where she now lives. I asked her, "Barbara, after all these years of tireless work on behalf of refugees, what do you think is the greatest difference you've made in the world?"

She looked over at me and boldly said, "The biggest differences I've made are the ones I don't even know about." The truth of her words struck me hard. "If you're working for justice and you're living with compassion and integrity, you are probably making a difference in people's lives every day. You just might not realize it."

The ride back from St. Cloud passes quickly, and my reflections are suddenly interrupted by my phone ringing. I feel around blindly on the front seat to find it. "Hello?"

"Hi, Tori. It's Ahmed."

"Hi, Ahmed. What's up?"

"I just wanted to make sure you made it back to St. Paul with no problems," he says.

"Yeah, I'm pulling up to my friend's house now," I say, putting the car into park.

"Good, I'm very glad to hear it," he says.

"Thanks for checking in, Ahmed. That's really sweet of you."

"No problem," he says. There's a long awkward pause on the phone. "And there's one more thing I wanted to say to you . . ." he goes on. "I wanted to say that your coming all this way to find me again just to say thanks, that meant so much to me. I never knew I changed your life like that. It shows me that it's the little things we do for others that make the most difference . . . even when we don't know we've done them."

My heart is glowing. "You're so right."

EPILOGUE

By THE TIME my search for Ahmed ended in September 2010, life felt beautiful. I'd gained solace in the realization that changing the world—one person at a time—is easier than I thought, I was starting a new life in the Netherlands, and my relationship with Mark was going well. I initially settled into our apartment in Amsterdam with a cozy, peaceful feeling that maybe my search for "the one" had finally ended. I became skilled at ignoring the persistent little voice in my heart that begged me to reconsider. Instead, I tried to relax into the idea that, despite our challenges, Mark was likely going to be the man I'd grow old with. In the year that followed, I lied to myself nonstop about my true feelings, overlooked the ways we were both altering who we were to suit each other, and kept trying to convince myself that I'd found my future husband. I hadn't.

If I'm honest with myself, I knew at month six of our relationship, after that difficult camper van trip through Europe, that I hadn't found "the one." The "something's missing" feeling that I had with Mark (which never went away) was too serious to ignore. But I made the mistake of focusing on the fact that we were 90 percent compatible, and that most days with him were beautiful. I failed to realize that within the misaligned 10 percent were some serious deal breakers. It took us a long time to finally admit that our core needs, the few things that absolutely *must* be present for us to be happy in a relationship, had always been incompatible. We loved each other beyond belief, but we were simply too different. Instead of admitting this sooner, though, my response was to dig my heels in deeper, intent to "save" the relationship. (Apparently wanting to "save" things is a common thread in my life. . . .) The lingering perfectionist in me refused to fail at love.

We lived mostly in harmony during those few months in Amsterdam before we eventually moved back to East Africa for his job. By the summer of 2011, a whole year had passed, I'd nearly finished writing this book, and during a short visit to the US, he and I both booked one-way tickets back to the Netherlands, where we intended to settle down for good. But I knew I couldn't keep ignoring my gut instinct, which meant I knew I couldn't get on that plane.

A friend of mine once told me during my first breakup with Mark, "Where there is doubt, there's no doubt." The endless uncertainties that plagued our entire relationship should have made it glaringly obvious that we weren't a match. Maybe even as you were reading this book you could see how blind I was being to the truth. But the love I had for Mark was so deep and so real that I refused to believe that love wasn't enough. Unfortunately, the fact of the matter was that the real Tori wasn't compatible with the real Mark.

Waking up to this reality happened almost overnight. It was as if my stubborn will to fix things suddenly evaporated, and I could finally be real about how much of myself I'd given up or changed in hopes of making the relationship work. I suddenly found myself on a familiar trajectory of disenchantment, humility, and acceptance—the same feelings I faced following Ahmed's comment to me so many years ago. Our mutual decision to break up, made somewhere along Route 81 on our way to visit the Smokey Mountains, was as devastating as it was freeing. It was, in a way, a testament to how strong our love for each other was that we were willing to try so hard for so long to save it.

Since then, I followed another gut instinct and moved to San Francisco to start a new life where I'm profoundly happy and finally feeling authentically *me* again. Mark meanwhile found love again with a nice Dutch woman. He and I are occasionally in touch, and we both look back at our time together with gratitude for all that we shared and the ways we helped each other grow. . . . And we both refuse to throw away those stacks of beautiful love letters.

In other news, Ahmed and his wife had a baby boy, and Ahmed is currently working as a taxi driver in Chicago to save up some money so he can eventually make his dream of going to college a reality. Osman was promoted to Principal at the Community Secondary School where he continues to proudly serve the students while waiting for his turn in the resettlement process. Jane and Duncan are now in Burma on an MSF field assignment, and last I heard they were on their way to Bangkok for the birth of their first baby. Meanwhile, the problems in Dadaab have escalated beyond belief since my last visit, with the population rising to nearly half a million, as fighting in Somalia has intensified. The aid agencies there are unequipped to provide sufficient relief to such a large population, and UNHCR is struggling to deal with the mounting demands for resources and space.

The majority of the people living in the internal displacement camp in Bududa, Uganda ended up returning to their original land, and the village where the landslide occurred has been completely rebuilt by the people, despite the continued threats of future landslides. Six hundred families from the area were eventually moved to a resettlement area 300 kilometers northwest of Bududa where they were apparently given 2.5 acres of land from the Ugandan government along with a permanent house.

The One Acre Fund in Rwanda has had continued success with their projects since I last saw them and are now serving 50,000 farmers in six districts, are doubling farmers' income per planted acre, and have reached over 80 percent financial sustainability. Meanwhile, UTEXRWA experienced quite the opposite. When the Board of Directors decided to discontinue UTEXRWA's social business initiatives to focus only on textile production, both the CEO and Prem decided to leave the company. Less than three months after the new director took control, all 500 workers staged a strike to protest the low salaries, poor working conditions, and reduced employee benefits. It's unclear whether or not things have improved.

Thanks in large part to the remarkable people I met on my journey and the level of reflection I went through in preparing to share this story with the world, my feelings about aid have shifted. I am no longer focused on critiquing a broken system. Instead, I'm using my time and energy to provide hope, guidance, and inspiration to the next generation of changemakers through my work. I'm grateful for the twists and turns my path has taken, and for the individuals along the way who changed my life.

The other day while riding the bus through the Tenderloin District of San Francisco, I saw the top of a building painted boldly with three words: *Love*, *Dignity*, and *Justice*. I felt like the words had been put there just for me; the final signpost representing a journey that has spanned the past decade of my life. Those three words pretty much sum it all up. Because I've learned that what really matters is the love we have for one another, whether the soulful kind like I had with Mark or the love and compassion we share in endless ways with friends, family, and complete strangers on a daily basis. It's about living our lives with dignity, humility, and integrity while also supporting individuals and organizations that promote dignity for others around the globe. And it's about recognizing injustice when confronted with it, the way I did as a teenager in Lebanon and later when faced with the truth of Ahmed's words. But, more importantly, it's about finding ways to appropriately respond to the injustices we see, holding strong in the belief that we all have the ability to affect change, one person at a time.

Be a Part of the Solution

Do you want to make a difference in the world? Here are some tips to help you get started.

Start with yourself. As Gandhi said, "Be the change you wish to see in the world." Before you try to help others, first ensure that you're living your own life with a deep level of authenticity, integrity, and love.

Help locally. No matter where you live in the world, there are local grassroots organizations doing excellent work in your own backyard that could use your help. If you're not already volunteering for a local organization that you care about, consider starting now. Visit volunteermatch.com or idealist.org to find volunteer opportunities in your own community.

Be a better donor. Rethink how, why, and where you donate your money. Not all aid organizations are created equal, so be sure to conduct your own due diligence before giving. A free comprehensive guide on how to be a better donor is available for download at www.beyondgoodintentions.com.

Change your lens. One of the greatest challenges to eradicating poverty is how we choose to see those who live within it. Instead of viewing less wealthy individuals through the lens of lack, desperation, and pity, choose to see them and their communities through the lens of strength, dignity, resourcefulness, and possibility.

Support the students of Dadaab. If you'd like to directly help the students you've read about in this book, Ahmed and Mohamed have recently set up a campaign to raise money for scholarships, learning materials, and teacher training in Dadaab refugee camp. They would love your support. Visit www.beyondgoodintentions.com for more information about how you can help.

Start a dialogue. Help spark a dialogue about aid effectiveness by hosting a discussion session on the topic, sharing this book and its message with those you know, or by using social media platforms to engage others in the conversation.

Learn more. Take time to explore the truth about the complicated challenges facing the world and the most effective ways to address them. You can get started by checking out the resources available at the Center for Global Development (cgdev.org), wiser.org, beyondgoodintentions.com, and the "Listening Project" (cdainc.com).

Advocate for better aid. Get involved with one of the many emerging campaigns to improve our approaches to helping the world. Write op-eds expressing your views on the subject, putting pressure on aid organizations to improve their transparency and impact. Write to your government representatives to voice your concerns about your country's foreign aid policies. If you're an aid worker, donor, or policy maker, start catalyzing change from the inside.

Thank someone who changed your life. Being able to thank Ahmed in person was a beautiful moment for me. If someone has made a difference in your life, find a way to let him or her know.

Never lose hope. As Osman demonstrated, one of the most important things we can do is to keep our sense of hope alive. Positive change is happening all over the world.

DISCUSSION GUIDE

1. After reading about Tori's journey across East Africa, have your views on international aid changed at all? If so, how?

2. A key theme of the book is the importance of gratitude, which is demonstrated in Tori's quest to thank Ahmed. If you could thank someone for the way he or she changed your life, who would you thank, and why? *(And what's stopping you?)*

3. Tori felt compelled to take action after she witnessed the injustices facing the refugees in Lebanon, and in particular after meeting Ahmed. Have you ever experienced a similar call to action? How did you respond?

4. If you were to donate to any of the organizations or individuals mentioned in the book, which would you donate to and why? What criteria do you use when deciding how to donate your money?

5. Tori was tempted to put a long list of ideas in the UNHCR "Suggestion Box" at Dadaab refugee camp. What suggestions would you put in the box after reading about life in the camp?

6. Do you believe in altruism? Is aid work ever truly "selfless"? Why or why not?

7. Osman and the rest of the "Tsunami Class" were full of hope. Where do you think that deep feeling of hope comes from, despite living in such difficult circumstances, and what effect does it have?

8. In chapter nine, Edwin confesses, "The donors still seem to have all the power. They're the ones setting the agenda." After reading about KARA's struggles with their major donors, do you think the traditional donor/NGO relationship needs to change? In what ways?

9. The majority of the people living in the displacement camp after the Bududa landslide were dishonestly collecting aid that wasn't meant for them. How did you feel when you read about this, and how could it be prevented in future relief efforts?

10. What do you feel are the pros and cons of international volunteerism? What conditions or requirements might enable volunteers to be more helpful to the organizations they're trying to serve?

11. What do you think was the primary cause for the ups and downs of Mark and Tori's relationship? Do you agree that sometimes love isn't enough? Also, what parallels did you notice about Tori's search for answers about love and her search for answers about aid?

12. What conditions do you think helped promote the self-reliance Tori witnessed in Kyarumba among the people

associated with the Bukonzo Joint Savings and Credit Cooperative? Do you think their success is replicable elsewhere? If so, how?

13. During her travels across Rwanda, Tori encountered an old woman begging at the window of the bus and didn't know how to respond. What would you have done? Why?

14. The One Acre Fund set up a system in which the farmers they serve are viewed as "clients" instead of "beneficiaries." How is that model different from traditional approaches to aid, and do you think it is effective?

15. What role do you think foreigners should play in international development? For example, how do you compare the roles and impact of the MSF doctors, the orphanage volunteers, Stan Burkey, and the One Acre Fund team?

16. Rwanda is leading the way as a model for how a country can take control of its own development. Do you think other countries should follow their example?

17. If you had the chance to meet any of the people mentioned in the book, who would you choose, and what would you talk about?

18. Tori's mentor, Barbara Harrell-Bond, told her, "If you're working for justice and you're living with compassion and integrity, you are probably making a difference in peoples' lives every day. You just might not realize it." Do you agree

with her? What are some of the ways you might have made a difference for others without being aware of your impact at the time?

19. Who are your world-changing heroes? What were their approaches to making a difference? Why were they successful?

20. Tori discovered that it's often the little things we do that ultimately make the biggest difference for others. What small step can you take today to help make the world a slightly better place?

To download the complete Reader's Discussion Guide featuring additional questions and resources, please visit www.beyondgoodintentions.com.

ACKNOWLEDGMENTS

GRATITUDE IS A beautiful thing. In fact, it was the motivating factor that prompted my search for Ahmed in the first place, and hence this story. And while a simple "thanks" might never feel like enough, I'm thrilled to be able to share my gratitude for all the people who have helped make this book possible.

First and foremost, I want to reiterate my endless gratitude for Ahmed and the way he unknowingly changed my life. That moment of truth back in 2002 was a crucial turning point in my path, and I will forever be grateful for his honesty and courage that day. I would also like to thank the members of the "Tsunami Class" of Hagadera Secondary School who continue to inspire me through their unwavering hope and perseverance.

An enormous amount of gratitude must also go to my beloved family. To my mom, Cathy, for always supporting my dreams (even when those dreams involved her baby girl heading off to the Somali border), and for her constant encouragement throughout the writing and editing process. I'm also grateful to my sister, Catherine Langford, for always making me laugh and for graciously proofreading my book only days before giving birth to my beautiful niece, Elise. And finally, to my dad, Rich, who was always one of my biggest fans but who sadly was taken from this earth much too soon. If there's a bookstore in heaven, I'm pretty sure he has proudly bought every copy up there to share with his friends.

Special thanks must also go to all the people who worked tirelessly to bring this book to life. To my devoted agent, Gary Morris, at the David Black Agency for believing in the power of this story from the very beginning, and for expertly guiding me through the publishing process. I'm also profoundly grateful to my publisher, Seal Press, for their incredible support and commitment. Special thanks must also go to my editors, Brooke Warner and Laura Mazer, whose feedback and diligence throughout the editing process was invaluable. Finally, to the entire staff of Seal Press and Perseus Books who have worked behind the scenes to make this book a reality including the marketing, design, and editorial teams, along with my publicist, Andie Atwood. I am endlessly grateful to you all for giving me the chance to share this story with the world.

It is with sadness that I must posthumously thank author and Wall Street Journal columnist, Jeff Zaslow. It was Jeff who convinced me that I had a story to tell in the first place, and without his encouragement this book may never have been written. I was devastated when I heard about his tragic death, as I had been eagerly looking forward to the day that I'd be able to beam with gratitude as I placed my finished book in his hands. I will forever be grateful for the inspiration and support he provided me.

I'd also like to thank all of the individuals and organizations whose stories appear in this book. Their willingness to share their experiences with me with such candor was truly remarkable. A special thanks should also go to all the aid organizations and recipients I've interacted with over the past decade who have helped shape my understanding of this field. Also, to my early mentors Barbara Harrell-Bond, Elizabeth Kiss, and Miriam Cooke whose wisdom and guidance helped set me on this path.

Finally, to my advanced readers Jennifer Lentfer, Pete Ondeng, Philippa Young, Britt Kringle, Pamela Howe, Catherine Langford, Saroj Yadav, and Sara LeHoullier: thank you for your priceless second set of eyes. And endless gratitude to all my dear friends and champions who have supported me in various ways including Henry Lippincott, Colin Scott, Kelsey Dunn, Tobias Schatton, Catie Liken, Ashley and Mark Younger, Charlene Chen, Jared Leiderman, Erin Katzelnick-Wise, Kambria Hooper, Paris Wallace, Kevin Moore, Joel Nunez, Kosta Gramatis, Sebastian Lindstrom, Alicia Sully, Matt Langford, Taylor Milsal, Wendy Walker, Amaya and Walker Whitworth, Anthony Sandberg, Nik Hesler, Hans Raffauf, Ida Tin, Crystal Costella Mendez, Edward Harran, Maya Lockwood, Jan Farley, Jennifer Cote, Cristina Lash, Kate Doyle, Lydia Barlow Faiia, Bill Younger, the entire Palomar5 crew, Max Marmer, Megan Collins, Paul Gleger, Rennie Walker, Wine Ngon, Rye Barcott, Sammy Riley, the Love-Spring community, Sara Dosa, Steffen Biersack, Terri Hinton, the Sandbox community, the Center for Public Leadership team, Catherine and Wayne Reynolds, the Dunn Family, Abby Falik, Eleni Pallas, the Rouffaers, Rick Boehlke, the Newell family, Dina Nayeri, and Becky Desjardins, among many, many others (you know who you are, I hope). And, of course, my gratitude goes out to Mark for his love and support.

A final thank you to all the beautiful souls who have changed my life, whether you know it or not.

About the Author

© SARAH DERAGON

Tori Hogan is the founder and director of Beyond Good Intentions, an organization that produces films and educational programs on the topic of international aid effectiveness. For more than a decade, Hogan has spent time immersed in the developing world as an aid worker, volunteer, researcher, filmmaker, and aid critic.

In 2006, frustrated by the lack of results she was witnessing while working with refugee populations in Africa and the Middle East, Hogan embarked on a yearlong round-the-world journey where she met with countless aid organizations and recipients to produce the ten-part Beyond Good Intentions film series on aid effectiveness. Since then, she has dedicated her time to educating young people worldwide about this topic.

Hogan received her B.A. from Duke University, served as a Fulbright Scholar in Egypt, and obtained an M.Ed. degree in International Education Policy from Harvard University. Born and raised in the Washington D.C. area, Hogan now lives in San Francisco but remains a global nomad at heart.